AAT

Level 4

Diploma for Professional Accounting Technicians

Management Accounting

Course Book

From September 2026

BPP
LYCEUM EDUCATION GROUP

First edition 2026

ISBN 9781 0355 4449 3

ISBN (for internal use only) 9781 0355 4069 3

eISBN 9781 0355 4470 7

British Library Cataloguing-in-Publication Data

A catalogue record for this book is available from the British Library

Published by

BPP Learning Media Ltd
BPP House, Aldine Place
142–144 Uxbridge Road
London W12 8AA

learningmedia.bpp.com

Your learning materials are printed on paper obtained from traceable sustainable sources.

We are grateful to the Association of Accounting Technicians for permission to reproduce past examination questions.

Contents

Introduction to the course

Syllabus overview

The role of the management accountant is becoming ever more central to the success of an organisation. Delivering relevant and business focused information to support the operational activities of the organisation is vital so that it can meet its objectives. This unit encompasses the key areas of planning, control, decision making and liquidity management.

This unit will allow students to understand how the budgetary process is undertaken. Students will be able to construct budgets and then identify and report both on areas of success and on areas that should be of concern to key stakeholders. Students will also gain the skills required to critically evaluate organisational performance.

Students will be equipped with the knowledge and skills across a range of areas that will help to enhance the control environment of the organisation. Appreciating the range of methods available and understanding how and when it is appropriate to use each of them, will allow them to advise a business in a range of situations.

Students will also gain an appreciation of the methods used to deal with the issues surrounding both short-term and long-term decision making. Understanding the techniques available for both forms of decision making and the fundamental differences between them is key to providing the organisation with appropriate information on which to make decisions.

The success of any organisation is not just reliant on its profitability but also on the effective management of its cashflow. This unit provides students with the skills to both monitor and manage liquidity.

Test specification for this unit assessment

Assessment method	Marking type	Duration of assessment
Computer-based assessment	Wholly computer marked	2 hours

Learning outcomes	Weighting
(1) Understand and implement the organisational planning process	25%
(2) Use cost and management accounting techniques to aid control	35%
(3) Use techniques to aid short-term and long-term decision making	20%
(4) Understand and manage organisational liquidity	20%
Total	**100%**

Assessment structure

Duration: 2 hours

Competency is 70%

The total number of marks for this assessment is 100.

Note. This is only a guideline as to what might come up, based on the AAT's sample. The format and content of each task may vary from what we have listed below.

Your assessment will consist of nine tasks.

The assessment will take the form of a computer-based test. The assessment will require computer marking and the results will be available instantly.

Task	Max marks	Response type	Expected content*	Chapter ref	Study complete
1	16	SFQ (short-form questions)	**Budgetary process and the preparation of budgets** A number of small exercises: Examples of areas that might be tested (this list is not exhaustive): • Selecting appropriate sources of information from various data sources • Selecting appropriate accounting treatment of cost items such as raw materials (direct cost) • Completing statements about budgets	1 Costing techniques 3 Budgetary control systems	

Task	Max marks	Response type	Expected content*	Chapter ref	Study complete
2	9	SFQ	**Forecasting where constraints exist** Examples of areas that might be tested (this list is not exhaustive): • Identification of components of time series data: Trend, Seasonal variation, Cyclical variation, Random variation • Application of seasonal adjustments to forecast future sales • Calculation of sales forecasts using trend and seasonal data • High-low method for cost estimation • Use of linear cost functions ($y = a + bx$) • Limiting (restricting) factors: identification of the limiting factor (eg materials, labour); calculation of contribution per unit; calculation of contribution per unit of scarce resource; ranking of products to determine optimal production plan • Identification of true/false statements relating to limiting factors and budgeting constraints	2 Forecasting techniques 11 Short-term decision making	

Task	Max marks	Response type	Expected content*	Chapter ref	Study complete
3	12	SFQ	**Flexed budgets** Examples of areas that might be tested (this list is not exhaustive): • Preparation of a flexed budget for a given level of activity • Adjustment of variable costs in line with actual output levels • Treatment of fixed costs within a flexed budget • Treatment of semi-variable costs (splitting into fixed and variable elements where required) • Calculation of sales, costs and operating profit in a flexed budget • Comparison of flexed budget to actual results • Calculation and identification of variances (favourable/adverse) • Understanding the purpose and use of flexed budgets in performance evaluation • Identification of limitations of flexed budgeting (eg difficulty splitting costs, assumptions about cost behaviour) • Identification of true/false statements relating to flexed budgeting and variance interpretation	6 Standard costing and flexed budgets 7 Variance analysis 8 Interpretation of variances	

<table>
<tr><th>Task</th><th>Max marks</th><th>Response type</th><th>Expected content*</th><th>Chapter ref</th><th>Study complete</th></tr>
<tr><td>4</td><td>11</td><td>SFQ</td><td>Standard costing
Examples of areas that might be tested (this list is not exhaustive):
• Preparation of a standard cost statement for direct materials
• Calculation of material variances: Material price variance, Material usage variance
• Identification of favourable and adverse variances
• Calculation of fixed overhead absorption rate per unit
• Calculation of fixed overhead variances: Expenditure variance, Volume variance
• Understanding and classification of types of standards
• Identification of causes of variances (eg material quality, labour inefficiencies)
• Identification of true/false statements relating to variance analysis and standard costing principles</td><td>6 Standard costing and flexed budgets
7 Variance analysis
8 Interpretation of variances</td><td></td></tr>
</table>

Task	Max marks	Response type	Expected content*	Chapter ref	Study complete
5	12	SFQ	**Management accounting techniques** Examples of areas that might be tested (this list is not exhaustive): • Calculation of overhead cost per unit using activity-based costing (ABC): Identification of cost drivers; calculation of cost per driver; allocation of overheads to products • Comparison of traditional absorption costing and activity-based costing • Understanding the implications of using ABC (eg impact on cost accuracy and decision making) • Life cycle costing: Identification and aggregation of costs over the full product life; calculation of total life cycle cost and cost per unit; inclusion of design, development and end-of-life costs • Target costing: Derivation of target cost from selling price and required margin • Identification of true/false statements relating to costing techniques • Understanding of when different costing approaches are appropriate	9 Activity-based costing 10 Target costing and life cycle costing	

Task	Max marks	Response type	Expected content*	Chapter ref	Study complete
6	10	SFQ	**Comparing short-term and long-term decision making, and relevant costing** Examples of areas that might be tested (this list is not exhaustive): • Understanding differences between short-term and long-term decisions (eg risk, level of investment, type of assets) • Identification of relevant and non-relevant costs: Opportunity costs, Avoidable vs unavoidable costs, Sunk costs • Application of relevant costing principles to decision scenarios • Make or buy (outsourcing) decisions: Calculation of relevant cost of internal production, Identification of costs to include/exclude, Comparison with external supplier cost • Unit cost calculations based on relevant costs only • Selection of the financially preferable option • Consideration of non-financial factors (eg quality, reliability, confidentiality) • Identification of true/false statements relating to decision-making principles	11 Short-term decision-making techniques 12 Long-term decision-making techniques	

Task	Max marks	Response type	Expected content*	Chapter ref	Study complete
7	10	SFQ and advanced questions	**Long-term decision-making** • Understanding the concept of time value of money • Calculation of non-discounted payback period: • Determining annual contribution • Deducting fixed costs/overheads • Calculating annual and cumulative cash flows • Identification of the year in which payback occurs • Application of decision rules (eg comparing payback period to target) • Calculation of net present value (NPV): • Applying discount factors • Calculating present value of cash flows • Determining overall NPV • Interpretation of NPV results (accept/reject decision) • Identification and matching of investment appraisal methods: • Payback period • Internal rate of return (IRR) • Accounting rate of return (ARR)	12 Long-term decision-making techniques	

Task	Max marks	Response type	Expected content*	Chapter ref	Study complete
8	12	SFQ	**Managing liquidity** Examples of areas that might be tested (this list is not exhaustive): • Calculate working capital cycle • Consequences of not paying suppliers on time • Calculation of working capital cycle components • Calculation and interpretation of the working capital cycle • Identification of changes in liquidity position (improvement/deterioration) • Understanding relationships between profit, cash and working capital • Basic financial awareness of borrowing and investment options • Understanding features of financial products • Identification of gearing-related impacts of financing decisions • Consequences of not paying suppliers on time • Weaknesses and limitations of cash budgets	13 Liquidity and working capital	

Task	Max marks	Response type	Expected content*	Chapter ref	Study complete
9	8	SFQ	**Calculating and identifying appropriate financing and investment options** Examples of areas that might be tested (this list is not exhaustive): • Calculate average interest rate on overdraft, monthly mortgage payments, total number of shares, dividend payable per share, dividend yield per share, total finance costs, net yield • Identify impact of market value on dividend yield per share, appropriate types of finance	14 Financing options 15 Investment options	

Skills bank

Our experience of preparing students for this type of assessment suggests that to obtain competency, you will need to develop a number of key skills.

1 Learning and applying the theory

2 Logical approaches to tasks

3 Effective use of your time in the assessment

Each of these key skills are analysed on the following pages.

What do I need to know to do well in the assessment?

This unit is one of the mandatory Level 4 units. *Management Accounting* is a broad syllabus that is examined by a mixture of computational questions that require the application of knowledge, multiple choice questions and true/false type questions. The questions are both theoretical and application based, which means that you need an overall broad knowledge of the syllabus alongside fairly detailed knowledge for some areas. You will also need an understanding of the techniques involved in approaching the computational questions.

The knowledge that you have to acquire includes the following:

Theoretical knowledge – the fundamental definitions and basic thinking behind different management accounting techniques. These will often be tested in narrative questions.

Practical knowledge – the application of techniques to 'real life' situations, which will be tested mostly in computational questions.

In this section we will look at approaches that you can take to help you learn the key elements of the knowledge in the syllabus and develop your application skills.

Assumed knowledge

Management Accounting is a mandatory unit. The unit builds on the fundamental concepts and techniques introduced in Level 2 and Level 3. The following topics were introduced and are also relevant to this assessment:

- Cost behaviour and cost classification
- Absorption costing principles
- Flexible budgeting and variance analysis
- Short-term decision-making techniques – in particular breakeven analysis, margin of safety and required profit

Assessment style

In the assessment you will complete tasks by:

(a) Entering narrative by selecting from drop down menus of narrative options known as picklists

(b) Using drag and drop menus to enter narrative

(c) Typing in numbers, known as gap fill entry

(d) Entering ticks

Introduction to the assessment

The question practice you do will prepare you for the format of tasks you will see in the *Management Accounting* assessment. It is also useful to familiarise yourself with the introductory information you **may** be given at the start of the assessment. For example:

You have 2 hours to complete this assessment.

- This assessment contains 9 tasks and you should attempt to complete every task.
- Each task is independent. You will not need to refer to your answers to previous tasks.
- The total number of marks for this assessment is 100.
- Read every task carefully to make sure you understand what is required.
- Where the date is relevant, it is given in the task data.
- Both minus signs and brackets can be used to indicate negative numbers unless task instructions state otherwise.
- You must us a full stop to indicate a decimal point. For example, write 100.57 not 100,57 or 10057.
- You may use a comma to indicate a number in the thousands, but you don't have to. For example, 10000 and 10,000 are both acceptable.
- You will need to double click to enter values into a gapfill or cell within a table.

(a) As you revise, use the BPP Passcards to consolidate your knowledge. They are a pocket-sized revision tool, perfect for packing in that last-minute revision.

(b) Attempt as many tasks as possible in the Exam Practice Kit. There are plenty of assessment-style tasks which are excellent preparation for the real assessment.

(c) Always check through your own answers as you will in the real assessment, before looking at the solutions in the back of the Exam Practice Kit and Course Book.

Key to icons

Key term

A key definition which is important to be aware of for the assessment.

Formula to learn

A formula you will need to learn as it will not be provided in the assessment.

Formula provided

A formula which is provided within the assessment and generally available as a pop-up on screen.

Activity

An example which allows you to apply your knowledge to the technique covered in the Course Book. The solution is provided at the end of the chapter.

Illustration

A worked example which can be used to review and see how an assessment question could be answered.

Assessment focus point

A high priority point for the assessment.

Open book reference

Where use of an open book will be allowed for the assessment.

Real life examples

A practical real life scenario.

AAT qualifications

The material in this book may support the following AAT qualifications:

AAT Level 4 Diploma for Professional Accounting Technicians.

Supplements

From time to time, we may need to publish supplementary materials to one of our titles. This can be for a variety of reasons, from a small change in the AAT unit guidance to new legislation coming into effect between editions.

You should check our supplements page regularly for anything that may affect your learning materials. All supplements are available free of charge on our supplements page on our website at:

learningmedia.bpp.com/pages/resources-for-students

Improving material and removing errors

BPP Learning Media do everything possible to ensure the material is accurate and up to date when sending to print. In the event that any errors are found after the print date, they are uploaded to the following website: learningmedia.bpp.com/pages/aat-errata

These learning materials are based on the qualification specification released by the AAT in November 2025.

Glossary of terms

It is useful to be familiar with interchangeable terminology including IFRS and UK GAAP (generally accepted accounting principles).

Below is a short list of the most important terms you are likely to use or come across, together with their international and UK equivalents.

UK term	International term
Profit and loss account	**Statement of profit or loss (or statement of profit or loss and other comprehensive income)**
Turnover or Sales	Revenue or Sales Revenue
Operating profit	Profit from operations
Reducing balance depreciation	Diminishing balance depreciation
Depreciation/depreciation expense(s)	Depreciation charge(s)
Balance sheet	**Statement of financial position**
Fixed assets	Non-current assets
Net book value	Carrying amount
Tangible assets	Property, plant and equipment
Stocks	Inventories
Trade debtors or Debtors	Trade receivables
Prepayments	Other receivables
Debtors and prepayments	Trade and other receivables
Cash at bank and in hand	Cash and cash equivalents
Long-term liabilities	Non-current liabilities
Trade creditors or creditors	Trade payables
Accruals	Other payables
Creditors and accruals	Trade and other payables
Capital and reserves	Equity (limited companies)
Profit and loss balance	Retained earnings
Cash flow statement	**Statement of cash flows**

Accountants often have a tendency to use several phrases to describe the same thing! Some of these are listed below:

Different terms for the same thing
Nominal ledger, main ledger or general ledger
Subsidiary ledgers, memorandum ledgers
Subsidiary (sales) ledger, sales ledger
Subsidiary (purchases) ledger, purchases ledger

1 Costing techniques

Learning outcomes

1.2	**Types of budgets and recommendations for their use** **To be able to:** Prepare operating budgets incorporating the following costs and revenue: • Direct • Indirect • Fixed • Variable • Semi-variable • Stepped • Capital • Revenue
2.3	**Activity-based costing** **To be able to:** • Calculate product costs using traditional absorption costing

Assessment context

Cost classification and behaviour is essential knowledge used in many management accounting techniques.

Business context

Grouping costs together is essential for a business to be able to analyse costs, prepare budgets and plan effectively.

Chapter overview

Costing techniques

Cost behaviour

- Fixed

- Stepped

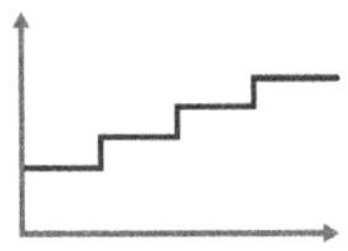

- Variable

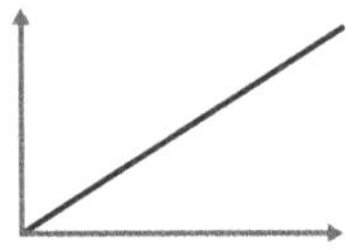

- Semi-variable

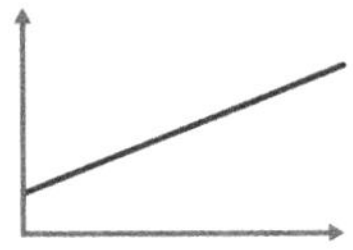

  - High-low method
    - Used to split fixed and variable elements
    - Find highest and lowest activity levels
    - Subtract Low from High
    - Use remainder to calculate variable cost
    - Substitute VC back into High or Low total cost formula to calculate fixed cost

Cost classification

Classification by function

- Production costs
  - Associated with the production of goods and services
  - Direct costs
    - Directly traced to product
  - Indirect costs
    - Incurred as a result of making a product but not directly traceable
- Non-production costs
  - All other costs in a business
  - Indirect costs

Dealing with indirect costs

- Absorption costing + ABC
  - Budget needs to be consistent with method employed by the business
  - Inappropriate attribution of cost can result in wrong decisions being taken by the business

Classification by type

- Capital expenditure
  - Purchase/improvement of noncurrent assets
- Revenue expenditure
  - Purchase goods resale
  - Maintenance
  - Expenses associated with running a business

Classification by nature

- Materials
- Labour
- Overheads

Introduction

One of the key concerns for the management of a commercial organisation is to know how much its products or services cost to manufacture or provide. This information is needed so the organisation can:

- Set the selling price
- Determine the quantities of production and sales
- Decide whether to continue or discontinue a product
- Control costs
- Appraise the performance of individual managers

To do this, management need to understand the nature of the costs that make up a cost unit, and find a suitable method of allocating overheads to the cost units.

1 Cost behaviour and output

Assessment focus point

A business needs to know how costs behave with output so that costs can be forecasted.

It is expected that costs will increase as production increases (ie as output increases), but the exact way costs behave with output may vary.

1.1 Types of cost behaviour

1.1.1 Variable costs

KEY TERM

Variable costs: Those costs that vary, ie rise and fall, with output (eg materials and labour costs vary with the number of units produced).

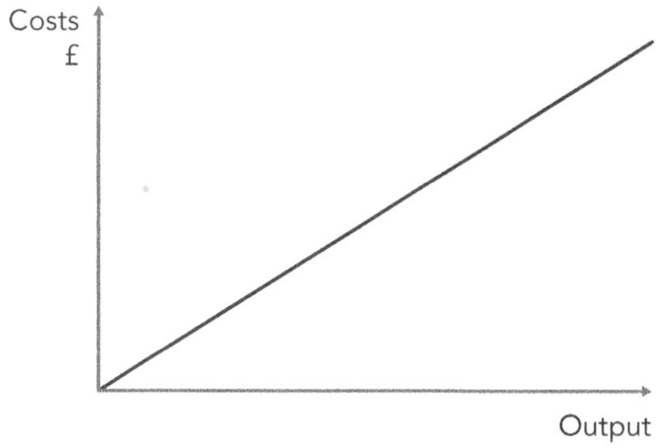

1.1.2 Fixed costs

KEY TERM

Fixed costs: Those costs that will not vary with output. These are often referred to as fixed overheads (eg rent and rates).

1.1.3 Stepped costs (sometimes called stepped fixed costs)

KEY TERM

Stepped costs: Costs that remain fixed for a certain level of output and then increase until a further level of output is reached. They then become fixed again until output levels reach another point, then increase again (eg supervisors' costs where a supervisor is required for every 20 members of staff and rent, which may increase with the addition of new facilities or space).

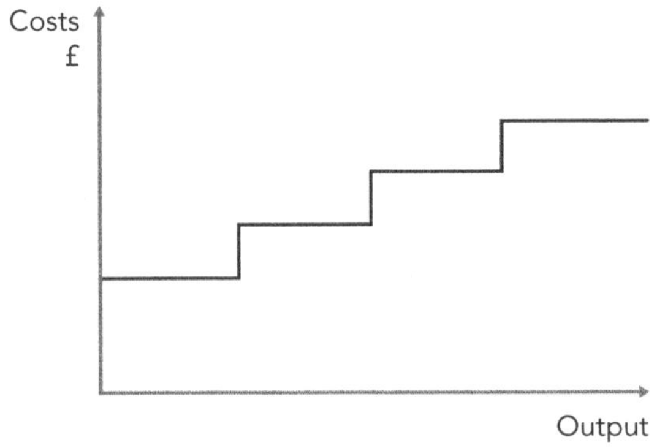

1.1.4 Semi-variable costs

KEY TERM

Semi-variable costs: Those costs which are part fixed and part variable and are therefore partly affected by changes in the level of activity (eg telephone bill, where there is a fixed line rental charge and a charge per call made).

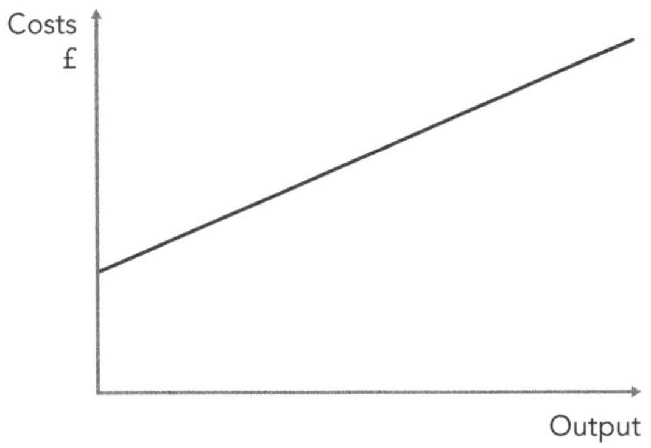

BPP

Remember, not all costs follow the textbook profiles. For example, production labour is often described as a variable cost. In reality, basic wages are often fixed and overtime is then paid at a higher rate, should it be required.

Illustration 1: Classification of costs by behaviour

Cameron Ltd produces one product, which requires the following inputs, in the forthcoming quarter:

Direct materials	1 kg @ £3.50 per kg
Direct labour	1 hour @ £12.00 per hour
Rent	£4,000 per quarter
Leased machines	£1,500 for every 4,000 units of production
Maintenance costs	£1,000 per quarter plus £1.00 per unit

Required

(a) Calculate the budgeted total cost of production and the budgeted cost per unit for each of the following production levels for the coming quarter:

(1) 4,000 units

(2) 10,000 units

(3) 16,000 units

Variable costs with a discount

Suppose now that the supplier of the materials offers a bulk purchasing discount of 6% for all purchases if an order is placed for more than 8,000 kg.

Required

(b) What is the direct materials cost in total and per unit at each level of production?

Solution

(a) **Direct materials** – this is a variable cost with a constant amount per unit (1 kg × £3.50 = £3.50). Therefore, the total cost is found by multiplying the number of units by the unit cost:

	£
£3.50 × 4,000 units =	14,000
£3.50 × 10,000 units =	35,000
£3.50 × 16,000 units =	56,000

Direct labour – another variable cost, with a unit cost of 1hr × £12 = £12:

	£
£12.00 × 4,000 units =	48,000
£12.00 × 10,000 units =	120,000
£12.00 × 16,000 units =	192,000

Rent – this is a fixed cost and therefore, provided we are still operating within the relevant range, it will remain at £4,000, whatever the production level.

Leased machines – this is a stepped cost and the number of machines leased will depend upon the quantity of production:

Units	Machine	£
4,000 =	1 =	1,500
10,000 =	3 =	4,500
16,000 =	4 =	6,000

Maintenance costs – this is a semi-variable cost with a fixed element of £1,000 and a variable cost of £1 per unit. The total cost for each activity level is:

Units		£
4,000 =	£1,000 + (4,000 × £1.00) =	5,000
10,000	£1,000 + (10,000 × £1.00) =	11,000
16,000	£1,000 + (16,000 × £1.00) =	17,000

Thus, the total costs of production are:

	Production level – units		
	4,000	10,000	16,000
	£	£	£
Direct materials (variable)	14,000	35,000	56,000
Direct labour (variable)	48,000	120,000	192,000
Rent (fixed)	4,000	4,000	4,000
Leased machines (stepped)	1,500	4,500	6,000
Maintenance costs	5,000	11,000	17,000
Total cost	72,500	174,500	275,000
Number of units	4,000	10,000	16,000
Cost per unit	18.13	17.45	17.19

The cost per unit will decrease if the production quantity increases. This is because the fixed cost and the fixed element of the semi-variable cost will then be spread over a larger number of units.

(b) **4,000 units**

		£
Total cost	4,000 × £3.50	14,000
Cost per unit	£14,000/4,000	3,50

10,000 units

		£
Total cost	10,000 × (£3.50 × 94%) =	32,900
Cost per unit	£32,900/10,000 =	3.29

16,000 units

		£
Total cost	16,000 × (£3.50 × 94%) =	52,640
Cost per unit	£52,640/16,000 =	3.29

The direct materials are now not a true variable cost, as the cost per unit falls once production is in excess of 8,000 units.

Activity 1: Cost behaviour

A manufacturer of a single product has supplied the budget information for the next quarter end:

Materials per unit	1.5 kg at £4.50 per kg
Rent per quarter	£6,500
Supervisor cost	£2,000 for every 2,500 units produced
Electricity	£1,250 per quarter plus £1.30 per unit

Required

Calculate the budgeted quarterly costs of production for the following activity levels to the nearest pound and classify each cost.

Cost	Quarterly production 2,000 units £	9,000 units £	Cost classification
Direct materials (W1)			▼
Rent (W2)			▼
Supervisors (W3)			▼
Electricity (W4)			▼

Picklist

- Fixed
- Semi-variable
- Stepped
- Variable

2 Determining the fixed and variable elements of semi-variable costs

In order to determine the semi-variable costs at a given level of activity, both the fixed element amount and the variable element rate must be known. Splitting out these elements is important as it will help the organisation forecast the cost at a future activity level.

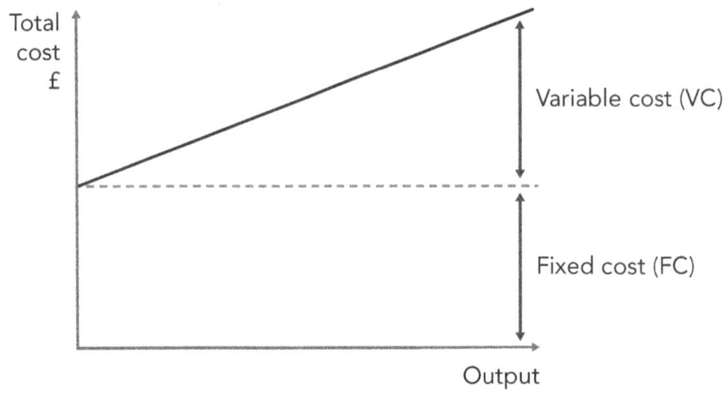

Formula to learn

Total cost = Fixed cost + (VC per unit × Output)

2.1 High–low method for semi-variable costs

Assessment focus point

This is a four-step method:

(a) Select the highest and lowest output level and their costs.

(b) Find the difference in the output and costs.

(c) Calculate the variable cost per unit.

(d) Calculate the fixed cost.

Illustration 2: High–low calculation 1

The total costs of a business for differing levels of output are as follows:

Output (units)	Total costs
10,000	27,000
12,000	31,000
14,000	35,000

The variable cost/unit and the fixed cost are calculated as follows:

	Output (units)	Cost £
Highest output	14,000	35,000
Lowest output	10,000	27,000
	4,000	8,000

Therefore VC/unit = £8,000/4,000 = £2

Substitute VC/unit back into highest (or lowest) level

	£
Total costs	35,000
Variable cost (14,000 units × £2)	(28,000)
Therefore Fixed cost	7,000

Care must be taken to determine the nature of the fixed cost base. In the assessment you may be presented with fixed costs that exhibit a stepped behaviour as demonstrated below.

Illustration 3: High–low method 2

The following data has been collected from a business:

Units produced	**5,000**	**7,500**	**10,000**
Total costs (£)	54,500	76,500	90,000

Total costs are made up of two elements, a fixed cost (that changes when the units exceed 7,000) and some variable costs, which remain constant per unit.

Here we calculate the total fixed costs at production levels below and above 7,000 units and the variable cost per unit.

High/low method above volume of 7,000 units.

	Output	Cost
Highest	10,000	90,000
Lowest	7,500	76,500
	2,500	13,500

Therefore VC/unit = £13,500/2,500 = £5.40

Note. This is constant at all volumes of output.

TC = FC + VC/unit × output

Substitute at lowest (or highest) level:

£76,500 = FC + £5.40 × 7,500

FC = £36,000 above output of 7,000 units

So at 5,000 units:

TC = FC + VC/unit × output

£54,500 = FC + £5.40 × 5,000

FC = £27,500 below output of 7,000 units

Activity 2: High–low method

You have been supplied with the following information about a factory's overheads.

Units produced	Total overheads £
15,000	250,000
19,000	290,000

The fixed portion of the overheads increases by £5,000 when more than 20,000 units are produced.

Due to the organisation obtaining bulk discounts from suppliers, variable costs reduce by £1.50 per unit if more than 22,500 units are produced.

Required

Calculate the total fixed and variable overheads for the following production levels.

Enter your answers to the nearest pound.

Units	Fixed £	Variable £
17,000		
25,000		

3 Cost classification

Cost classification is the arrangement of cost items into logical groups, for example, by their **type** (capital and revenue expenditure), their **function** (eg administration, production) or by their **nature** (eg materials, labour).

The eventual aim of costing is to determine the cost of producing a product/service.

3.1 Capital expenditure vs revenue expenditure

Capital expenditure includes:

- The purchase of non-current assets
- The improvement of the earning capability of non-current assets

Revenue expenditure includes:

- The purchase of goods for resale
- The maintenance of the existing earning capacity of non-current assets
- Expenditure incurred in conducting the business

Capital expenditure is shown as a non-current asset in the statement of financial position, while revenue expenditure is charged as a cost in the statement of profit or loss.

3.2 Cost classification by function

A company may also arrange cost items into groups by function (ie which part of the business the cost relates to). At the highest level of classification, there could be groups of production costs and groups of non-production costs.

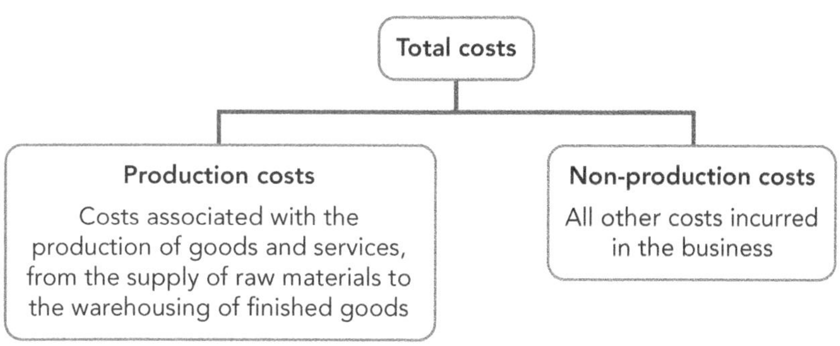

3.3 Cost classification by nature

Production costs can then be broken down further by their nature (ie the category of cost that has been incurred).

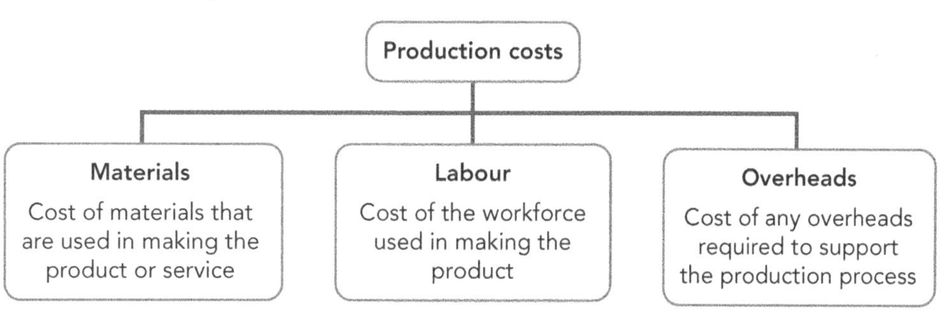

Non-production costs can also be broken down further by their nature to aid analysis.

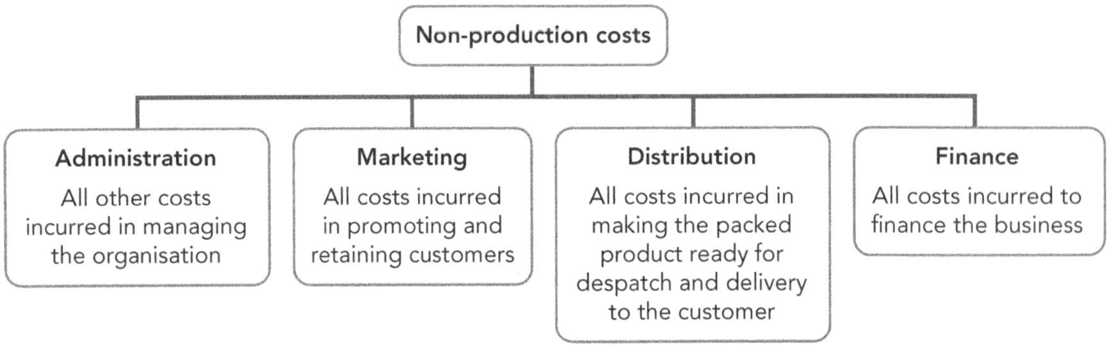

Illustration 4: Classifying costs

The following items of expenditure can be classified by the headings below:

Administration	Marketing and distribution	Capital expenditure	Cash flow
Depreciation charge of office equipment	Sales staff salaries	Factory extension	Payments to suppliers
Finance director's salary	Advertising	Van purchase	
Accounts staff salaries	Drivers' salaries		
Office staff salaries	Packing materials		
	Lorry repairs		

3.4 Direct and indirect costs

Costs can be further split into direct costs and indirect costs.

3.4.1 Direct costs

KEY TERM

Direct costs: Costs which can be specifically identified with, and allocated to, a single cost unit.

Direct costs are often variable (eg materials cost per unit) but can sometimes be fixed (eg tool hire for a specific cost).

The majority of direct costs are production costs, but some non-production costs could also be classified as direct (eg sales commission per unit sold).

Once all the direct costs are identified for a cost unit, the **prime cost** can then be calculated.

KEY TERM

Prime costs: Total of all direct costs in manufacturing a product/providing a service.

3.4.2 Indirect production costs

KEY TERM

> **Indirect costs:** Incurred in the course of making a product/service, but which cannot be identified with a particular cost unit.

Indirect production costs are often referred to as production overheads. Indirect costs are largely fixed costs, but some variable costs could also be indirect (eg oil for machinery).

Illustration 5: Identifying direct and indirect costs

Here are some of the costs involved in making chocolate bars, grouped by direct and indirect costs:

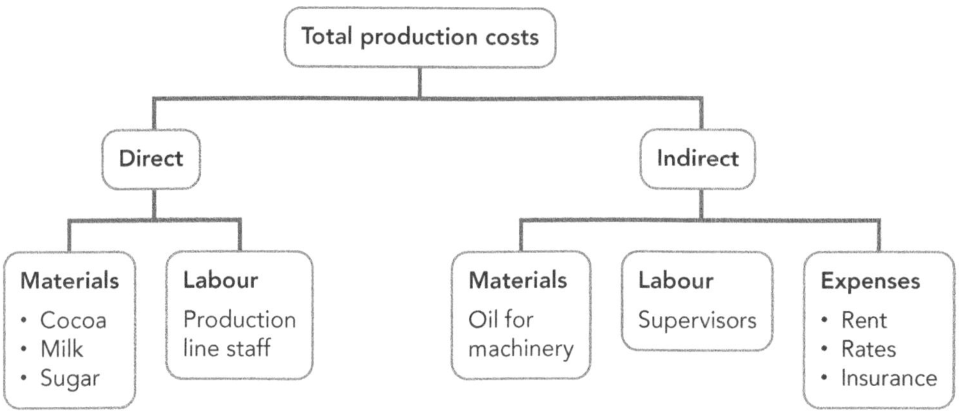

4 Methods of costing

There are three main methods of calculating a cost per unit. These allocate overheads in different ways. You will have covered these in earlier studies, but we will recap these here.

KEY TERM

> **Absorption costing:** A method whereby all production costs are included in the costing of a cost unit, both variable and fixed, direct and indirect. This method of costing distinguishes between production and non-production costs.
>
> **Marginal costing:** Under this method only the variable costs of production are included in the cost per unit. The fixed overheads are treated as period costs and not as part of the cost unit. Instead, the fixed overheads are charged to the statement of profit or loss as an expense for the period.
>
> **Activity-based costing:** A method of absorption costing which uses more sophisticated methods of allocating overheads to cost units. This method is covered later in this Course Book.

Assessment focus point

In the assessment you may be required to calculate the overhead cost per unit under both absorption and activity-based costing principles.

Make sure you are confident with how each method works and how to apply the overhead calculations.

5 Absorption costing

Absorption costing is a method of costing whereby all production costs (direct materials, direct labour, variable production overheads and fixed production overheads) are included in the costing of a cost unit.

Note that even when applying absorption costing, it is usually only the production overheads of the production and service cost centres that are absorbed. Administrative overheads (eg the salaries of the finance team, the depreciation of the office building) or selling overheads (eg the cost of an advertising campaign) will remain outside the cost units.

Absorption costing calculates an overhead absorption rate (OAR) that can be used to absorb the production overheads into each cost unit.

KEY TERM

Overhead absorption rate: An estimated amount of fixed overhead which can be used to calculate the overhead cost incurred to produce one cost unit.

To calculate the OAR the following method is used:

(a) Allocate and apportion overheads to each production and service cost centre.

(b) Re-apportion service cost centres cost to production cost centres to find total production cost.

(c) Absorb into production using an overhead absorption rate. This can be calculated as follows:

$$\frac{\text{Total production overheads}}{\text{Total activity level}}$$

The activity level chosen is the one that best reflects how the overhead is incurred, although there is no rule regarding which should be used. The most commonly used activity levels are:

- Total machine hours – This activity level is often used if the production process is machine intensive.
- Total labour hours – This activity level is often used if the production process is labour intensive.
- Budgeted cost units – This activity level is used if the difference between machine and labour hours is negligible, or if only one type of product is manufactured by the organisation.

Assessment focus point

You may be asked to calculate an OAR or a cost per unit using absorption costing.

Illustration 6: Absorption costing

Fenton Partners produce one product, the Fenton. The factory has two production departments, assembly and packing.

The expected costs of producing 100,000 units in the next quarter are as follows:

Direct materials	£24.00 per unit
Direct labour	2 hours assembly @ £11.00 per hour
	1 hour packing @ £16.00 per hour
Total assembly production overheads	£470,000
Total packing production overheads	£290,000

Overheads are absorbed on the basis of labour hours.

Production overheads

	Assembly £	Packing £
Total overheads	470,000	290,000
Number of labour hours	200,000	100,000
Absorption rate	£2.35 per labour hour	£2.90 per labour hour

Interpretation:

For every one hour that the product is worked on in the assembly department, it is charged with a £2.35 share of the overheads incurred.

For every one hour that the product is worked on in the packing department, it is charged with a £2.90 share of the overheads incurred.

Unit cost

	£
Direct materials	24.00
Direct labour	
Assembly 2 hours × £11.00	22.00
Packing 1 hour × £16.00	16.00
Overheads	
Assembly 2 hours × £2.35	4.70
Packing 1 hour × £2.90	2.90
Unit cost (total absorption costing)	69.60

Activity 3: Product cost calculation

Company M manufactures two products, X and Y, using traditional absorption costing based on direct labour hours. The following information is provided.

	X	Y
Forecast production	4,000	3,000

Budgeted production overheads

- Total overheads £297,000
- Absorbed using a labour-hour rate

Direct cost information per unit

	X	Y
Direct materials kg (@ £5 per kg)	3 kg	4 kg
Direct labour hours (@£20 per hour)	3 hours	5 hours

Required

Calculate the overhead cost per unit using traditional absorption costing and the total product cost per unit for Products X and Y.

Enter your answers to the nearest pound.

	X £	Y £
Direct materials		
Direct labour		
Overhead cost		
Total product cost per unit		

6 Marginal costing

Although marginal costing is not examined in MNAC, the concept of contribution (sales minus variable cost) is essential for decision-making topics covered later in this Course Book. Therefore, this section provides a brief recap of the idea without going into the full marginal costing method.

Marginal costing (also known as variable costing) is a costing system that measures only the variable (or marginal) cost of cost units (direct material, direct labour and variable overheads). This differs from absorption costing which considers both the variable and fixed costs of production.

In marginal costing, fixed costs are treated as a charge against profit in each time period, and are therefore subtracted off in full from profit within the period.

6.1 Contribution

A key term in marginal costing is contribution.

KEY TERM

> **Contribution:** The amount of money generated by a cost unit to contribute towards fixed costs incurred in a period in order to make a profit.

Contribution is calculated as follows:

> **Formula to learn**
>
> **Contribution = Sales revenue – All variable costs**

Note that contribution can be calculated either at a unit level, or in total within an accounting period.

Contribution is an important concept, and we will look at the use of contribution for decision making in a later chapter.

Chapter summary

- The nature of costs must be determined to correctly plan and control resources, and to perform a better assessment of manager performance.
- Costs are either capital or revenue in nature. Revenue expenditure is included in the cost of a product, but capital expenditure is not. Capital expenditure is converted to revenue expenditure in the form of depreciation.
- Direct costs are costs that can be related directly to a cost unit, whereas indirect costs (or overheads) cannot be attributed directly to a cost unit and instead are initially allocated or apportioned to a cost centre.
- Costs are often classified according to their behaviour as activity levels change – the main classifications are variable costs, fixed costs, stepped costs and semi-variable costs.
- There are three main methods of attributing indirect costs to production units – absorption costing, marginal costing and activity-based costing (ABC).
- Absorption costing is where the production overheads are included in the cost of each cost unit. An overhead absorption rate (OAR) is calculated to estimate the amount of production overhead used by each cost unit.
- Contribution = Sales revenue – All variable costs.

Activity answers

Activity 1: Cost behaviour

Cost	Quarterly production 2,000 units £	9,000 units £	Cost classification
Direct materials (W1)	13,500	60,750	Variable
Rent (W2)	6,500	6,500	Fixed
Supervisors (W3)	2,000	8,000	Stepped
Electricity (W4)	3,850	12,950	Semi-variable

Workings

1 As the cost per kg will vary with production, it is a variable cost

@ 2,000 units: 1.5kg × £4.50 × 2,000 = £13,500

@ 9,000 units: 1.5kg × £4.50 × 9,000 = £60,750

2 The rent cost will be unaffected by the volume of units produced, so is a fixed cost.

3 As the cost will increase at a certain production volume, this is a stepped cost.

@ 2,000 units:

2,000 units / 2,500 = 0.8 = 1 supervisor required

& Cost = £2,000

@ 9,000 units:

9,000 / 2,500 = 3.6 = 4 supervisors required

& Cost = 2,000 × 4 = £8,000

4 Electricity has a part fixed and part variable element, so is a semi-variable cost.

@ 2,000 units: £1,250 + (£1.30 × 2,000) = £3,850

@ 9,000 units: £1,250 + (£1.30 × 9,000) = £12,950

Activity 2: High–low method

Units	Fixed £	Variable £
17,000	100,000	170,000
25,000	105,000	212,500

	Units	£
High	19,000	290,000
Low	15,000	250,000
	4,000	40,000

Variable cost per unit = £40,000 / 4,000 = £10 per unit

@ 19,000 units:

	£
Total cost	290,000
Total variable cost (£10 × 19,000)	(190,000)
Fixed cost	100,000

@ 17,000 units

	£
Fixed cost	100,000
Variable cost (£10 × 17,000)	170,000
Total cost	270,000

@ 25,000 units

	£
Fixed cost (£100,000 + £5,000)	105,000
Variable cost ((£10 – £1.50) × 25,000)	212,500
Total cost	317,500

Activity 3: Product cost calculation

	X £	Y £
Direct materials	15	20
Direct labour	60	100
Overhead cost	33	55
Total product cost per unit	108	175

OAR = Budgeted overheads / Budgeted labour hours

Budgeted labour hours = (3 × 4,000) + (5 × 3,000) = 27,000 labour hours

OAR = £297,000 / 27,000 = £11 per labour hour

Product X

Material cost per unit = £5 × 3 kg = £15 per unit

Labour cost per unit = £20 × 3 hours = £60 per unit

Overheads = £11 × 3 hours = £33 per unit

Product Y

Material cost per unit = £5 × 4 kg = £20 per unit

Labour cost per unit = £20 × 5 hours = £100 per unit

Overheads = £11 × 5 hours = £55 per unit

Test your learning

1 The direct materials cost for 10,000 units is estimated to be £43,600 and for 12,000 it is estimated to be £52,320. This is a variable cost.

Required

True or false? Tick the correct answer.

	✓
True	
False	

2 A business expects to incur fixed costs of £64,000 in the following month.

Required

Complete the table below to show the total fixed cost and the fixed cost per unit at each of the following activity levels.

Activity level	Total fixed cost £	Fixed cost per unit £
3,000 units		
10,000 units		
16,000 units		

3 A business makes 3,500 units per month with the following costs:

Direct materials	£5 per unit
Direct labour	£10 per unit
Rent	£10,000 per month
Supervisor costs	£7,500 per month for every 5,000 units of production

Required

The full production cost per month is

£ [ ]

4 Given below are the activity levels and production costs for the latest six months for a factory:

	Activity level Units	Production cost £
July	103,000	469,000
August	110,000	502,000
September	126,000	547,000
October	113,000	517,000
November	101,000	472,000
December	118,000	533,000

Required

(a)

The variable element of the production cost is

£ [ ] per unit

The fixed element of the production cost is

£ [ ]

(b) **Complete the following table to show the estimated production costs at each of the following levels of production.**

Level of production	Production cost £
120,000 units	
150,000 units	

5 A manufacturing business has two production departments P1 and P2. P1 is a labour-intensive department, while P2 is highly mechanised with relatively few machine operatives. Budgeted figures are as follows:

	P1	P2
Overheads apportioned	£50,000	£60,000
Machine hours	800	4,000
Labour hours	2,500	600

Required

(a) **The overhead absorption rate for department P1 is:**

	✓
£62.50	
£20.00	
£15.00	
£100.00	

(b) **The overhead absorption rate for department P2 is:**

	✓
£62.50	
£20.00	
£15.00	
£100.00	

6 The budgeted overheads apportioned to two production cost centres, X and Y, together with the budgeted labour hours and machine hours, are given here:

	X	Y
Overheads	£260,000	£380,000
Direct labour hours	20,000	120,000
Machine hours	100,000	10,000

Production cost centre X involves a highly mechanised process, with only a few machine workers. Production Y involves a highly labour-intensive process.

Required

(a) **Complete the table to calculate separate departmental overhead absorption rates for each production cost centre using an appropriate basis.**

Department	Overhead absorption rate
X	
Y	

Each unit of Product A utilises the following hours in each production department.

	X	Y
Direct labour hours	1	4
Machine hours	5	2

Required

(b) **The overhead to be included in the cost of each unit of product A is**

£ [ ]

7 Given below is the budgeted information about the production of 60,000 units of a single product in a factory for the next quarter:

Direct materials	£12.50 per unit
Direct labour	
Assembly apprentice	4 hours @ £8.40 per hour
Finishing apprentice	1 hour @ £6.60 per hour
Assembly production overheads	£336,000
Finishing production overheads	£84,000

It is estimated that 60% of the assembly overhead is variable cost and that 75% of the finishing overhead is variable cost.

Required

Complete the table below to show the budgeted cost of the product using absorption costing.

Method of costing	Budgeted cost £
Absorption costing	

2 Forecasting techniques

Learning outcomes

1.3 **Calculate forecasts**

Understand:

- The elements of a time series
- The simple regression equation

Be able to:

- Use moving averages to calculate the seasonal variations and trend from a time series
- Use the simple regression equation to calculate total cost
- Calculate forecasts of future performance based on historical data

Assessment context

You could be asked to use statistical techniques to forecast costs and revenues in the assessment.

Business context

Businesses use a variety of models and techniques to help forecast their performance.

Chapter overview

Forecasting techniques

- **Time series analysis**
  - Trend
  - Seasonal variations
  - Cyclical
  - Random
  - TS = T + SV
- **Linear regression**
  - Y = a + bx

Introduction

A business may collect data about its previous activities, costs and sales revenues. This data can then be used to forecast future costs and revenues in order to plan and budget forthcoming periods. This chapter considers a number of statistical techniques that can be used to produce forecasts from historical data.

1 Time series analysis

KEY TERM

Time series: A series of figures or values recorded over time.

A time series analysis may be used if an organisation has collected data about costs and revenues over an extended period of time. Examples of this type of data include:

- Output at a factory each day for the last month
- Total costs per annum for the last ten years
- Monthly sales over the last five years

A time series analysis is an analysis of past patterns of data. Any pattern found in the data is then assumed to continue into the future and a forecast can be produced.

1.1 Components of a time series (TS)

KEY TERM

Trend: The underlying movement over time in the values of the data recorded.

Seasonal variation (SV): The regular short-term fluctuations in recorded values due to circumstances that affect results at different times of the year, on different days of the week or at different times of the day.

Trend (T)

A trend is the general movement of a time series over a long period of time. It can often be attributed to the impacts of sales growth or decline, or inflation. If the trend was plotted on a graph it would show as a smooth line or curve.

The trend can be found through the calculation of moving averages, or through linear regression analysis.

Examples of a trend include a steady decline in the average sales of a national daily newspaper, or a steady increase in sales of a smart phone.

Seasonal variation

A seasonal variation is a predicted movement away from the trend. These variations are due to repetitive events which occur over a short but fixed period of time (for example weekly or quarterly).

Examples of seasonal variations include sales of tabloid newspapers being higher on Mondays and Saturdays than other days due to the extra sports coverage, or sales of ice cream being higher in summer than in winter.

Cyclical variations

These are recurring patterns over a longer period of time, not generally of a fixed nature. For example, changes in employment linked to the business cycle.

Random variations

These are non-recurring unpredictable variations caused by unforeseen circumstances. For example, storms, strikes, sudden machine failures.

Assessment focus point

You will only be required to perform calculations using the **trend** and **seasonal variations** in the assessment. However, the words cyclical variation and random variation may appear in multiple-choice or picklist options (as shown in Activity 3). Knowing roughly what they mean is helpful, but you will not be asked to calculate them.

1.2 The additive model

Under the additive model, components are assumed to add together to give the forecast sales.

Formula to learn

TS = T + SV

where:

TS = Time series forecast (sometimes called seasonally adjusted value)

T = Trend (sometimes called underlying cost or moving average)

SV = Seasonal variations

The seasonal variations in time series analysis can be expressed as additions to, or subtractions from, the trend.

Assessment focus point

An assessment task may ask you to calculate the seasonal variation from given actual and trend information. You therefore need to be comfortable with re-arranging the additive formula to find the seasonal variation as follows:

SV = TS – T

1.3 Moving average

The main method for calculating a trend from a time series is the calculation of a **moving average**, which is the average of the results of a fixed number of periods and relates to the mid-point of the overall period.

Let's consider plotting the sales figures generated by a business into a graph:

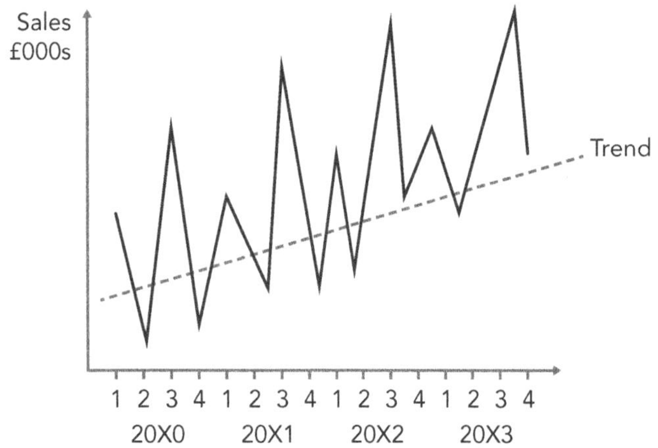

In the above graph, there would appear to be a large seasonal variation in demand, but there is also a basic upward trend. A series of moving averages are therefore calculated to determine what the general movement of the data set is.

Once the trend has been established, a forecast can be determined using the formula TS = T + SV, where TS can be equal to either costs or sales revenue.

Illustration 1: Moving average

The sales figures for a business for the first six months of the year are as follows:

	£
January	35,500
February	37,500
March	34,500
April	40,000
May	42,000
June	39,000

It is felt that the sales cycle is on a quarterly basis – ie the seasonal variations repeat themselves every three months. What is required, therefore, is a three-month moving average. This is done by first totalling the figures for January, February and March and then finding the average:

$$\frac{35{,}500 + 37{,}500 + 34{,}500}{3} = £35{,}833$$

Then we move on by one month, and the average for February, March and April sales is calculated:

$$\frac{37{,}500 + 34{,}500 + 40{,}000}{3} = £37{,}333$$

Then, the average for March, April and May would be calculated as follows:

$$\frac{34{,}500 + 40{,}000 + 42{,}000}{3} = £38{,}833$$

Finally the average for April, May and June can be determined:

$$\frac{40{,}000 + 42{,}000 + 39{,}000}{3} = £40{,}333$$

Now we can show these moving averages, together with the original figures – the convention is to show the moving average next to the middle month of those used in the average.

The seasonal variation can then be calculated by subtracting the moving average from the actual data.

	Actual data £	Moving average – trend £	Seasonal variation £
January	35,500		
February	37,500	35,833	+1,667
March	34,500	37,333	–2,833
April	40,000	38,833	+1,167
May	42,000	40,333	+1,667
June	39,000		

Activity 1: Moving averages

Given below are the production costs for a factory for a six-month period.

Required

Complete the table to show the three-month moving average for these figures.

Month	Actual £	Three-month moving average £
March	226,504	
April	251,600	
May	238,200	
June	247,600	
July	240,500	
August	262,800	

1.4 Centred moving average

If the moving average is based on an even number of periods, then there is no central time period to place the moving average against. A further average – the centred moving average – is required in order to find the trend.

Illustration 2: Centred moving average

The quarterly sales figures for Wrigley Partners for the last two years are given below:

20X6

	£
Quarter 1	88,900
Quarter 2	100,300
Quarter 3	63,800
Quarter 4	75,200

20X7

	£
Quarter 1	91,600
Quarter 2	103,700
Quarter 3	66,100
Quarter 4	76,400

The sales figures exhibit seasonal variations over the four quarters of a year. In order to find the trend, a four-quarterly centred moving average must first be calculated.

We start by calculating the average of quarters 1–4 in 20X6:

$$\text{First average: } \frac{88{,}900 + 100{,}300 + 63{,}800 + 75{,}200}{4} = 82{,}050$$

Next, move on by one quarter, and calculate the moving average for Q2–Q4 20X6 and Q1 20X7:

$$\text{Second average: } \frac{100{,}300 + 63{,}800 + 75{,}200 + 91{,}600}{4} = 82{,}725$$

Once all moving averages are calculated, they will be displayed as follows:

20X6

	Actual £	Moving average £
Quarter 1	88,900	
Quarter 2	100,300	
		82,050
Quarter 3	63,800	
		82,725
Quarter 4	75,200	
		83,575

20X7

	Actual £	Moving average £
Quarter 1	91,600	
		84,150
Quarter 2	103,700	
		84,450
Quarter 3	66,100	
Quarter 4	76,400	

As the moving average being calculated is an even number, it is shown in between the second and third quarter for each quarterly average – the middle of the four quarters.

In order to obtain a trend line the centred moving average must now be calculated.

To do this we take each consecutive pair of moving average figures and in turn average them, and show them against the third quarter.

$$\text{First average: } \frac{82{,}050 + 82{,}725}{2} = 82{,}388$$

$$\text{Second average: } \frac{82{,}725 + 83{,}575}{2} = 83{,}150$$

$$\text{Third average: } \frac{83{,}575 + 84{,}150}{2} = 83{,}863$$

$$\text{Fourth average: } \frac{84{,}150 + 84{,}450}{2} = 84{,}300$$

20X6

	Actual £	Moving average £	Centred moving average (Trend) £
Quarter 1	88,900		
Quarter 2	100,300		
		82,050	
Quarter 3	63,800		82,388
		82,725	
Quarter 4	75,200		83,150
		83,575	

20X7

	Actual £	Moving average £	Centred moving average (Trend) £
Quarter 1	91,600		83,863
		84,150	
Quarter 2	103,700		84,300
		84,450	
Quarter 3	66,100		
Quarter 4	76,400		

Activity 2: JB Ltd

JB Ltd is planning ahead and wishes to forecast the cost of its main ingredient used in the manufacture of product X.

Required

(a) **Complete the table below by entering the missing figures. Use minus signs for negative figures.**

20X6	Jan £	Feb £	Mar £
Underlying cost per kg (£)	180		240
Seasonal variation (£)		12	–18
Seasonally adjusted cost (£)	220	222	

(b) **Assuming the trend continues to increase at the same monthly rate as in part (a) above, complete the table below to show the projected costs for the first quarter of 20X7. Use minus signs for negative figures.**

20X7	Jan £	Feb £	Mar £
Underlying cost per kg (£)			
Seasonal variation (£)			
Seasonally adjusted cost (£)			

1.5 The multiplicative model

Assessment focus point

You may be presented with seasonal variations as a percentage movement away from the trend rather than in absolute figures. To find the time series, the multiplicative model is used.

Under the multiplicative model, the components of the time series are multiplied together rather than added together. The time series can then be determined as follows:

Formula to learn

TS = T × SV

Illustration 3: Multiplicative model

The trend figures for sales in units for Earthware Design for the four quarters of 20X0 are given below:

Quarter 1	158,400
Quarter 2	159,900
Quarter 3	161,500
Quarter 4	163,100

The seasonal variations are expressed as follows:

Quarter 1	+8%
Quarter 2	–5%
Quarter 3	–17%
Quarter 4	+14%

Required

What are the forecast sales for each of the quarters of 20X0?

Solution

Quarter 1	158,400 × 1.08	=	171,072
Quarter 2	159,900 × 0.95	=	151,905
Quarter 3	161,500 × 0.83	=	134,045
Quarter 4	163,100 × 1.14	=	185,934

Activity 3: Time series

(a) Complete the sentences using the picklists.

(1) ▼ equals actual costs for a month less seasonal variation for a month.

The impact of the economic cycle is known as a (2) ▼ .

Picklist 1

- Cost
- Time series
- Trend

Picklist 2

- Cyclical variation
- Random variation
- Seasonal variation

You are preparing a forecast and have been given the following information.

Period	Sales trend 20X6 (£)	Seasonal variation
October to December	1,690,000	-10%
January to March	1,760,000	-6%
April to June	1,830,000	+12%
July to September	1,900,000	+18%

This trend is expected to continue into 20X7.

Required

(b) Calculate the sales forecast for 20X7.

Period	Sales forecast £
October to December	
January to March	
April to June	
July to September	

2 Linear regression

KEY TERM

Linear regression: A technique for forecasting costs or sales using the equation of a straight line.

Linear regression analysis involves the prediction of the value of one variable, for example total cost, given the value of another variable, such as the volume of output. It assumes that there is a linear relationship (straight line on a graph) between the two variables.

2.1 The equation of a straight line

To find the straight line on a graph the following **equation** is used:

y = a + bx

Both a and b are constants and represent specific figures:

- a is the point on the graph where the line intersects the y axis
- b represents the gradient of the line (how steep it is)

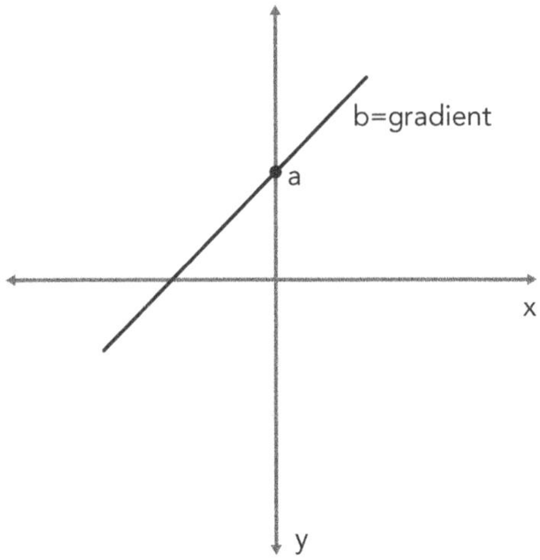

Linear regression can be used for the following purposes:

- Calculation of a future semi-variable cost using historic cost values
- Calculation of a sales trend for use in time series analysis

2.2 Using the equation to forecast semi-variable costs

To forecast the amount of a semi-variable cost at a given production level, the components of the linear regression equation represent the following:

a = Fixed costs

b = Variable cost per unit

y = Total costs

x = Number of units of activity or output

Illustration 4: Linear regression – costs

The linear regression equation for the canteen costs (y) of a business for a month is as follows:

$y = 20{,}000 + 45x$

The variable x represents the number of employees using the canteen.

It is anticipated that the number of employees using the canteen in the next three months will be as follows:

	Number of employees
January	840
February	900
March	875

Required

What are the forecast canteen costs for each period?

Solution

		£
January	20,000 + (45 × 840)	57,800
February	20,000 + (45 × 900)	60,500
March	20,000 + (45 × 875)	59,375

2.3 Using the equation to forecast sales

To forecast future sales volumes or sales revenue using the linear regression equation, the components represent the following:

y = Total sales

x = The time period in the time series (for example, the year number)

b = The increase in sales each time period (for example, each year)

a = A constant value, which has no specific meaning

Illustration 5: Linear Regression – sales

The trend for sales volume for one of Trinket Ltd's products is given:

$y = 16.5 + 0.78x$

Where y is the volume of sales in thousands in any given time period and x is the time period. The first quarter of 20X1 is deemed to be time period 1.

Required

Calculate the forecast trend sales volume for the four quarters of 20X4.

Solution

Step 1

Find the values of x for the four quarters in 20X4.

Q1	20X1	x = 1
Q2	20X1	x = 2
Q3	20X1	x = 3
Q4	20X1	x = 4
Q1	20X2	x = 5

And so on until:

Q1	20X4	x = 13

Step 2

Calculate the trend for each quarter using the linear regression equation.

20X4	x value	y = 16.5 + 0.78x '000 units
Q1	13	26.64
Q2	14	27.42
Q3	15	28.20
Q4	16	28.98

Assessment focus point

You do not need to commit the equation of a straight line to memory. You will be given this equation in the assessment and asked to find values of its components from given information.

Activity 4: Linear regression – costs

The linear regression equation for production costs (y) for a business is:

$y = 63{,}000 + 3.20x$

Where x = the number of production units.

Required

Calculate the production costs if production is expected to be 44,000 units in the next quarter.

The production costs will be £ [ ] .

Activity 5: Linear regression – sales

The linear regression equation for the trend of sales in thousands of units based upon time series analysis of the monthly figures for the last two years is:

$y = 4.8 + 1.2x$

Required

Calculate estimated sales trend for each of the first three months of next year.

Month 1	
Month 2	
Month 3	

2.4 Determining a and b

Assessment focus point

The high–low method (covered in Chapter 1) is a quicker version of the linear cost equation $y = a + bx$. With only two data points, both methods produce the same cost function, because both methods find the straight line that fits those two points.

If you are asked to calculate the values for a and b in the assessment, you are usually given a range of values for x and y. The a and b variables can then be found by using the high–low method.

Activity 6: a and b

A company's selling and distribution costs vary in a linear manner, and can be expressed using the regression equation y = a + bx, where x = number of units sold.

The total delivery costs for 400 units and 4,000 units are £10,000 and £28,000 respectively.

Required

Calculate the values of a and b.

Value of a: ____________

Value of b: ____________

3 Extrapolation and interpolation

All of the techniques discussed in this chapter aim to derive future forecasts from historical data sets, meaning that both interpolation and extrapolation is used to determine what the future values should be.

KEY TERM

Interpolation: Forecasts data within the historical data range.

Extrapolation: Forecasts data outside of the historical data range.

As an organisation's forecasting looks towards the future, and therefore outside of historical data ranges, extrapolation is the most often used method. This is especially true when extending the trend line in linear regression analysis. When extrapolating data, an underlying assumption is therefore made that current trends will continue into the future.

Chapter summary

- Statistical techniques can be used to forecast sales revenue and cost data. These forecasts are then use as the basis of planning resources and budgeting.
- Time series analysis can be used to estimate the trend for future periods and then apply seasonal variations to find the forecast sales or cost figures.
- Linear regression analysis can be used to estimate either semi-variable costs at a particular activity level or future sales volumes at a particular point in time, based on the assumption of a linear trend in sales.
- The linear regression line, $y = a + bx$, will always be given to you in an assessment and you will not need to remember it. However, care should be taken with the variables x and y; x is always the independent variable and y is the dependent variable.
- You may also need to calculate y given values for a, b and x, or a value for x given values for a, b and y. You may also be required to apply the high–low method to calculate values for a and b given two pairs of values for x and y.
- All of these methods of forecasting data use a process of extrapolation outside of the historical data set to predict data in future periods.

Activity answers

Activity 1: Moving averages

Month	Actual £	Three-month moving average £
March	226,504	
April	251,600	238,768
May	238,200	245,800
June	247,600	242,100
July	240,500	250,300
August	262,800	

Activity 2: JB Ltd

(a) 20X6 – cost per kg

20X6	Jan £	Feb £	Mar £
Underlying cost per kg (£)	180	(222 – 12) 210	240
Seasonal variation (£)	(220 – 180) 40	12	–18
Seasonally adjusted cost (£)	220	222	(240 – 18) 222

(b) 20X7 – cost per kg

20X7	Jan £	Feb £	Mar £
Underlying cost per kg (£)	540	570	600
Seasonal variation (£)	40	12	–18
Seasonally adjusted cost (£)	580	582	582

Trend is increasing by £30 per month. There are 12 periods between January 20X6 and January 20X7

Therefore Jan 20X7 trend = 180 + (30 × 12) = 540

(Alternatively, you could start from March and add 10 months: Jan 20X7 trend = 240 + (30 × 10) = 540.)

Activity 3: Time series

(a) [Trend] equals actual costs for a month less seasonal variation for a month.

The impact of the economic cycle is known as a cyclical variation .

(b) Sales trend for 20X7

Period	Sales forecast £
October to December	1,773,000
January to March	1,917,600
April to June	2,363,200
July to September	2,572,400

Trend for 20X6 = Increase in £70,000 per quarter.

Sales forecasts:

October – December 20X6 = (1,900,000 + 70,000) × 90% = £1,773,000

January – March 20X7 = (1,900,000 + 70,000 × 2 quarters) × 94% = £1,917,600

April – June 20X7 = (1,900,000 + 70,000 × 3 quarters) × 112% = £2,363,200

July – September 20X7 = (1,900,000 + 70,000 × 4 quarters) × 118% = £2,572,400

Activity 4: Linear regression – costs

The production costs will be £ 203,800 .

63,000 + 3.2 × 44,000

Activity 5: Linear regression – sales

Month 1	x = 25: y = 4.8 + 1.2(25) = 34.8 ie 34,800 units
Month 2	x = 26: y = 4.8 + 1.2(26) = 36.0 ie 36,000 units
Month 3	x = 27: y = 4.8 + 1.2(27) = 37.2 ie 37,200 units

y = 4.8 + 1.2x

The first two years account for x = 1 to x = 24

Therefore the x values in which we are interested are x = 25, 26, 27

Activity 6: a and b

Value of a: 8,000

Value of b: 5

Units	£
4,000	28,000
(400)	10,000
3,600	18,000

Variable cost per unit (value of b): £18,000/3,600 units = £5.00

@ 4,000 units

	£
Total cost	28,000
Total variable cost (£5 × 4,000)	(20,000)
Fixed cost (value of a)	8,000

Test your learning

1 Given below are the production cost figures for a business for the last year.

Required

Complete the table to calculate a three-month moving average for these figures.

	Actual £	Three-month moving average £
July	397,500	
August	403,800	
September	399,600	
October	405,300	
November	406,100	
December	408,500	
January	407,900	
February	410,400	
March	416,000	
April	413,100	
May	417,500	
June	421,800	

2 Given below are the quarterly sales figures for a business for the last three and a half years.

Required

Complete the table to calculate a four-quarter moving average, the trend using a centred moving average and the seasonal variations.

		Actual £	Four-quarter moving average £	Centred moving average = TREND £	Seasonal variations £
20X5	Quarter 1	383,600			
	Quarter 2	387,600			
	Quarter 3	361,800			
	Quarter 4	328,600			
20X6	Quarter 1	385,900			
	Quarter 2	392,400			
	Quarter 3	352,500			
	Quarter 4	338,800			
20X7	Quarter 1	392,500			
	Quarter 2	410,300			
	Quarter 3	368,900			
	Quarter 4	344,400			
20X8	Quarter 1	398,300			
	Quarter 2	425,600			

3 The total production costs of a business are £15,000 if 1,000 units are produced, and £25,000 if 2,000 units are produced.

The linear regression equation can be used to forecast the production costs where y is the total production cost and x is volume of production:

$y = a + bx$

Required

Calculate a and b, and then the production costs if 1,400 units are produced.

4 The linear regression equation for costs of the stores department of a business is given as follows:

$y = 13{,}000 + 0.8x$

where x is the number of units produced in a period.

The anticipated production levels for the next six months are given below.

Required

Complete the table to calculate the forecast stores department costs for the next six months.

	Production Units	Costs £
January	5,400	
February	5,600	
March	5,700	
April	6,000	
May	5,500	
June	6,100	

5 A time series analysis of sales volumes each quarter for the last three years, 20X6 to 20X8, has revealed that the trend can be estimated by the equation:

$y = 2{,}200 + 45x$

where y is the sales volume and x is the time period.

The seasonal variations for each quarter have been calculated as:

Quarter 1	–200
Quarter 2	+500
Quarter 3	+350
Quarter 4	–650

Required

Use the table below to estimate the sales volume for each quarter of 20X9.

	Value of x	Trend	Seasonal variation	Forecast sales
Quarter 1 20X9				
Quarter 2 20X9				
Quarter 3 20X9				
Quarter 4 20X9				

3 Budgetary control systems

Learning outcomes

1.1	**The budgetary process** **Understand:** • Purposes of a budget • The budget cycle • Sources of data for budgeting • The role of the budget committee • The participatory alternatives: top-down and bottom-up
1.3	**Types of budgets and recommendations for their use** **Understand:** • The features of the following budget methods: incremental, zero-based, rolling • The comparative advantages of each budget method • The circumstances in which each budget method should be recommended
1.5	**Impact of internal and external factors** **Be able to:** • Advise on the reliability of forecasts

Assessment context

It is important to understand the uses of budgetary control and to be prepared to break budgets down into, for example, monthly or weekly periods.

Business context

A core part of any business is to determine its objectives and come up with a plan of how it will achieve these objectives (strategy). Budgeting provides detail of how the business should operate in order to achieve its objectives.

Chapter overview

Budgetary control systems

- **Budget, plans and forecasts**
  - Purposes of budgeting
  - Planning and control cycle

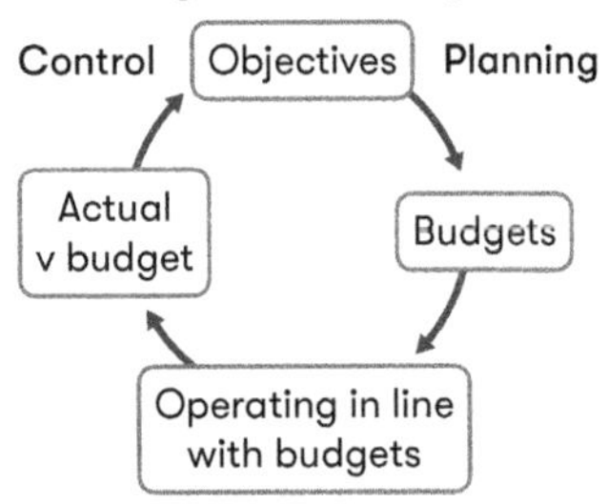

- **Uses of budgetary control**
  - Planning
  - Co-ordinating
  - Authorising
  - Cost control
- **Budget co-ordination**
  - Budget committee
  - Budget accountant
  - Budget manual
  - Budget holders
  - Master budget
- **Methods of budgeting**
  - Incremental
  - Zero based
  - Rolling budgets
- **Behavioural aspects**
  - Motivation
    - Top-down budgeting
    - Bottom-up budgeting
    - Managers should be evaluated only on those items within their control.
    - Level of standard – attainable is the best level to motivate
  - Participation

Introduction

In this chapter we will look at the uses of budgeting, and a high-level view of budget setting. In later chapters we will consider the detail of how budgets are prepared.

1 Budgetary control systems

Budgetary control involves several key activities:

- Setting budgets
- Coordinating departments
- Assigning responsibilities
- Comparing actual results with plans
- Taking action to improve profits

1.1 Cycle of planning and control

The planning and control cycle of a budgetary control system can be summarised by the following diagram.

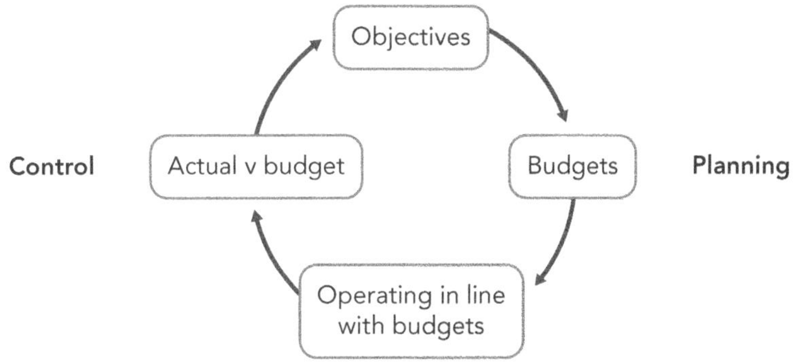

This diagram shows that the strategic objectives of a firm drive the budgets that are set.

Objectives and budgets: Strategic objectives are generated from the strategic plan of the business, which itself considers the long-term direction of the business. Once this plan and the subsequent objectives are set, shorter-term plans are produced in order to meet those objectives. These shorter-term plans are then converted into financial budgets.

Operating in line with budgets and comparing actual results against budget: The company will then aim to operate within these budgets. This is measured by comparison of actual and budgeted results. Action can then be taken to improve performance, and this can feedback into the strategic objectives. This creates a cycle of continuous improvement in the organisation.

Illustration 1: Strategic plans to budgets

A business has a strategic plan to update the technology used on one of its products in order to improve the quality of the product, which has fallen behind that of its competitors.

Required

How would this strategy be reflected in the budget for the coming year?

Solution

Budgets set within the business may include the following:

- A reduced sales price per unit of the existing product if competitor's products are superior
- Reduced sales volumes as customers may source the product from competitors
- Reduced production cost budget as a result of the reduced sales volumes
- High research and development cost budget for the development of the new technology

These budgets would then be monitored throughout the coming year, and any action taken to improve performance. For example, if actual sales revenue was lower than that budgeted, despite the decrease in revenue originally budgeted, then management would need to establish the reasons behind this. It may be that technology has advanced so much over the year that the product is becoming obsolete much more quickly than expected.

This investigation would then feedback into the strategic objectives of the business, which may adapt to a greater emphasis on research and development.

1.2 Purposes of a budget

Budgetary control relies on maintaining an appropriate balance between **planning, co-ordination, authorisation** and **control**. Over-emphasising any one of these areas can create conflict or unintended consequences, so it is important that they work together as part of an integrated system of financial management.

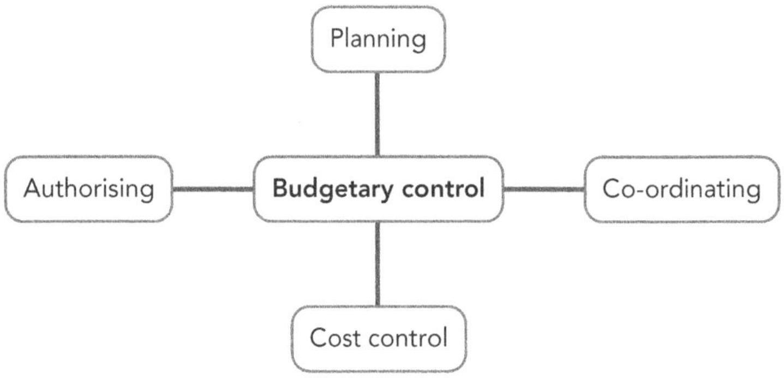

1.2.1 Planning

Planning is a primary purpose of a budget. It allows a business to plan revenue and costs for future periods, and to plan the resources needed to achieve the revenue and cost targets.

It is also important that the budget set is aligned to the overall strategic objectives of the organisation, as explained above.

1.2.2 Co-ordination

The activities of different departments need to be co-ordinated to ensure everyone in an organisation is working towards the same goals. This means, for example, that the purchasing department should base its budget on production requirements and that the production budget should, in turn, be based on sales expectations.

1.2.3 Authorisation

Agreeing a budget with each department's manager gives the responsibility to that manager for meeting the budget, and the authorisation to make decisions within the constraints set in the budget. For example, a manager may choose to invest in new equipment as the cost of doing so would have been agreed within their capital budget for the period.

1.2.4 Control

Budgets act as a benchmark against which actual performance is monitored. Control over actual performance is provided by the comparisons of actual results against the budget plan. Departures from budget can then be investigated and the reasons for any departures can be divided into controllable and uncontrollable factors; and action taken to improve performance.

1.2.5 Potential for conflict

Emphasis on any one of these areas can damage the business elsewhere, so care needs to be taken to ensure that a balance between them is maintained.

For example, over-emphasis on cost control could prevent business growth as new opportunities are not authorised because they are not in the original budget.

Illustration 2: Conflict in budgeting

A sales director may be concerned about controlling the costs within her budget, and so limits the petrol costs of her sales team. This may mean potential customers at greater distances from the company's base are not visited, and the sales growth being sought is thereby restrained. This is an example of cost control conflicting with planning.

Activity 1: Conflict in budgeting

A production manager does not invest in machinery to manufacture a new product as his capital budget limits his authorisation to purchase such equipment. This action risks sales falling if the organisations competitors have made such investment. Sales growth is part of the organisations strategic plan.

Required

Which two purposes of budgeting conflict in this scenario?

	✓
Planning	
Co-ordination	
Authorisation	
Control	

2 Sources of data

Data required for forecasting may be obtained from either an internal source or from an external source. Note that in this Course Book, we will use the terms data and information interchangeably, although technically, data is unprocessed facts and figures, and information is data that has been processed into a useable form.

Primary data is data that is used for the purpose for which it was originally collected. For example, a business designing and running its own customer survey to understand satisfaction levels is using primary data.

Secondary data is data that is being used for a purpose different from the one for which it was originally collected, or data that has been collected by someone else and then reused. For example, a company analysing Office for National Statistics (ONS) datasets is using secondary data.

Note. The distinction between primary and secondary data depends on how the data is **used** not the format or method of collection.

The results of the same customer survey used to illustrate primary data could become secondary data if later used by someone else to answer a different question from the one the survey was designed for.

Likewise, for the ONS itself, the data they collect is primary. It is only when an external user re-uses it for their own purposes that it becomes secondary.

2.1 Internal data

KEY TERM

Internal data: Data collected from inside the business such as internal documents or sources.

These could include: financial accounting records, purchase invoices, payroll information, sales information, inventory records, production information, published accounts and historical records.

Internal data source	Examples of data	How it is used in budgeting
Historical financial records	Previous sales, costs, profits, cash flows	Used to identify trends, set realistic sales targets, estimate future costs, and forecast cash requirements.
Sales reports	Sales volumes, customer orders, pipeline activity	Used to prepare sales budgets, production budgets, staffing needs and purchasing requirements.
Production and operations data	Machine capacity, labour hours, wastage rates, downtime	Helps determine production budgets, resource needs, bottlenecks and cost-efficiency targets.
Purchasing and inventory records	Supplier prices, inventory levels, reorder points	Used to budget for material costs and plan inventory levels for production or retail activity.
Payroll and human resources (HR) information	Staff numbers, wage rates, overtime levels	Used to estimate labour costs, plan recruitment and forecast payroll expenses.
Internal strategic plans	Growth objectives, expansion plans, new products	Used to align the budget with long-term strategy and plan for new investments or market initiatives.
Management accounts	Monthly performance, variances	Helps identify performance issues, adjust assumptions and refine the next budget cycle.

2.2 External data

KEY TERM

External data: Data collected from sources outside the business.

These could include: the internet, market research, interviews, online questionnaires (primary external data), government statistics eg consumer price index (CPI), national statistics, banks, newspapers, trade journals, reference manuals, consultancies, libraries and advice and information bureaux.

External data source	Examples of data	How it is used in budgeting
Office for National Statistics (ONS)	Inflation rates, wage statistics, economic growth forecasts	Used to adjust cost forecasts, plan wage increases, estimate price changes and set realistic growth assumptions.
Industry and market reports	Competitor performance, market demand, sector trends	Helps forecast sales volumes, identify market opportunities and adjust pricing or production strategy.
Supplier and contractor information	Price lists, contract terms, delivery times	Used to budget for materials, negotiate costs and identify potential cost increases.
Government policy and regulation	Tax changes, minimum wage updates, compliance costs	Helps adjust labour budgets, tax estimates, and cost assumptions for regulation-driven changes
Economic forecasts (banks, trade bodies)	Interest rates, exchange rates, economic outlook	Used to forecast financing costs, import/export costs, and investment decisions
Customer feedback and market research	Customer preferences, willingness to pay	Supports sales budgeting, product planning and pricing decisions
Competitor analysis	Competitor pricing, new products, market share	Helps refine pricing strategies and anticipate shifts in market demand
Technology and innovation trends	Automation opportunities, cost-saving technologies	Helps budget for capital investment, efficiency improvements and long-term cost savings.
Trade associations	Industry statistics, benchmark reports, market growth data, sector trends	Helps set realistic sales forecasts, compare performance with industry averages, anticipate sector-wide cost changes and support strategic budgeting decisions

2.3 Limitations of secondary external sources of data

Secondary external sources of data have four limitations:

- Users will be unaware of any limitations in the data
- Data may not be relevant to the needs of the business
- It may be out-of-date
- The geographical area covered may not be appropriate

Activity 2: Sources of information 1

Match the information requirement to its appropriate source.

Information required	Source
Inflation	Market research
Sales demand	National Statistics Office
Competitor wage rates	Bank
Cost of debt	Stock listing in financial press
Share prices	Trade association

Activity 3: Sources of information 2

You are constructing a budget and require the following pieces of information.

Required

Match the information requirement to its appropriate source.

Information required	Source
Population figures for areas in the UK	HM Revenue & Customs
VAT rates	Financial Times newspaper
Possible sales prices achievable in the market place	Office for National Statistics
	Trade journal
	Purchasing manager
	Market research

3 Co-ordination of the setting of budgets

There are many functional budgets that need to be set and many of these are interrelated. Operational planning and budget-setting all takes place over a considerable period of time and often requires the involvement of many managers and staff of all levels. Therefore, it is important that budget setting is co-ordinated if meaningful budgets are to be produced.

3.1 Budget committee

KEY TERM

Budget committee: A committee of senior executives who oversee the preparation of budgets.

The **budget committee** is responsible for co-ordinating, administering, reviewing and authorising all of the individual budgets, and the subsequent master budget. Each function of the business should be represented on the budget committee in order to ensure that there is full communication between all areas of the business.

KEY TERM

Budget accountant: An accountant who helps the budget committee in the preparation of budgets.

Budget manual: A set of instructions as to how the budget is to be prepared.

Budget holder: A member of staff, usually a manager, who is responsible for the budget for a particular area of the business.

Activity 4: Budget committee

Identify whether the following statements are true or false.

Statement	True or false
The budget committee is responsible for coordinating the overall budgeting process across the organisation	▼
The budget committee is responsible for preparing detailed budgets for each department	▼

Picklist

- False
- True

4 Motivation

A budget is used to monitor and evaluate performance, by comparing budgeted and actual performance, in order to drive improved performance across an organisation. Since managers and their staff are accountable for the actual performance compared with the budget, budgets can be used as a tool to motivate.

4.1 Motivation vs control

Often a budget includes elements which are outside the control of a manager responsible for that budget. For example, a budget may contain a depreciation cost. This cost is an accounting adjustment, and the manager cannot take any action to reduce this cost.

It is therefore important to assess the controllability of items within a manager's budget. Items which are unaffected by the control actions of the manager should be ignored when assessing that manager's performance. The manager should therefore only be assessed on items that are within their control. A failure to do so may impact on the manager's motivation for achieving budgetary targets.

4.2 Top-down budgeting

KEY TERM

> **Top-down budgeting:** A budgeting system in which the budget is set and imposed by senior management.

In a top-down budgeting system, senior management are made solely responsible for the setting of the budgets. These budgets are then imposed upon lower-level managers, who are in turn responsible for meeting the targets set within the budgets.

Advantages:

- Senior management will incorporate the strategic plans into all of the budgets.
- The resource (or cost) budgets will all be in harmony with each other.
- Senior management has an overview of all of the resources of the business.
- The budget should be produced more quickly.
- Input from junior management, who may not have the skills or knowledge necessary for the budgeting process, is eliminated.

Disadvantages:

- Managers may become demotivated by the prospect of working to meet targets that someone else has set.
- The managers' detailed knowledge of a particular resource is ignored.
- The initiative of lower-level management may be stifled.
- Managers may resent other departments for being allocated a proportionally greater share of the budget of the organisation, leading to rivalry between departments.

4.3 Bottom-up budgeting

KEY TERM

> **Bottom-up budgeting:** A budgeting system in which operational managers have a degree of input into the budget. It is a form of negotiated budgeting in which operational and senior management negotiate the final budget.

In a bottom-up budgeting system, budgets are prepared by functional managers based upon their detailed knowledge of a particular resource and the costs associated with it. In practice, these budgets are then normally reviewed by the budget committee and a process of negotiation then takes place in which the requirements of senior management are balanced against what managers believe is possible.

Advantages:

- Budgets are based on the detailed working knowledge of managers.
- The motivation of the managers to achieve a budget which they have set should be increased.
- The managers' commitment to the strategic plans of the company should be increased (greater goal congruence).

Disadvantages:

- The outcome of negotiations with the budget committee may cause dissatisfaction.
- The budgeting process will take more time and involve more personnel.
- There may be a lack of co-ordination between resource budgets that must be corrected.
- Managers may be tempted to introduce budgetary slack in order to ensure that when the actual results are compared to the budget, the outcome is favourable.

KEY TERM

> **Goal congruence:** Where the goals of individual functions or departments are consistent with the overall goals and strategy of the organisation.

Budgetary slack: An extra amount of cost built into a budget, by budget holders, in order to make the targets easier to meet.

5 Methods of budgeting

In Chapter 4, we will look more closely at the details of setting up each of the budget types, but in this chapter, we will consider the overall methods that might be adopted to set the resource (ie cost) budgets for each period.

5.1 Incremental budgeting

One of the most common methods of setting the budget for a period is **incremental budgeting**.

KEY TERM

Incremental budgeting: A method of budgeting whereby the previous budget is adjusted for changes in prices and activity levels.

To compile an incremental budget, the budget for the forthcoming period is set by taking the budget for the previous period and adding on a percentage to reflect any increases in prices or changes in activity level since the last budget was set.

Incremental budgeting would be appropriate for those businesses whose costs are not expected to change significantly.

The advantages of incremental budgeting are:

- It is a fairly simple procedure that will not require too much management time.
- The budget is stable and changes are only gradual.
- Co-ordination of budgets is made easier.

However the disadvantages are:

- Any inefficiencies in the original budget are repeated each period.
- There is no incentive to reduce costs or develop new ideas.
- The budgets may become out of date.
- There may be budgetary slack built into the budget, meaning that meeting the budget is easier for managers as this slack remains each year.

Illustration 3: Incremental budgeting

A Rugby Club's advertising budget last year was £100,000. This year, it is anticipated that 20% more advertising will be made and that inflation has been 2%.

The advertising budget for this year would be: £100,000 × 20% = £120,000 – for the additional advertising

£120,000 × 1.02 = £122,400 – for inflation

5.2 Zero-based budgeting (ZBB)

KEY TERM

Zero-based budgeting: A method of budgeting whereby the budget for each cost centre is looked at from scratch for each period.

Every item of expenditure within a zero-based budget must be justified before it can be included. This will often be approached from an activity-based perspective on the basis that, in general, it is activities that incur costs.

For each item of activity that leads to an expense, a decision package is compiled in which the following questions must be asked and answered:

- Is the activity necessary?
- Are there alternatives to this activity (eg outsourcing)?
- What are the costs of the alternative?
- What would happen if the activity were not carried out?
- Is the expense of the activity worth the benefit?

By asking such questions, the activity and its related expenditure can be justified for inclusion in the budget; or a cheaper alternative found.

ZBB is not particularly useful for production departments where costs are largely dependent upon the levels of production and sales. However, it can be a useful technique for service department costs such as the maintenance or personnel departments. It can also be a useful method for factoring in discretionary costs such as advertising and training.

The advantages of ZBB are:

- It challenges existing operations and forces an organisation to examine alternative activities and existing expenditure levels.
- Any budgetary slack in the budget in one period is not automatically reproduced in the budget for the next period.
- Inefficient practices can be removed.
- The cost effectiveness of work practices and procedures is constantly being monitored.

The disadvantages of the method are:

- It is time consuming, complex and costly.
- Short-term benefits are emphasised which may be detrimental in the long term.

5.3 Rolling budgets

KEY TERM

> **Rolling budgets:** Are continually updated in order to project a continual amount of time into the future.

A rolling budget is compiled by adding the next accounting period when the current accounting period is over. By doing this, a set amount of time is always included within the budget.

For example, a budget is set on a quarterly basis for the next year. The January to March budget is set out in detail while the budget for the period from April to December is usually less detailed. At the end of March, the detailed budget is created for April to June, along with an additional outline budget for the quarter from January to March of the following year, which is added in later.

This has the advantage of giving budget holders and the budget committee an opportunity to react to changes in circumstances. It will also enable a more accurate budget to be produced if any items could not be accurately forecast when the original budget was set. However, it also means that budgeting will tend to be done more frequently, and take up more management time.

Rolling budgets are one of the methods of dealing with uncertainty inherent in budgeting.

5.4 Fixed and flexed budgets

KEY TERM

> **Fixed budgets:** Budgets that are set in advance of a period and their purpose is to provide a single achievable target for the entire organisation to work towards. This target level of activity means that all areas of the business will be co-ordinated towards achieving this goal.
>
> **Flexible budgets:** Budgets which, by recognising different cost behaviours, are designed to change as the volume of activity changes.
>
> **Flexed budgets:** Budgets that are prepared at the actual activity level that was achieved during the period, in order to show what the standard costs should have been at that particular activity.

Fixed and flexed budgets are covered in more detail in Chapter 7.

6 External factors affecting cost forecasts

6.1 Market considerations

In addition to considering where the individual products of a business are in their life cycle when producing sales forecasts, it is also important to consider the overall market for a particular product. Is it a new, emerging market for a new product, an established market for a long-standing product, or a declining market for a product which is no longer of great interest to consumers?

For example, no matter how technologically advanced a DVD player is, online streaming and other on-demand TV and movie services mean that demand for DVD players is in sharp decline.

Furthermore, the level of competition in the market for products will affect the demand and price for those products. These considerations need to be taken into account when forecasting sales, and therefore costs of sales.

6.2 Market analysis

The general state of the environment in which the business operates can also impact on its sales and cost forecasts. This can often be efficiently done by carrying out a PEST analysis. Using PEST, the environment is examined under the following categories:

- **P**olitical
- **E**conomic
- **S**ocial
- **T**echnological

6.2.1 Political factors

Political factors may affect a forecast of future sales and, in turn, costs. This might particularly be the case if the business is an exporter, as the political development of other countries can either help or hinder the export drive.

In the UK, legislation such as health and safety and minimum wage requirements, might have an effect on the cost of producing products.

6.2.2 Economic factors

The general economic climate will have a huge effect on the sales and costs of a business. All economies have stages, the four main ones being:

- **Recession** – Employment, consumer confidence and consumer spending start to fall
- **Depression** – Heavy unemployment and low consumer demand are typical in this phase, though very often economies go straight from recession to recovery without experiencing depression.
- **Recovery** – Investment and employment start to regenerate and consumer spending rises
- **Boom** – Consumer spending is rising fast

These factors will affect the future forecast for sales, and therefore costs, of a business. For example, if the trend of sales has been taken from historical data collected in a recovery period followed by a boom period, and a period of recession is about to follow, then the projected trend figure will be completely misleading as sales demand forecasts will be too optimistic.

6.2.3 Social factors

The way in which society operates and changes can have a fundamental effect on the sales of a business, and therefore costs. Factors such as family sizes, lifestyle expectations, divorce rates and average life span can all affect, in the medium to long term, the prospects for sales of a particular product. Other factors such as fashion and health concerns can also impact upon the future sales of a business product.

6.2.4 Technological factors

Technological factors are probably one of the most important factors in the current high-tech consumer market place. Product life cycles can be significantly reduced; advances in technology happen continuously and can potentially make current product lines outdated much quicker. This has a huge impact on potential sales demands.

For example, the launch of PlayStation 3 virtually ended sales of PlayStation2; PS4 had the same effect on its predecessor.

The availability of faster machinery may make it difficult to use current output levels as a basis for forecasting future production output due to increases in production efficiency.

Technological advances can also change the nature of production. The advent of advanced manufacturing technology is changing the cost structure of many firms. Direct labour costs are reducing in significance, while fixed manufacturing costs are increasing. This causes forecasting difficulties because of the resulting changes in cost behaviour patterns.

6.3 Impact on forecast reliability

All these market and environmental factors affect not only the levels of future sales and costs, but also the reliability of the forecasts. Where markets are volatile, technology is rapidly changing, or economic conditions are uncertain, forecasts become less reliable because historical data may no longer be a good predictor of future performance. Forecasters should therefore treat projections with caution and consider carrying out sensitivity or scenario analysis to understand the range of possible outcomes.

Activity 5: Sales forecasting

In which situation is a sales forecast most likely to be unreliable?

	✓
The product is in a stable market with little recent change	
The product is being launched into a new market where demand patterns are uncertain	
There is lots of historical data available, but it may not fully reflect current conditions	
Technology in the market tends to change gradually rather than rapidly	

Activity 6: Using past data

A business uses sales figures from a recent 'boom' period to predict next year's sales.

Required

What is the main risk?

	✓
The forecast may be too low	
The forecast may be too high if the economy is starting to slow down	
The forecast will always be accurate	
The forecast will automatically adjust for changes in society	

Activity 7: Regular reviews

Why should a business review its forecasts regularly?

	✓
The law requires most businesses to update forecasts monthly	
Forecasts rely on facts, so assumptions are not needed	
There may have been changes in technology, competitors or rules	
Reviewing forecasts automatically reduces production costs for the business	

Chapter summary

- Budgets can help management in their planning and control functions, in authorising and co-ordinating departments and functions, and in motivating employees.
- The first stage of the planning process is to determine the strategic plan of the business and identify and choose strategies that will meet that strategic aim.
- Once the strategic plan is in place the operational plans or shorter-term budgets can be set with the aim of meeting those strategic aims.
- The budget manual and budget committee are usually essential elements of control within the budgeting process.
- There are various ways of implementing a budgetary control system, each of which is likely to have behavioural effects on management. These include top-down and bottom-up budgeting.
- Budgets can be set using a variety of different methods including incremental budgeting, zero-based budgeting and rolling budgets.
- External factors such as political, economic, social and technological changes can all affect the reliability of a business's forecasts.

Activity answers

Activity 1: Conflict in budgeting

The correct answers are:

	✓
Planning	✓
Co-ordination	
Authorisation	✓
Control	

New machinery means that new products can be produced, extending the business product range, both growing sales and stopping customers going to competitors. This will enable the business to meet its strategic objective of sales growth. Not authorising spend on new machinery therefore conflicts with the organisation's strategic plans.

Activity 2: Sources of information 1

The correct answers are:

Information required	Source
Inflation	National Statistics Office
Sales demand	Market research
Competitor wage rates	Trade association
Cost of debt	Bank
Share prices	Stock listing in financial press

Activity 3: Sources of information 2

The correct answers are:

Information required	Source
Population figures for areas in the UK	Office for National Statistics
VAT rates	HM Revenue & Customs
Possible sales prices achievable in the market place	Market research

Activity 4: Budget committee

Statement	True or false
The budget committee is responsible for coordinating the overall budgeting process across the organisation	True
The budget committee is responsible for preparing detailed budgets for each department	False

The first statement is true. The budget committee oversees and co-ordinates the entire budgeting process, ensuring consistency and alignment across departments.

The second statement is false. Departments prepare their own budgets and the budget committee reviews, challenges and approves them, but does not prepare them.

Activity 5: Sales forecasting

The correct answer is:

	✓
The product is in a stable market with little recent change	
The product is being launched into a new market where demand patterns are uncertain	✓
There is lots of historical data available, but it may not fully reflect current conditions	
Technology in the market tends to change gradually rather than rapidly	

New or 'emerging' markets lack reliable past data, and customer demand is harder to anticipate. This makes forecasts much less dependable than in markets where behaviour is already understood.

Although stable markets, gradual technological change or the presence of historical data can all introduce some uncertainty, they still provide far more information to base a forecast on than a market with no established demand patterns.

Activity 6: Using past data

The correct answer is:

	✓
The forecast may be too low	
The forecast may be too high if the economy is starting to slow down	✓
The forecast will always be accurate	
The forecast will automatically adjust for changes in society	

If the economy moves from a boom into a slowdown or recession, sales usually fall. Using strong boom-year numbers might give an unrealistically high forecast.

Activity 7: Regular reviews

The correct answer is:

	✓
The law requires most businesses to update forecasts monthly	
Forecasts rely on facts, so assumptions are not needed	
There may have been changes in technology, competitors or rules	✓
Reviewing forecasts automatically reduces production costs for the business	

External factors change all the time. Small changes in competition, technology or regulations can make old forecasts inaccurate, so reviewing them keeps them up to date.

Test your learning

1 **Which of the following is primarily a purpose of a budget?**

	✓
To record past financial performance	
To plan future financial activity and support decision making	
To comply with statutory reporting requirements	
To calculate tax liabilities	

2 **Top-down budgeting can be faster but may reduce manager commitment. True or false?**

	✓
True	
False	

3 **Select the appropriate person to contact in each of the following situations:**

The draft budget is ready for review: [▼]

The managing director needs help in interpreting the draft budget: [▼]

Picklist

- The budget accountant
- The budget committee
- The budget holder

4 **Match the budget method to its advantage:**

Helps eliminate outdated assumptions: [▼]

Saves time where activity is stable: [▼]

Keeps forecasts up-to-date: [▼]

Picklist

- Incremental budget
- Rolling budget
- Zero-based budget

5 **Zero-based budgeting is most suitable when:**

	✓
The organisation has stable operations year-to-year	
The organisation wants to challenge existing spending patterns	
The organisation wants a quick, low effort budget	
Market conditions are highly predictable	

4 Preparing operating budgets

Learning outcomes

1.2	**Types of budgets and recommendations for their use** **Be able to:** • Prepare operating budgets incorporating the following costs and revenue: direct, indirect, fixed, variable, semi-variable, stepped, capital and revenue • Prepare production budgets incorporating the following schedules: production plan – inventory and sales, material usage, material purchases, labour costs, labour hours, plant utilisation
1.4	**Budgeting where resource constraints exist** **Understand:** • The principal budget factor
1.5	**Impact of internal and external factors** **Understand:** • The key planning assumptions used in the budget • The potential threats to budget achievement - market trends, competition, external events • When a budget revision is appropriate **Be able to:** • Calculate the impact of changes to planning assumptions and forecasts • Recalculate budgets accordingly

Assessment context

Budget preparation is usually examined through numerical tasks in this assessment. However, you may also be asked short narrative questions. For example, questions on budgeting terminology such as the principal budget factor, or questions about the impact of internal and external factors.

Business context

A core part of any business is to determine its objectives and come up with a plan of how they will achieve these objectives (strategy). Budgeting provides detail of how the business should operate in order to achieve its objectives.

Chapter overview

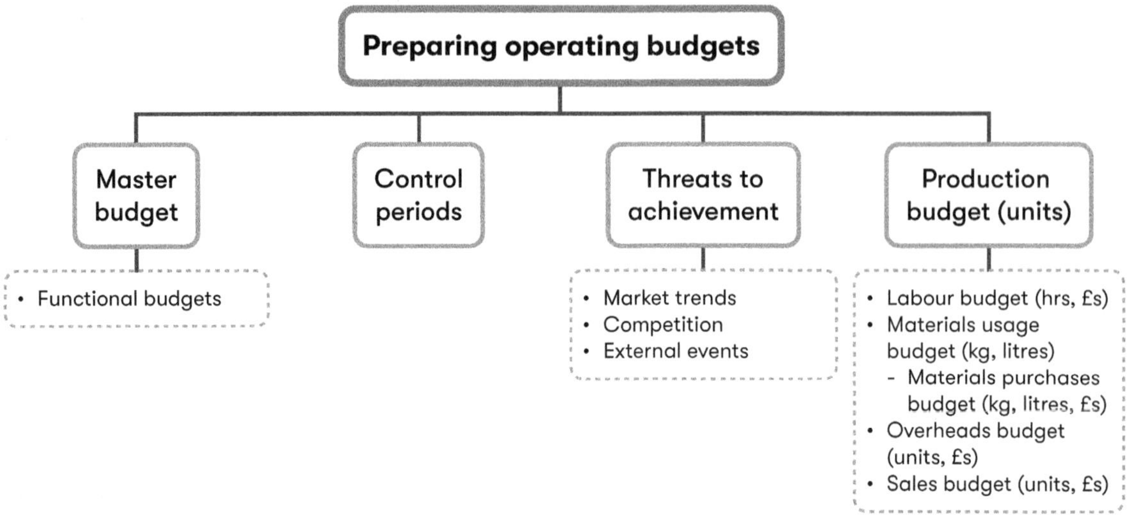

Introduction

In Chapter 2 we looked at the forecasting techniques used to construct budgets. In this chapter we will consider how the managers or heads of different departments prepare specific budgets for their areas. This involves preparation of the physical plans (materials requirements, labour needs, production volumes, etc) on which the financial budgets are built.

1 Preparing sales and resource budgets

KEY TERM

Principal budget factor: This is the resource or condition that restricts the activities of an organisation and therefore limits what can be included in the budget.

The process of preparing sales and resource budgets involves:

(a) Determining the **principal budget factor** (also known as the key budget factor), which is the factor that limits activity for the period. For the purposes of this chapter, it is assumed that the principal budget factor is sales demand – the business would not want to produce more units than it can sell, so sales demand limits production activity, which in turn limits the amount of material and labour required in the period. Other limiting factors are considered in Chapter 11.

(b) Compiling 'physical' plans for each production resource aligned with sales forecasts eg determining quantities of material required, labour hours or machine hours necessary.

(c) Taking these physical plans and creating financial plans, ie converting the physical quantities into costs using standard costs. This gives specific resource budgets.

(d) Combining all resource budgets, sales (income) budgets, capital and cash budgets to create a master budget for the organisation.

An overview of the budget setting process is demonstrated in the diagram below:

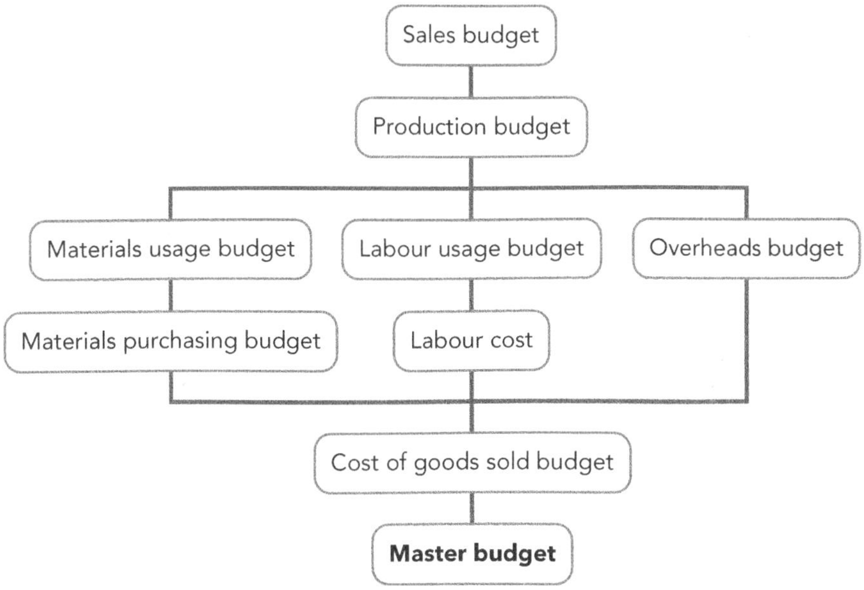

1.1 Sales budget

The sales budget will normally be in two parts. There will be a forecast for the number of units that it is anticipated will be sold, and a **sales revenue budget** calculated by multiplying the estimated unit sales by the expected selling price per unit.

Forecasting the quantity of sales for future periods was considered in Chapter 2. Once the expected quantity of sales has been determined, then the anticipated price to be charged for the products or services can be applied to this forecast. This gives us the budgeted income, usually referred to as the sales revenue budget (in £). From the sales budget, the resource budgets for production can then be prepared.

Illustration 1: Sales budget

Oliver Engineering produces a single product, the Stephenson. The forecast sales quantities for the first five periods of 20X0 are as follows:

Period 1 Units	Period 2 Units	Period 3 Units	Period 4 Units	Period 5 Units
10,000	12,000	15,000	13,000	11,000

The current selling price of the Stephenson is £40, although it is anticipated that there will be a 10% price increase in Period 4.

The sales revenue budget can now be prepared.

	Forecast revenue £
Period 1 (10,000 × £40)	400,000
Period 2 (12,000 × £40)	480,000
Period 3 (15,000 × £40)	600,000
Period 4 (13,000 × £44)	572,000
Period 5 (11,000 × £44)	484,000
	2,536,000

2 Production budget

Once the sales budget has been prepared, the next stage is to prepare the **production budget** in finished goods units. We need to consider whether any **changes in inventory levels** of finished goods are anticipated.

2.1 Changes in finished goods inventory levels

If all goods produced can be sold, and there is to be no change in the levels of finished goods held in inventory, then the amount that must be produced is the same as the quantity of forecast sales.

However, if the level of finished goods held in inventory is to change, then this will affect the quantity that is to be produced.

Once the sales quantity has been determined, then the production quantity will be calculated as:

Sales quantity	X
Less opening inventories of finished goods	(X)
Add closing inventories of finished goods required	X
Production quantity	X

The opening inventories of finished goods are deducted from the sales quantity as we already have these in inventory and therefore do not need to make them.

Illustration 2: Production budget

Oliver Engineering's forecast sales quantities are as follows:

Period 1 Units	Period 2 Units	Period 3 Units	Period 4 Units	Period 5 Units
10,000	12,000	15,000	13,000	11,000

Closing inventories of finished goods are to be enough to cover 25% of sales demand for the next period. The inventory of finished goods at the start of Period 1 is expected to be 3,000 units.

Required

Prepare production budgets for periods 1 to 4.

Solution

The finished goods inventory levels are determined by finding 25% of sales demand for the next period:

			Units
Period 1	12,000 units × 25%	=	3,000
Period 2	15,000 units × 25%	=	3,750
Period 3	13,000 units × 25%	=	3,250
Period 4	11,000 units × 25%	=	2,750

We can now start to forecast the production quantities that are required for the first four periods of next year.

Production budget

	Period 1 Units	Period 2 Units	Period 3 Units	Period 4 Units
Sales quantity	10,000	12,000	15,000	13,000
Less opening inventories	(3,000)	(3,000)	(3,750)	(3,250)
Add closing inventories	3,000	3,750	3,250	2,750
Production quantity	10,000	12,750	14,500	12,500

Activity 1: Production budget

A business has budgeted sales for the following period of 3,500 units. The inventories at the start of the period are 800 units and these are to be reduced to 600 units at the end of the period.

Required

What is the production quantity for the period?

[ ] units

3 Materials usage budget

The next stage is to determine the amount of material required for each unit of the product for the purposes of calculating the **materials usage budget**. This will normally come from the standard cost card.

The standard quantity per unit will then be applied to the number of units to be produced, in order to determine the amount of material required to be used in production in each period.

Illustration 3: Materials usage budget

Continuing the Oliver Engineering example, we know the production quantities required for each of the first four periods of the year. From the standard cost card, each unit of production requires 2 kg of material X.

The materials usage budget can now be prepared:

Materials usage budget

	Period 1	Period 2	Period 3	Period 4
Quantity of production (units)	**10,000**	**12,750**	**14,500**	**12,500**
Materials usage (qty × 2 kg)	20,000 kg	25,500 kg	29,000 kg	25,000 kg

4 Materials purchases budget

Once the materials usage budget has been calculated, it can be used to prepare the **materials purchases budget**.

To determine how many units of material must be purchased, the opening and closing inventories of materials must be considered. This ensures that enough material is available to meet budgeted usage while achieving the desired closing inventory level.

The quantity of purchases will be determined as follows:

Materials usage	X
Less opening inventory of materials	(X)
Add closing inventory of materials	X
Quantity to be purchased	X

Once the required purchase quantity has been calculated, the budgeted purchase price can be applied. This gives the materials purchases budget in monetary terms.

Illustration 4: Materials purchases budget

We know the materials usage budget for Oliver Engineering is as follows:

Materials usage budget

	Period 1	Period 2	Period 3	Period 4
	kg	kg	kg	kg
Materials usage	20,000	25,500	29,000	25,000

It is the policy of the company to hold enough materials to cover 50% of the following period of production. The inventory level at the start of Period 1 is 12,000 kg of material and the materials usage in Period 5 is calculated as 28,000 kg.

First, we must determine the inventory levels of materials required at the end of each period. This has to be enough to cover 50% of production for the next period.

The closing inventories of materials are as follows:

			kg
Period 1	25,500 kg × 50%	=	12,750
Period 2	29,000 kg × 50%	=	14,500
Period 3	25,000 kg × 50%	=	12,500
Period 4	28,000 kg × 50%	=	14,000

Now the materials purchases budget can be prepared, first in units.

Materials purchases budget

	Period 1 kg	Period 2 kg	Period 3 kg	Period 4 kg
Materials usage	20,000	25,500	29,000	25,000
Less opening inventories of materials	(12,000)	(12,750)	(14,500)	(12,500)
Add closing inventories of materials	12,750	14,500	12,500	14,000
Materials to be purchased	20,750	27,250	27,000	26,500

The cost of each kg of material X has been, and will continue to be, £5. Therefore, the value of the materials purchases budget can also be set by taking the quantity to be purchased for each period and applying the unit price. For example, for Period 1, 20,750 kg must be purchased at a cost of £5 per kg = £103,750.

Materials purchases budget

Period 1 £	Period 2 £	Period 3 £	Period 4 £
103,750	136,250	135,000	132,500

Activity 2: Materials purchases budget

A business requires 124,000 litres of a material for production in month 3. The material costs £2.60 per litre and current inventories are 14,000 litres. The business aims to increase its inventory levels by 15% by the end of the month.

Required

What is the budgeted cost of materials for month 3?

£ [ ]

5 Labour usage (hours) budget

Once the production budget has been set, then it is necessary to determine the number of hours of labour that are required for the production level in the **labour usage budget**. This can be determined by applying the standard labour hours per unit to the number of units to be produced as per the production budget.

Illustration 5: Labour usage budget

The standard cost card for the Stephenson, produced by Oliver Engineering, shows that the standard time for production of one unit is 1.5 Grade A labour hour.

Production budget

	Period 1 Units	Period 2 Units	Period 3 Units	Period 4 Units
Quantity of production	10,000	12,750	14,500	12,500

Labour usage budget

	Period 1	Period 2	Period 3	Period 4
Labour hours (qty × 1.5 hours)	15,000 hrs	19,125 hrs	21,750 hrs	18,750 hrs

6 Labour cost budget

Once we know the number of hours to be worked in each period, then the **labour cost budget** (in £) can be set by applying the standard wage rate to the number of hours. However, care must be taken with any overtime hours that are to be worked.

Illustration 6: Labour cost budget

The labour usage budget for Oliver Engineering is as follows:

Labour usage budget

	Period 1	Period 2	Period 3	Period 4
Labour hours	15,000 hrs	19,125 hrs	21,750 hrs	18,750 hrs

The Grade A labour are paid at a rate of £21 per hour but only 19,000 hours can be worked within the normal working hours. Any hours above 19,000 are overtime hours that are paid at time and a third.

We will now produce the figures for the **labour cost budget**:

		£
Period 1	15,000 hours × £21	315,000
Period 2	(19,000 hours × £21) + (125 hours × £28)	402,500
Period 3	(19,000 hours × £21) + (2,750 hours × £28)	476,000
Period 4	18,750 hours × £21	393,750

The labour cost budget will look like this:

Labour cost budget

Period 1 £	Period 2 £	Period 3 £	Period 4 £
315,000	402,500	476,000	393,750

7 Overheads budget

Budgets must also be set for the **overheads** and production facilities related costs, which can include, for example, factory rent and costs of running machinery. Overheads will also include depreciation charges.

As we have already seen in Chapter 1, overheads may be variable, semi-variable, fixed or stepped costs.

Illustration 7: Overheads budget

Oliver Engineering is now trying to produce estimates for its overheads for the first four periods of the year.

The cost of machine power is considered to be a true variable cost and it has been estimated that each Stephenson uses £2.40 of machine power.

The cost of the maintenance department has been estimated at £12,000 if 8,000 units are produced; and £16,000, if 12,000 units are produced.

The factory rent is £8,000 for each period.

The cost of production supervisors depends upon the level of activity within the factory. For an activity level of up to 12,000 units, the production supervisors' costs are £2,000 per period; for up to 14,000 units, this increases to £3,000; and for activity up to 16,000 units, the cost rises to £4,000 per period.

Before we can prepare the overhead budget, we must use the high low method to determine the variable and fixed elements of the maintenance department costs.

Maintenance department costs

	Production level Units	Total cost £
Level 1	8,000	12,000
Level 2	12,000	16,000
Increase	4,000	4,000

Variable cost = £4,000/4,000 units = £1 per unit

At 8,000 units:

	£
Variable cost 8,000 × £1	8,000
Fixed element (bal fig)	4,000
Total cost	12,000

We can produce the budgeted figures for each of these overheads based as usual on the production budget:

Machine power is a variable cost = units × £2.40

Maintenance department is a semi-variable cost = (units × £1) + £4,000

Rent is a fixed cost = £8,000 per period

Supervisors' costs are a stepped cost:	≤ 12,000 units	= £2,000
	≤ 14,000 units	= £3,000
	≤ 16,000 units	= £4,000

Production budget

	Period 1 Units	Period 2 Units	Period 3 Units	Period 4 Units
	10,000	12,750	14,500	12,500

Overhead budget

	Period 1 £	Period 2 £	Period 3 £	Period 4 £
Machine power @ £2.40/unit	24,000	30,600	34,800	30,000
Maintenance department @ £1/unit + £4,000	14,000	16,750	18,500	16,500
Rent – £8,000 per period	8,000	8,000	8,000	8,000
Supervisors' costs	2,000	3,000	4,000	3,000
	48,000	58,350	65,300	57,500

8 Plant utilisation budget

The plant utilisation budget is a plan of the plant and machinery usage required for budgeted production.

Illustration 8: Plant utilisation budget

Company Y manufactures three products: A, B and C.

Product	Units	Machine hours per unit
A	500	1.5
B	380	2
C	750	0.5

There are three machines in the department. Additional machines can be hired if required. Each machine can be used for 500 hours in the month of December.

The machine hours needed to manufacture these in December are calculated as follows:

Product	Units	Hours per unit	Hours required
A	500	1.5	750
B	380	2	760
C	750	0.5	375
Total			1,885

Three machines, each operating for 500 hours = 1,500 machine hours. 1,885 hours are required, therefore **one** extra machine must be hired.

9 How to complete materials and labour working schedules

In the exam, you may be given a production budget and a small set of notes, and then asked to complete the materials and labour working schedules.

This type of task will usually involve turning the information you are given (such as units produced, material per unit, labour time per unit, opening and closing inventories, and pay rates) into a set of completed working schedules. You can follow a standard approach: calculate materials used, apply the inventory formula to find purchases, work out the labour hours required, split them into basic and overtime and then value each line correctly. The example below shows you exactly how to do this step by step.

Illustration 9: Working schedules

Oliver Engineering is preparing resource budgets for Period 1. The following information is available:

Production budget

Item	Units
Opening inventory of finished goods	9,000
Production	150,000
Sub-total	159,000
Sales	145,000
Closing inventory of finished goods	14,000

Notes.

1 **Materials**

Each finished unit requires 0.5 kg of material.

Closing inventory of material is valued at the budgeted purchase price.

2 **Labour**

Each unit takes 6 minutes to produce.

Basic hours available = 11,000 hours

Overtime is paid at 40% above the hourly rate.

Required

(a) Complete the materials working schedule:

Working schedule – materials	Kg	£
Opening inventory	3,200	4,160
Purchases @ £1.30 per kg	(b)	(c)
Used in production	(a)	(d)
Closing inventory	2,800	3,640

(b) Complete the labour working schedule:

Working schedule – labour	Hours	£
Basic time @ £20	(b)	(d)
Overtime	(c)	(e)
Total	(a)	(f)

Solution

(a)

Step 1 Calculate materials used in production

150,000 units × 0.5 kg = **75,000 kg (a)**

Step 2 Use the materials used and the formula to calculate purchases in kg

Materials usage – opening inventory of materials + closing inventory of materials = Purchases

75,000 kg – 3,200 kg + 2,800 kg = **74,600 kg (b)**

Step 3 Value purchases

74,600 kg × £1.30 = **£96,980 (c)**

Step 4 Calculate the value of materials used in production

We used a total of 104,400 kg

We used the opening inventory = £4,160 (3,200 kg)

And we used 75,000 kg - 3,200 kg = 71,800 newly purchased kg (@ £1.30 = £93,340)

Total value = £4,160 + £93,340 = **£97,500 (d)**

The completed working schedule looks like this:

Working schedule – materials	Kg	£
Opening inventory	3,200	4,160
Purchases @ £1.30 per kg	74,600	96,980
Used in production	75,000	97,500
Closing inventory	2,800	3,640

(b)

Step 1 Calculate the total labour hours needed

150,000 units × 6/60 = **15,000 hours (a)**

Step 2 Split between basic hours and overtime hours

Basic hours available = **11,000 hours (b)**

Overtime hours = 15,000 – 11,000 = **4,000 hours (c)**

Step 3 Value labour cost

Basic rate = £20 per hour. Overtime rate = £20 × 140% = £28 per hour

Basic cost = 11,000 × £20 = **£220,000 (d)**

Overtime cost = 4,000 × £28 = **£112,000 (e)**

Total labour cost = **£332,000 (f)**

The completed working schedule looks like this:

Working schedule – labour	Hours	£
Basic time @ £20	11,000	220,000
Overtime	4,000	112,000
Total	15,000	332,000

Activity 3: Working schedules – Treble

Treble Ltd is preparing its resource budgets for December. You have been given the following data:

Production budget – December	Units
Opening inventory of finished goods	3,000
Production	20,000
Sub-total	23,000
Sales	16,000
Closing inventory of finished goods	7,000

Each unit produced requires 0.75 kg of material.

Closing inventory to be valued at budgeted purchase price.

It takes 15 minutes to make each item. 25 staff work 160 basic hours each in the period. Overtime is paid time and a half (50% above basic rate).

Required

Complete the workings schedules below:

Working schedule – materials	Kg	£
Opening inventory	2,000	4,750
Purchases @ £2.50 per kg		
Used in production		
Closing inventory	1,000	2,500

Working schedule – labour	Hours	£
Basic time @ £12 per hour		
Overtime		
Total		

Overhead	Hours	£
Variable @ £2 per hour		
Fixed		7,750
Total		

Variable overhead is recovered on total labour hours.

10 Master budget

Once the budget committee has agreed all the resource budgets with the budget holders, they will then be incorporated into the **master budget**, which normally takes the form of a budgeted statement of profit or loss, budgeted statement of financial position and a cash budget.

11 Control periods within a budget

It is usual for an organisation to complete a budget which covers a full year. However, depending on the needs of the organisation, the budget will also be broken down into smaller time periods (or control periods) such as quarters, months, weeks or even days.

Such a breakdown is required because the comparison of the budgeted figures and the actual performance achieved by a business is used by management to monitor and control. What they find out from this evaluation may lead them to take decisions which may alter their initial plans. Suitable time intervals for making such decisions may correspond to the pattern by which a business generates income and incurs costs.

It is important that the behaviour of costs is correctly reflected in the split of control periods. If a particular cost is likely to vary from month to month, it would not be accurate to split the annual budgeted cost evenly by twelve months.

Illustration 10: Control periods

A business has a seasonal variation that means sales demand is highest in the month of May. It has prepared the following annual budgets for production, direct labour and fixed overheads:

Budgeted units

	Units
Units produced	700,000

Budget in £

Cost of production	£
Direct labour	840,000
Fixed production overhead	600,000

The business monitors its performance on a monthly basis, so is now attempting to break down the annual budget into monthly control periods.

In the month of May it is anticipated that 85,000 units will be produced to meet the sales demand for the month.

The business has also provided the following information:

- 7,500 direct labour hours are available
- Each unit requires 6 minutes of direct labour time
- The direct labour rate is £20 per hour and an overtime premium is paid at half of basic rate
- Fixed production overheads are incurred at a steady monthly rate across the year

Required

Calculate the direct labour and fixed overhead budgets for May.

Solution

Fixed overheads budget

We are able to split the fixed overheads evenly over the 12 months for the year, as they are incurred at a steady monthly rate across the year.

The fixed overheads budget for May is therefore:

£600,000 / 12 months = £50,000

Direct labour cost budget

If the labour cost was split evenly over the year, the labour cost budget would be:

£840,000 / 12 = £70,000

This would not be an accurate figure – because of the seasonal variation, more production activity takes place in May. It is therefore logical to assume that more of the direct labour cost would be incurred in May than in other months of the year.

To accurately calculate May's direct labour cost, we need to take into account the standard time per unit, rate per hour and the overtime rate.

There are 7,500 labour hours available, but this won't be enough to meet total production.

Overtime hours are therefore:

	Hours
Direct labour hours available	7,500
Labour hours required for production (6 mins × 85,000 units) / 60	8,500
Overtime required	1,000

The direct labour budget is therefore:

	£
Standard labour hours (7,500 hrs × £20)	150,000
Overtime hours (1,000 hrs × £20 × 1.5)	30,000
Total labour budget	180,000

The logic used to break down the labour cost budget can be used for other resource budgets where there is a shortage in the month, for example materials or machine capacity.

Activity 4: Control periods

A business has provided the following information:

- Each unit requires 9 minutes of direct labour time costing £17.00 per hour
- Each unit is made from 1.5 kg of material costing £2.50 per kg
- 75,000 kg of material is available within July. Additional material can be purchased at a cost of £3.00 per kg
- Variable production overhead relates to labour hours
- Fixed production overheads are incurred at a steady monthly rate across the year

Budgeted units

	Annual	July
Units sold	530,000	48,000
Units produced	550,000	52,000

Required

Calculate the sales revenue budget and the production cost budget for July using the information provided.

Budget in £

	Annual £	July £
Sales revenue (W1)	5,830,000	
Cost of production		
Materials used (W2)	2,062,500	
Direct labour (W3)	1,402,500	
Variable production overhead (W4)	330,000	
Fixed production overhead (W5)	480,000	
Total production cost	4,275,000	

12 Planning and agreeing draft budgets

In order to achieve budget integrity, the following steps should be taken.

- Draft budgets should be planned and then agreed with all parties. In Chapter 3, we considered the budget setting process, with budgets being reworked perhaps a number of times. The final version should be agreed by both the senior management and the manager of the department concerned.
- The managers of the department should check and reconcile figures in the budget to ensure their accuracy and consistency. This may require revisions to the budget throughout the period to which it refers. Revisions may be required if actual results highlight an unrealistic plan or if the underlying forecasts or planning assumptions have to change because of external factors. The budgets must then be recalculated.

Forecasts and budgets should be updated when necessary to take account of new relevant information, such as changes in inflation or increases/decreases in predicted sales demand. Regular reforecasting and re-budgeting can help to mitigate the inherent risks relating to the assumptions made when budgeting.

Once the draft budgets have been agreed, the budget should be submitted for approval.

12.1 Threats to budget achievement

Market trends

Market trends refer to general movements in customer behaviour, demand patterns or industry direction that can influence whether a budget remains realistic. Trends such as increasing demand, declining interest in a product, shifts towards substitute products, or seasonal patterns can all affect forecast accuracy.

When market trends point to rising demand, budgets may need to be revised to include higher production volumes, additional labour demand or increased materials purchases. Conversely, if demand is weakening, the business may need to scale back production, reduce overtime or revise revenue assumptions. Monitoring market trends ensures that budgets remain in line with the current environment.

Competitive pressures

Competitive pressures arise when rival businesses change their pricing, introduce new products, enhance quality or take actions that affect market share.

If competitors lower prices, an organisation may need to revise its own selling price assumptions or prepare for reduced sales volume. When a new competitor enters the market or an existing one expands capacity, sales forecasts may need to be adjusted downward, affecting production, materials usage and labour budgets. Alternatively, if a competitor exits the market, an organisation may revise its budgets upwards to reflect the opportunity for increased demand.

Factoring in competitive pressures ensures budgets remain realistic.

External events

External events include factors outside the organisation's control, such as changes in regulation, economic conditions, supply chain disruptions, inflation, interest rates or unexpected events like extreme weather or geopolitical developments. These events can directly influence costs (eg higher material prices), sales (eg reduced consumer spending) or operational capacity (eg transport delays or staff shortages).

When external events alter the assumptions on which the budget was built, the organisation must reassess the reliability of its forecasts and update the budget accordingly.

Recognising the impact of external events helps management maintain budgets that reflect current risk and operating conditions.

13 Uncertainty in the budget setting process

The very nature of forecasting future costs, revenues and sales volumes means that there is uncertainty inherent in the budgeting process.

13.1 Methods of dealing with uncertainty

- Planning models – enable management to highlight the most critical variables
- Regular re-forecasting – using data collected over time to enhance forecasting models, for example through time series models
- Re-budgeting – updating budgets periodically and when new information comes to light (see section below)
- Rolling budgets (covered in Chapter 3)

Chapter summary

- The sales budget will normally be the first budget to be prepared, if it is the principal budget factor, showing the anticipated sales in both units and value.
- From the sales budget, the production budget will be prepared, taking into account planned changes in inventory levels for finished goods.
- The production budget is then used to prepare the materials and labour budgets in terms of both units and value.
- The materials usage budget is based upon the production for the period.
- The materials purchases budget is based upon the materials usage budget but with adjustments for planned changes in inventories of materials – once the quantities of purchases are known, then they can be valued by applying the anticipated purchase price per unit.
- The labour usage budget is based upon the production budget and the standard hours for each unit. Once the hours have been determined, the labour cost budget can be calculated using the hourly rates of labour, taking account of any overtime hours required.
- Budgets will also be set for overheads – in order to try to estimate the expected overhead or expense, the behaviour of the cost must be taken into account: variable, semi-variable, fixed or stepped.
- A master budget is completed by adding a budgeted statement of financial position and a cash budget to the budgeted operating statement.
- Budgets are broken down into smaller time periods to enable monitoring of performance and subsequent actions to take place on a timely basis. The intervals of the budget may correspond to the income and expenditure pattern of the organisation.
- Uncertainty exists when budgeting. Methods to address this include planning models, regular re-forecasting, re-budgeting and the use of rolling budgets.
- Budgets can be revised to reflect changing circumstances.

Activity answers

Activity 1: Production budget

3,300 units

Working

	Units
Sales	3,500
Less opening inventories of finished goods	(800)
Add closing inventories of finished goods	600
Production quantity	3,300

Activity 2: Materials purchases budget

£ 327,860

	Litres
Materials usage	124,000
Less opening inventory	(14,000)
Add closing inventory (14,000 × 1.15)	16,100
Materials purchases	126,100

Cost of purchases 126,100 × £2.60 = £327,860

Activity 3: Working schedules – Treble

Working schedule – materials	Kg	£
Opening inventory	2,000	4,750
Purchases @ £2.50 per kg	14,000	35,000
Used in production	15,000	37,500
Closing inventory	1,000	2,500

Working schedule – labour	Hours	£
Basic time @ £12 per hour	4,000	48,000
Overtime	1,000	18,000
Total	5,000	66,000

Overhead	Hours	£
Variable @ £2 per hour	5,000	10,000
Fixed		7,750
Total		17,750

Variable overhead is recovered on total labour hours.

Activity 4: Control periods

Budget in £

	Annual £	July £
Sales revenue (W1)	5,830,000	528,000
Cost of production		
Materials used (W2)	2,062,500	196,500
Direct labour (W3)	1,402,500	132,600
Variable production overhead (W4)	330,000	31,200
Fixed production overhead (W5)	480,000	40,000
Total production cost	4,275,000	400,300

Workings

1 £5,830,000 / 530,000 units × 48,000 units = £528,000

	kg
Material required (52,000 units × 1.5 kg)	78,000
Material available	(75,000)
Additional material required	3,000

	£
Basic material (75,000 kg × £2.50)	187,500
Additional material (3,000 kg × £3.00)	9,000
Total labour cost	196,500

2 £1,402,500 / 550,000 units × 52,000 units = £132,600 Or (52,000 × 9 mins) / 60 × £17 = £132,600

3 £330,000 / 550,000 units × 52,000 units = £31,200 Or (52,000 × 9 mins) / 60 × £4 – £31,200

4 £480,000 / 12 = £40,000

Test your learning

1 A company forecasts sales of 12,000 units for quarter 2.

Opening finished goods inventory = 2,500 units.

Closing inventory must cover 20% of next quarter's sales.

Quarter 3's sales are forecast to be 15,000 units.

Required

What is the production budget for quarter 2?

[ ] units

2 **Complete the following production budget for the product of an organisation. Closing inventory is to be 30% of the next period's sales. Sales in Period 4 will be 4,200 units.**

	Period 1 Units	Period 2 Units	Period 3 Units
Opening inventory	1,140		
Production (bal fig)			
Units required			
Sales	3,800	4,000	4,500
Closing inventory			
Units required			

3 Budgeted sales of Product P for the next quarter are 42,000 units.

Finished goods in inventory at the start of the quarter are 7,000 units and closing inventory will be 8,334.

The standard cost card indicates that each unit should take 3.5 labour hours.

Required

The production budget for the quarter is [ ] units.

The labour usage budget for the quarter is [ ] hours.

4 The production budget is as follows:

Quarter 2	Quarter 3
16,020 units	17,850 units

The details of overheads are:

Light and heat – this is estimated at a rate of £4.80 per unit of production in each quarter.

Maintenance department – previous periods have shown that at a production level of 13,000 units, the maintenance department costs totalled £68,500; and at a production level of 17,000 units, the costs totalled £86,500.

Leased machinery – some of the machinery is leased, and for production levels up to 17,000 units, the leasing cost is £15,600 per quarter. However, if production exceeds this level, then a further machine must be leased at a quarterly cost of £4,800.

Rent and rates – the rent and rates are £84,000 per annum.

Required

Complete the following:

Overhead cost	Quarter 2 £	Quarter 3 £
Light and heat		
Maintenance		
Leasing		
Rent and rates		

5 Sales of a product in the next four-week period are expected to be 280 units. At the beginning of the period, 30 units are held in inventory, although the budgeted closing inventory is expected to be five units.

Each unit of the product requires two hours of Grade O labour and three hours of Grade R labour. Grade O labour is paid £15 per hour, whereas Grade R labour (16 workers) receives a guaranteed weekly wage of £280.

A unit of the product requires 7 kg of material. The expected price per kg of the material is £50.

Required

For the following four-week period, what is the:

Production budget? [ ] units

Materials usage budget? [ ] kg costing £ [ ]

Labour cost budget? £ [ ]

6 Two products, J and K, are produced from the same material. The data below relates to Period 1.

(a)	Budgeted production	J	450 units
		K	710 units
(b)	Material requirements per unit	J	25 kg
		K	40 kg
(c)	Opening inventory of material	40,000 kg	
(d)	Closing inventory of material	27,359 kg	

Required

The purchases budget (in kg) for Period 1 is [ ] kg

7 Two products, X and Y, are manufactured. Budgeted production levels in Period 7 are 420 units of X, and 590 units of Y.

Each X requires five labour hours; each Y, four labour hours.

There are 25 production workers, each of whom works a 35-hour week. There are five weeks in each period.

The rate of pay per hour for production employees is £10. Any overtime is paid at 125% of basic rate.

Required

What are the budgeted labour hours to be worked during Period 7, including any overtime? What is the cost of labour budget for Period 7?

Budgeted labour hours: [ ] hours

Cost of labour budget for Period 7: £ [ ]

5 Preparing cash budgets

Learning outcomes

1.2	**Types of budgets and recommendations for their use** **Be able to:** • Prepare cash flow forecasts/budgets allowing for: time lags, changes in receivables, changes in payables, changes in inventory, prompt payment discounts, irrecoverable debts, exchange rate movements, taxation, non-current assets, loans, profit distributions, inflation.

Assessment context

Preparation of cash budgets is likely to be tested in the assessment.

Business context

Management of cash resources is very important for any business; accurate cash forecasting is part of this.

Chapter overview

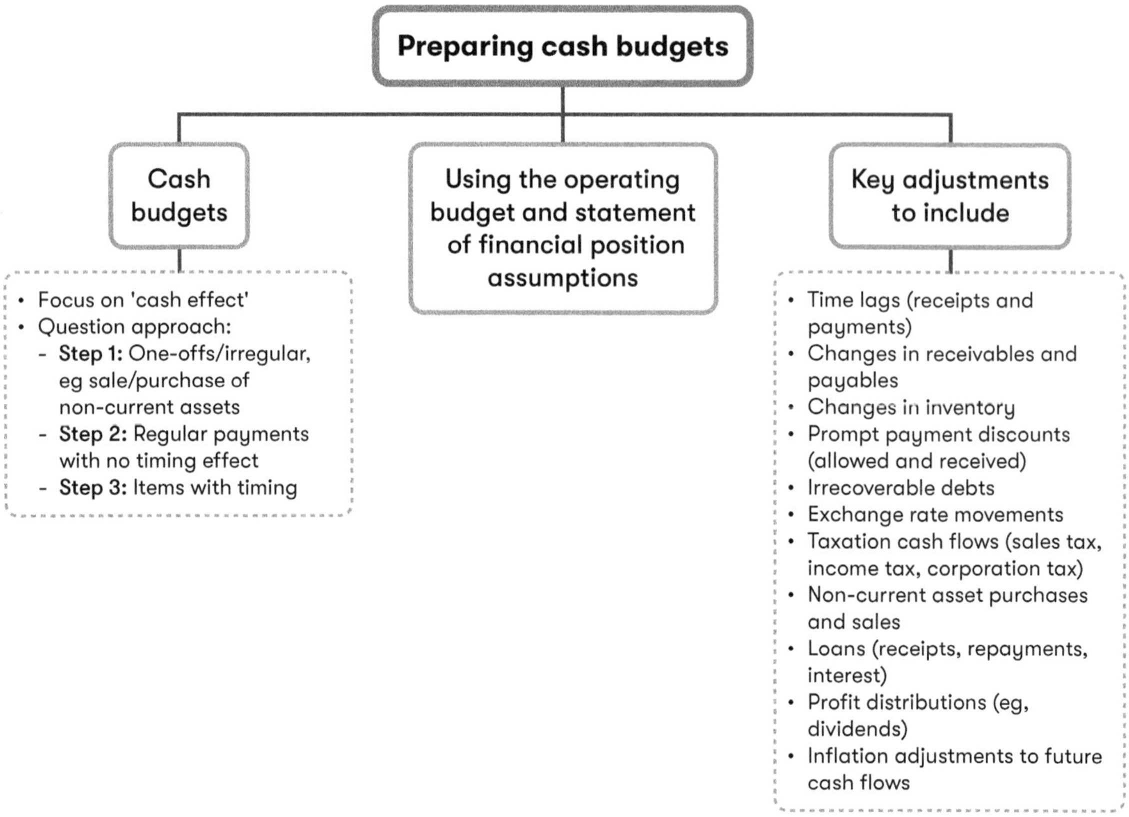

Introduction

Cash is as important to the survival of a business as profit. Management therefore need to plan and control cash flows, not just income and expenditure. This is done by preparing a **cash budget**.

Cash budgets can give management an indication of any cash surpluses or shortages expected.

Management can then make decisions on financing any expected cash shortage or investing any cash surpluses.

1 Cash budgets

Cash budgets consider the cash element of business transactions, whereas the income statement (profit or loss account down to operating profit) records all transactions on an accruals basis, regardless of when cash is received or paid.

KEY TERM

> **Cash budgets:** Methods of determining the expected net cash flow for a future period, and the expected cash balance at the end of that future period.

1.1 Presentation of a cash budget

The net cash flow is determined by deducting the payments from the receipts. This net movement is applied to the opening cash balance in order to find the anticipated closing balance.

XYZ Ltd: Cash budget for the three months ended 31 March 20X7

	Jan	Feb	Mar
Cash receipts			
Sales receipts	X	X	X
Sale of non-current assets	X		
Loan receipt		X	
	X	**X**	**X**
Cash payments			
Purchase payments	X	X	X
Wages	X	X	X
Overheads	X	X	X
Purchase of non-current assets		X	
Loan repayments	X	X	X
Dividend			X
	X	**X**	**X**
Net cash flow	**X**	**(X)**	**X**
Opening balance	X	X	(X)
Closing balance	**X**	**(X)**	**X**

Assessment focus point

If you are asked to prepare a cash flow forecast, you will be given a proforma to use, similar to the one above.

2 Forecasting cash receipts and cash payments

In this section, we look at two methods of deriving receipts and payments from the budgeted operating statement (operating budget):

(a) Using the operating budget and changes in statement of financial position balances

(b) Using the operating budget and allowing for time lags

2.1 Using the operating budget and statement of financial position assumptions

Sales recorded in a month will not usually equal cash received for that month, because most businesses will have a mixture of cash sales and sales on credit.

Therefore, some cash will not be received until after the month that the sale occurred.

If business sales include credit sales, the cash received in a month is calculated by adjusting the sales figure by the change in the receivables balance.

Illustration 1: Cash budget 1

The cash received and cash paid for January can be worked out from the operating budget and assumptions on the change in the receivables balance as follows:

	£
Receivables b/fwd per statement of financial position	450
Sales (on credit) per operating budget	1,200
Receivables c/fwd per statement of financial position	(500)
Cash received	1,150

This can also be expressed as:

	£
Sales (on credit) per operating budget	1,200
Increase in receivables – from start to end of month per statement of financial position	(50)
Cash received	1,150

The same method applies to cash paid.

Purchase payments

	£
Payables b/fwd per statement of financial position	340
Purchases (on credit) per operating budget	760
Payables c/fwd per statement of financial position	(320)
Cash paid	780

This can also be expressed as:

	£
Purchases (on credit) per operating budget	760
Decrease in payables – from start to end of month per statement of financial position	20
Cash paid	780

An alternative approach is to calculate the cash effect due to changes in receivables, payables and inventory balances.

An increase in these balances will affect cash flows of the business as follows:

- If receivables balances increase, less cash is received into the business generating a lower cash inflow
- If payables balances increase, less cash has been paid out of the business generating a lower cash outflow
- If inventory balances increase, the business has not yet sold these goods and has therefore not yet received the revenue from these sales, generating a lower cash inflow

Assessment focus point

This method is a common way in which cash budgets are tested. Make sure you work through the following illustration and activity to fully prepare yourself for the assessment.

Illustration 2: Cash budget 2

Terra Ltd is currently preparing its cash budget for the forthcoming period. Its operating budget is as follows:

Operating budget

	£	£
Sales revenue		22,000
Expenditure		
Materials	5,600	
Labour	9,500	
Other costs	3,800	18,900
Operating profit		3,100

Terra has made the following statement of financial position assumptions:

- Receivables will increase by £1,100
- Material payables will decrease by £800
- Labour costs are paid in the period in which they are incurred
- Other payables will increase by £350

Required

What is the expected cash flow for Terra for the period?

Solution

To answer this, we need to understand the impact that the change of balances will have on the cash received or paid out by the business.

Receivables

Since receivables have increased, Terra has not collected £1,100 of cash from its customers. This makes the cash inflow from sales revenue lower than the sales revenue on the operating budget as follows:

	£
Sales revenue per operating budget	22,000
Cash not collected from customers	(1,100)
Total cash inflow	20,900

Materials

Since materials payables have decreased, Terra has paid £800 more cash over to their suppliers. This makes the cash outflow from materials higher than the materials cost on the operating budget as follows:

	£
Materials cost per operating statement	5,600
Additional cash paid to suppliers	800
Total cash outflow	6,400

Labour

Labour is paid in the same month that the cost is incurred. Since no balances are held for labour, this means that the cash outflow from labour will be the same as the cost stated on the operating statement. The cash outflow is therefore £9,500.

Other costs

Since other payables has increased by £350, Terra has not yet paid those suppliers. This makes the cash outflow lower than the value of other costs on the operating statement as follows:

	£
Other costs per operating statement	3,800
Cash not yet paid to suppliers	(350)
Total cash outflow	3,450

Using these figures, we can now put together the cash budget:

Cash budget	£	£
Sales receipts		20,900
Payments		
Materials	6,400	
Labour	9,500	
Other costs	3,450	19,350
Cash flow		1,550

Activity 1: Cash budget – Aqua Ltd

Aqua Ltd is trying to forecast its cash position. Its operating budget is as follows:

Operating budget	£	£
Sales revenue		43,250
Expenditure		
Materials	12,500	
Labour	15,000	
Other costs	4,250	31,750
Operating profit		11,500

Aqua has made the following statement of financial position assumptions:

- Receivables will decrease by £2,300
- Material payables will increase by £1,400
- Labour costs are paid in the period in which they are incurred
- Other payables will decrease by £900

Required

Prepare the cash flow forecast from the operating budget and statement of financial position assumptions. Enter receipts and payments as positive figures.

Show a net cash outflow as a negative, eg –500.

Cash budget	£	£
Sales receipts		
Payments		
Materials		
Labour		
Other costs		
Cash flow		

2.2 Using the operating budget and allowing for time lags

KEY TERM

Lagged receipt: If cash is received at a later time to when the sale was recorded, there is a lagged receipt.

Lagged payment: If cash is paid at a later time to the recording of the purchase or expense, it is a lagged payment.

Irrecoverable debt: Invoiced amounts that it is considered will never be received in cash.

From the total budget sales a certain amount will be cash sales, and the remainder will be credit sales. Cash received for cash sales are received at the time of sale.

For credit sales, the receipt of payment occurs at a time after the sale; there is a **time lag** between the sale and receipt of payment. We need to account for lagged payments and receipts, therefore assumptions are made about the time lag between the sales/purchases and cash received/paid. Unfortunately, sometimes a customer does not pay, and has no prospect of being able to. This debt is known as an irrecoverable debt and should be excluded from cash flow forecasts.

Illustration 3: Time lags and irrecoverable debts

The fuel division of SC Fuel and Glass is preparing its quarterly cash flow forecast for the three months of October, November and December.

The sales of the fuel division for these three months are expected to be as follows:

October	£680,000
November	£700,000
December	£750,000

Of these sales, 20% are cash sales and the remainder are sales on credit. Experience has shown that, on average, the receivables for credit sales pay the money according to the following pattern:

The month after sale	20%
Two months after sale	50%
Three months after sale	25%
Irrecoverable debts	5%

Therefore, the cash for October credit sales will be received in November, December and January. If we are preparing the cash flow forecast for the period from October to December, then some of the cash inflows will be from credit sales in earlier months. Therefore, you also require information about the credit sales for these earlier months.

The total sales in July to September for the fuel division (again 20% of these were cash sales) are:

July	£600,000
August	£560,000
September	£620,000

We can now start to piece together the information required to prepare the cash budget from sales for October to December:

Cash budget – October to December

	October £	November £	December £
Cash receipts:			
Cash sales (20% of month sales)	136,000	140,000	150,000

Now we need to deal with sales on credit, which are more complicated and will require a working:

Workings – Cash from credit sales

	October £	November £	December £
July sales			
(80% × 600,000 × 25%)	120,000		
August sales			
(80% × 560,000 × 50%)	224,000		
(80% × 560,000 × 25%)		112,000	
September sales			
(80% × 620,000 × 20%)	99,200		
(80% × 620,000 × 50%)		248,000	
(80% × 620,000 × 25%)			124,000
October sales			
(80% × 680,000 × 20%)		108,800	
(80% × 680,000 × 50%)			272,000
November sales			
(80% × 700,000 × 20%)			112,000
Cash from credit sales	443,200	468,800	508,000

Cash budget – October to December

	October £	November £	December £
Cash receipts:			
Cash sales	136,000	140,000	150,000
Cash from credit sales	443,200	468,800	508,000

Activity 2: Cash budget – Kookaburra

Kookaburra has prepared the following budgeted data.

	March £	April £	May £	June £	July £
Sales	4,250	4,600	5,000	5,350	5,400
Purchases	1,200	1,300	1,500	1,600	1,750
Wages	800	800	850	850	850
Other overheads	650	650	675	675	675
Capital expenditure			3,000	1,000	

Additional information:

- 30% sales are for cash. The remaining sales are on credit and customers pay one month later.
- Purchases are paid for after one month.
- Wages and other overheads are paid in the current month. Other overheads include £400 of depreciation each month.

Required

Prepare a monthly cash flow forecast for Quarter 2.

Monthly cash flow forecast for Quarter 2

	April £	May £	June £	Total Qtr 2 £
Receipts				
Cash sales				
Credit sales				
Total receipts				
Payments				
Purchases				
Wages				
Other overheads				
Capital expenditure	–			
Total payments				
Net cash				
Opening cash balance	750			
Closing cash balance				

2.3 Prompt payment discount

If the business offers prompt payment discounts (also known as settlement discounts) to customers who pay early, the cash budget must reflect the reduced amount of cash received. Customers who take the discount will pay sooner, but they will only pay the invoice amount minus the discount. For example, if a 3% discount is offered on credit sales payable in the month of sale, the cash receipt from those customers will be 97% of the invoiced amount.

Similarly, if the business receives a prompt payment discount from its suppliers for paying early, the cash budget must show the lower cash payment. In this case, the business settles the liability earlier, but pays less than the full invoice amount because the supplier's discount reduces the cash outflow. Therefore, both discounts allowed (on sales) and discounts received (on purchases) must be incorporated into the forecast to ensure that cash receipts and payments reflect the actual cash expected to flow in and out.

Activity 3: Effect of discounts on receipts

George has forecast sales as follows: December £10,000; January £10,000; February £12,000; March £15,000.

Sales are partly for cash and partly on credit, as follows:

- 40% for cash (no discount)
- 60% on credit

For credit sales, a 5% discount is offered for payment within the month of sale and 25% of credit customers take up this option. The remaining credit customers pay in the month after sale.

Required

What are the cash receipts for each of January to March?

	January £	February £	March £
Cash sales			
Credit sales			
Pay in same month			
Pay in next month		4,500	5,400
Cash received			

2.4 Exchange rate movements

Where a business expects to receive or make payments in a foreign currency, exchange rate movements can affect the **actual amount of cash** received or paid once the transaction is converted into the home currency. This is known as **transaction risk**. If the home currency becomes stronger before an overseas customer pays, the same foreign-currency receipt will convert into **less** cash, reducing the inflow. Conversely, if the home currency weakens before the business pays a foreign-currency supplier, the payment will cost **more** in the home currency, increasing the cash outflow. For example, a UK business expecting to receive €1,000 when the exchange rate is €2:£1 would expect £500, but if the pound strengthens to €2.50:£1 by the time the cash is received, the business will only receive £400. For this reason, all foreign-currency receipts and payments must be converted at the **expected rate** for the month in which the cash flow occurs and included in the cash budget at that sterling amount.

Activity 4: Exchange rate movements

A UK business is due to receive €50,000 from a European customer in one month. The current exchange rate is €1.25:£1, but the business expects the pound to strengthen by 10% by the time the cash is received.

Required

What is the expected sterling cash receipt to include in the cash budget (rounded to the nearest whole thousand)?

£ ____________

2.5 Taxation

Taxation can create significant cash outflows for a business, and these must be included in the cash budget in the period they are expected to be paid. Common tax-related cash flows include **corporation tax, sales tax payments or refunds**, and **income tax payments** for employees. These items do not appear in the operating profit figure, but they can have a major impact on the cash position. Only the **actual cash amount** payable should be included. For example, corporation tax is usually paid some months after the end of the financial year, while sales tax is paid or refunded quarterly. These payments reduce the closing cash balance and must be planned for in the relevant month to ensure the business has enough cash available.

2.6 Non-current assets and cash receipts or payments

When making capital purchases, the cash outflow often matches the amount shown as an addition in the statement of financial position. Alternatively, the payment may be made in instalments.

However, on the sale of an asset, the profit (or loss) that is recorded in the statement of profit or loss is not a cash amount. For the purposes of the cash budget, the proceeds on sale must be calculated. This can be done using the profit (or loss), provided the carrying amount of the asset in the books of the business is known (ie in the statement of financial position) at the date of sale.

Cash inflows on sale of non-current assets = proceeds

Proceeds =	Carrying amount (ie net book value)
	plus
	Profit on sale (or minus loss)

Activity 5: Sale of a non-current asset

AC Ltd sold machinery in February for a profit of £5,000. The carrying amount in February was £20,000.

Required

What were the proceeds from the sale of the machinery?

The sales proceeds were £ ____________

2.7 Loans

Loans can create both cash inflows and cash outflows, and both must be shown in the cash budget in the period they occur. When a business **takes out a new loan**, the amount borrowed is recorded as a **cash receipt**, increasing the cash balance for that month. However, loans also lead to future **cash payments** in the form of regular repayments of capital and, in some cases, interest. These repayments reduce cash in the periods in which they are due. For example, if a business receives a £50,000 loan in August and then makes monthly repayments of £1,000 from the end of that month, the cash budget must show a **£50,000 receipt in August** and **£1,000 payments in each repayment month**. Only the actual cash movements are included, not the remaining loan balance.

2.8 Profit distributions

Profit distributions represent amounts paid out of the business's profits to its owners, such as dividends to shareholders or drawings in a sole trader or partnership. These distributions are cash outflows and must be included in the cash budget in the period in which they are actually paid. They do not affect the operating profit figure, but they do reduce the closing cash balance. For example, if a company declares a dividend of 10p per share and has 100,000 shares in issue, the cash budget must include a payment of £10,000 in the month the dividend is due to be paid. Only the cash element is included, and dividends are always shown as a separate payment line in the cash-flow forecast.

Formula to learn

Dividend payment = Number of shares × Dividend per share

Activity 6: Profit distributions

Company B has issued 150,000 ordinary shares. The company plans to pay a dividend of 8p per share on 30 September.

Required

What is the cash payment that should be included in the cash budget for this dividend?

	✓
£8,000	
£10,000	
£12,000	
£15,000	

2.9 Inflation

The increase in prices of goods and services over a period of time. In a cash budget, it may affect the values of:

- Selling prices
- Purchase prices
- Expenses
- Cost of non-current assets
- Labour costs

A business may have information about a **one-off increase** in sales price or an **annual increase** in the hourly rate paid to the workforce. These increases should be built into the cash budget.

KEY TERM

Inflation: Increase in prices of goods and services over time.

Activity 7: Inflation

Edward is a manufacturer of teddy bears and is preparing the cash budget for the next three months. The selling price of the bears has been £20 per unit for some time and it has been decided to increase this price by 5% per unit every month from 1 February.

The workforce are currently paid at a rate of £7 per hour and each bear requires 3 hours of labour. From 1 March, there is to be a 2.5% increase in the hourly wage rate.

Sales and production for the three months of January to March are estimated as follows:

	Sales Bears	Production Bears
January	3,500	3,600
February	4,100	3,900
March	4,000	4,200

Required

What figures should be used in the cash budget for sales and for wages costs?

	Workings	£
Sales		
January		
February		
March		
Wages		
January		
February		
March		

Chapter summary

- A cash budget or cash flow forecast allows an organisation to plan and control future cash flows in and out, and the expected cash or overdraft balance at the end of future periods.
- Receipts from cash sales will take place at the same time as the sale, but receipts from credit sales may be spread over a number of subsequent months.
- The movement in receivables during a period can be used with the budgeted sales to find the budgeted cash inflow (receipts) from sales during the period.
- Payments for purchases on credit will similarly be typically spread over a number of future months.
- The movement in payables during a period can be used with the budgeted purchases to find the budgeted cash outflow (payment) for purchases during the period.
- If prompt payment discounts are offered or received, the cash budget must include only the actual cash received from customers or paid to suppliers after deducting the discount.
- Any sales expected to become irrecoverable should be excluded from cash receipts, because these amounts will never be received in cash.
- Foreign-currency receipts and payments must be converted using the expected exchange rate for the month of payment, as movements in exchange rates change the sterling cash flow.
- Tax payments such as corporation tax, sales tax, and income tax must be included in the cash budget in the period they are due to be paid, as they represent significant cash outflows.
- Any non-cash flows such as depreciation charges must be excluded from the cash flow forecast.
- The proceeds on the sale of non-current assets can be found by adding the profit on sale to (or by subtracting the loss on sale from) the carrying amount of the asset.
- Loan cash flows include the initial loan received as a cash inflow and the subsequent repayments of capital and interest as cash outflows in the months they fall due.
- Profit distributions such as dividends must be shown as cash outflows in the period they are paid, calculated as number of shares × dividend per share.
- Expected inflation must be reflected by adjusting future sales prices, costs, wages or overheads before including them in the cash budget, so that cash flows use realistic future values.

Activity answers

Activity 1: Cash budget – Aqua Ltd

Cash budget	£	£
Sales receipts		45,550
Payments		
Materials	11,100	
Labour	15,000	
Other costs	5,150	31,250
Cash flow		14,300

Activity 2: Cash budget – Kookaburra

Monthly cash flow forecast for Quarter 2

	April £	May £	June £	Total Qtr 2 £
Receipts				
Cash sales	1,380	1,500	1,605	4,485
Credit sales	2,975	3,220	3,500	9,695
Total receipts	4,355	4,720	5,105	14,180
Payments				
Purchases	1,200	1,300	1,500	4,000
Wages	800	850	850	2,500
Other overheads	250	275	275	800
Capital expenditure	–	3,000	1,000	4,000
Total payments	2,250	5,425	3,625	11,300
Net cash	2,105	(705)	1,480	2,880
Opening cash balance	750	2,855	2,150	750
Closing cash balance	2,855	2,150	3,630	3,630

Activity 3: Effect of discounts on receipts

	January £	February £	March £
Cash sales (40%)	4,000	4,800	6,000
Credit sales			
Pay in same month (25% × 60% × 95% of sales)	1,425	1,710	2,138
Pay in next month (75% × 60% of sales)	4,500	4,500	5,400
Cash received	9,925	11,010	13,538

Activity 4: Exchange rate movements

£ 36,000

- If the pound strengthens by 10%, the euro becomes weaker.
- New exchange rate = €1.25 × 1.10 = **€1.375:£1**
- Sterling receipt = €50,000 ÷ 1.375 = **£36,363**, rounded to **£36,000** for AAT purposes.

Strengthening home currency → **foreign receipts convert to fewer pounds**, so the cash budget must show the reduced sterling inflow.

Activity 5: Sale of a non-current asset

The sales proceeds were £ 25,000

Profit + carrying amount = 5,000 + 20,000 = £25,000

Activity 6: Profit distributions

The correct answer is:

	✓
£8,000	
£10,000	
£12,000	✓
£15,000	

Dividend = number of shares × dividend per share = 150,000 × £0.08 = £12,000, which must be shown as a cash outflow in the period the dividend is paid.

Activity 7: Inflation

	Workings	£
Sales		
January	(3,500 × £20)	70,000
February	(4,100 × £20 × 1.05)	86,100
March	(4,000 × £20 × 1.05^2)	88,200
Wages		
January	(3,600 × 3 hrs × £7)	75,600
February	(3,900 × 3 hrs × £7)	81,900
March	(4,200 × 3 hrs × £7 × 1.025)	90,405

Test your learning

1 A business has estimates of the following sales figures:

	£
October	790,000
November	750,000
December	720,000
January	700,000
February	730,000
March	760,000

The business expects to receive cash from these sales as follows:

- 10% of the total sales for each month is received immediately in the month of sale (cash sales).
- 40% of the total sales for each month is received in the month after the sale.
- 45% of the total sales for each month is received two months after the sale.
- 5% of the total sales for each month is never received (irrecoverable debts).

Required

Complete the following:

Forecast cash receipts

	January £	February £	March £
Budgeted cash receipts from sales			

2 A business has estimates of the following sales figures:

	£
October	790,000
November	750,000
December	720,000
January	700,000
February	730,000
March	760,000

The business operates at a standard gross profit margin of 25%. Purchases are all made in the same month as the sale and are all on credit. 20% of purchases are offered a 2% discount for payment in the month after purchase and the business takes all such discounts. A further 65% of the purchases are paid for two months after the month of purchase; and the remaining 15% are paid for three months after the date of purchase.

Required

Complete the following:

	January £	February £	March £
Budgeted payments			

3 A business is about to prepare a cash flow forecast for the quarter ending 31 December.

Gross wages are expected to be £42,000 each month and are paid in the month during which they are incurred. General overheads are anticipated to be £30,000 for each of September and October, increasing to £36,000 thereafter. 80% of the general overheads are paid for in the month during which they are incurred; and the remainder, the following month. Included in the general overheads figure is a depreciation charge of £5,000 each month.

The business has planned to purchase new equipment for £40,000 in November; and in the same month, to dispose of old equipment, with estimated sales proceeds of £4,000.

Required

Complete the following extracts from the cash budget for the three months ending 31 December.

Cash budget for the quarter ending 31 December

	October £	November £	December £
Cash receipts			
Sales proceeds from equipment			
Cash payments			
Wages			
General overheads (W1)			
New equipment			

4 Make-it Ltd intends to sell an industrial unit, making a budgeted profit of £58,000. The carrying amount of the unit is £212,000.

Required

What are the budgeted cash inflows on the sale of the unit, ie the proceeds?

	✓
£58,000	
£154,000	
£212,000	
£270,000	

6 Standard costing and flexed budgets

Learning outcomes

2.1	**Flexed budgeting** **Understand:** • The purpose of budget flexing as part of the control process • The limitations of budget flexing **Be able to:** • Flex budgets, adjusting each element of the budget according to the original budget assumptions about revenue and cost behaviour
2.2	**Standard costing** **Understand:** • Different types of standard (basic, current, target, ideal) • The purpose of standard cost cards • How different types of standards can impact the level of the variance • How the use of standard costing can complement budgetary control **Be able to:** • Calculate the value of items to be included in standard cost cards

Assessment context

Standard costing and flexing budgets form the basis of variance analysis (covered later in this Course Book). It is therefore important that you can accurately calculate standard costs and flex budgets.

Business context

Many manufacturing organisations and some service industries make use of standard costing systems. Standard costs provide management with information to aid planning, decision making and controlling the business operations. Flexed budgets are used to improve the analysis of actual results compared to the budgeted results by ensuring like-for-like comparisons are made.

Chapter overview

Standard costing and flexed budgets

- **Bases of standards**
  - Basic
  - Current
  - Target
  - Ideal
- **Fixed budget**
  - Budget set in advance
  - Does not change
- **Flexed budget**
  - Restate budget based on actual volumes
  - Useful for control
  - Like for like comparison and meaningful variances

Introduction

A **standard costing system** is used in organisations that produce standardised products or services. Each unit of output is expected to use the same quantity of direct materials and requires the same amount of time to make.

The **standard cost** is the planned or predetermined unit cost of producing one unit of a product or service. It represents the expected cost of materials, labour and overheads for a single unit and provides a benchmark against which actual performance can be measured.

1 Standard cost card

KEY TERM

Standard cost: An estimated unit cost.

Standard cost card: Shows full details of the standard cost of each product.

A **standard cost** is calculated from management expectations of:

- Usage and efficiency levels of materials and labour
- Prices of materials, labour and overheads
- Budgeted overhead costs and budgeted levels of activity

A standard cost is a predetermined calculation of how much costs should be under specified working conditions. To aid control, it is important that the standard cost is accurate and reviewed regularly.

The standard cost of each unit is set out in a **standard cost card**, which is then used for control within an organisation.

Illustration 1: Standard cost card

A standard cost card for Product A:

	£	£
Direct materials		
Material X – 3 kg at £4 per kg	12.00	
Material Y – 9 litres at £2 per litre	18.00	
		30.00
Direct labour		
Grade A – 3 hours at £14 per hour	42.00	
Grade B – 4 hours at £16 per hour	64.00	
		106.00
Prime cost		136.00
Variable production overhead – 7 hours at £1 per hour		7.00
Fixed production overhead – 7 hours at £9 per hour		63.00
Standard full production cost		206.00

This cost card can then be used when setting budgets and controlling production of Product A.

Activity 1: Latt

Latt expects to make 5,000 units of production in the coming year.

The following has been estimated:

Each unit will require 3 kg of material with a total cost of £15.

Each unit will require 2 hours of labour paid at £12 per hour.

Fixed overheads are expected to be £50,000 and are absorbed on a labour-hour basis.

Required

Complete the standard cost card below:

Unit	Quantity (kgs or hours)	Rate £	Unit cost
Material			
Labour			
Fixed overheads	2		
Total			

1.1 The uses of standard costing

KEY TERM

Standard costing: A control technique which compares standard costs and revenues with actual results to obtain variances which are used to improve performance.

Standard costing has a variety of uses but the two principal ones relevant to this assessment are as follows:

- **Planning** – Standard costing allows for prediction of the use of resources so that budgets can be set. For example, the standard quantities of materials and labour can help the construction of the production budget. Standard costing can therefore improve the accuracy of budgets set.
- **Control** – To act as a control device by establishing standards (planned costs), highlighting (via variance analysis, which we will cover in the next chapter) activities that are not conforming to plan and thus alerting management to areas which may be out of control and in need of corrective action.

We will be concentrating on the **control and variance analysis** aspect of standard costing.

Activity 2: Press Co

The budgeted and actual results for Press Co for the month of February 20X1 are as follows:

	Budget		Actual	
Production (units of C06)		12,000		15,000
Direct materials	21,000 kg	£63,000	26,000 kg	£79,000
Direct labour	2,400 hours	£36,000	3,100 hours	£47,000
Fixed overheads (absorbed on a unit basis)		£54,000		£60,000
Total		£153,000		£186,000

Required

Complete the following sentences:

(a)

The standard quantity of labour per unit is [ ] minutes.

(b)

The budgeted quantity of materials needed to produce 15,000 units of C06 is [ ] kg.

(c)

The budgeted labour hours to produce 15,000 units of C06 is [ ] hours.

(d)

The budgeted labour cost to produce 15,000 units of C06 is £ [ ] .

(e)

The budgeted overhead absorption rate per unit is £ [ ] .

Standard costing therefore involves the following:

- The establishment of predetermined estimates of the costs of products or services
- The collection of actual costs
- The comparison of the actual costs with the predetermined estimates

Differences between actual and standard costs are called variances. A **favourable variance** happens when performance is better than expected. An **adverse variance** happens when performance is worse than expected.

2 Types of standard

2.1 Basic standards

KEY TERM

> **Basic standards:** Standards that have been unaltered over a long period of time.

- Reflect historical working patterns of the organisation.
- Very easy to set.
- Likely to be out of date as they will not have taken account of changes in inflation or working practices.
- Variances generated will usually be large.

2.2 Current standards (also sometimes known as normal standards)

KEY TERM

> **Current standards:** Standards based on current working conditions.

- Allow for current levels of wastage and inefficiency.
- Do not attempt to improve on current levels, so are deemed more short-term.
- Frequent revisions of the standard are necessary to ensure that current conditions are reflected.
- Variances are small to moderate in size and a mix of favourable and adverse.
- Good for motivating staff and monitoring performance.

2.3 Target standards

KEY TERM

Target (or attainable) standards: Standards that incorporate some improvement but allow for some inefficiency.

- Make allowances for some wastage and inefficiency.
- Achievable because target standard better reflects realistic working conditions.
- Target standard can only be met if operations are carried out effectively and efficiently, so it contains some element of improvement.
- Deemed more motivational for managers and staff than ideal standards, as they are not as difficult as ideal standards.
- Can result in some favourable variances if the operations of the organisation are more efficient than expected.
- May result in adverse variances if wastage and inefficiency was greater than anticipated.

2.4 Ideal standards

KEY TERM

Ideal standards: Standards set on the basis that perfect working conditions apply at all times.

- No allowance is given for wastage, inefficiencies or idle time when setting the standard.
- Standard doesn't reflect real conditions, so budgets based on it are likely to be inaccurate.
- Variances are large and mostly adverse.
- Harder for staff to meet; therefore, can be demotivational.

Activity 3: Types of standard

Identify whether the following statements are true or false.

Statement	True ✓	False ✓
Current or target standards are a better basis for budgeting because they represent the level of productivity which management will wish to plan for.		
Basic standards may provide an incentive to greater efficiency even though the standard cannot be achieved.		
Ideal standards usually lead to large adverse variances because they assume perfect efficiency.		
A target standard can motivate employees by encouraging improved efficiency.		

3 Budgetary control

3.1 Fixed budgets

KEY TERM

Fixed budgets: Budgets that are set in advance of a period and their purpose is to provide a single achievable target for the entire organisation to work towards. This target level of activity means that all areas of the business will be co-ordinated towards achieving this goal.

The control element of the budgeting system lies in the comparison of the actual results for a period to the budgeted figures. However, if the actual activity levels turn out to be significantly different from the target set in the fixed budget, then comparison of the actual results to the fixed budget will be fairly meaningless, as we will not be comparing like with like.

3.2 Flexible and flexed budget

KEY TERM

Flexible budgets: Budgets which, by recognising different cost behaviours, are designed to change as the volume of activity changes.

A flexible budget has two uses within an organisation:

- **Planning** – For example, a business may expect to sell 10,000 units in the forthcoming period, but research has identified that output and sales might be as low as 8,000 units or as high as 12,000 units. The business may therefore prepare contingency plans at each of these activity levels, and then assess the possible outcomes. This contingency plan is a flexible budget.
- **Control** – Flexible budgets can be used to prepare a flexed budget to which actual results can be compared.

KEY TERM

Flexed budgets: Budgets that are adjusted to reflect the actual activity level that was achieved during the period, showing what costs and revenues should have been at that particular activity level using standard rates.

3.3 Factors to consider when preparing flexible and flexed budgets

When preparing flexible and flexed budgets, attention needs to be paid to stepped and semi-variable costs:

- Separation of costs into fixed and variable elements – variable elements will increase as the activity level increases
- Fixed costs may behave in a stepped fashion as activities increase/decrease

Illustration 2: Fixed vs flexed budget

Martin Engineering prepares detailed budgets for each quarter of the year. The budget for Quarter 4 of 20X0 was set as follows:

Sales volume 1,000 units	Quarter 4 budget £
Sales revenue	40,000
Materials	(10,000)
Labour	(12,000)
Production overhead	(3,000)
Gross profit	15,000
General expenses	(8,000)
Operating profit	7,000

This budget was set on the basis of both production and sales of 1,000 units and no opening or closing inventories.

It is now the first week in January 20X1 and the actual results for Quarter 4 are being compared to the budget:

Original budget 1,000 units		Actual 1,200 units
£		£
40,000	Sales revenue	45,600
(10,000)	Materials	(12,480)
(12,000)	Labour	(13,800)
(3,000)	Production overhead	(3,200)
15,000	Gross profit	16,120
(8,000)	General expenses	(9,080)
7,000	Operating profit	7,040

Variance report

Original budget 1,000 units		Actual 1,200 units	Variance
£		£	£
40,000	Sales revenue	45,600	5,600 Fav
(10,000)	Materials	(12,480)	2,480 Adv
(12,000)	Labour	(13,800)	1,800 Adv
(3,000)	Production overhead	(3,200)	200 Adv
15,000	Gross profit	16,120	1,120 Fav
(8,000)	General expenses	(9,080)	1,080 Adv
7,000	Operating profit	7,040	40 Fav

The results show a mixed picture: sales and profit appear favourable, while all cost categories show adverse variances. However, these figures cannot be directly compared because the original budget assumed production and sales of 1,000 units, whereas the actual level of activity was 1,200 units.

To make a fair comparison, we need to **flex the budget** to reflect the actual output of 1,200 units.

Sales

Budgeted selling price	=	£40,000/1,000 units
	=	£40 per unit

The details of the cost behaviour of each of the costs are given below:

Materials	The materials cost is totally variable.
Labour	Each employee can only produce 250 units each quarter – the cost of each employee is £3,000 each quarter.
Production overhead	The production overhead is a totally fixed cost.
General expenses	The general expenses are made up of a budgeted fixed cost of £5,000 and a variable element.

Therefore, the budgeted sales revenue for 1,200 units is:

Sales	=	1,200 × £40
	=	£48,000

Materials are totally variable.

Budgeted materials per unit	=	£10,000/1,000 units
	=	£10 per unit
Budgeted materials cost for 1,200 units	=	1,200 × £10
	=	£12,000

Labour is a stepped cost.

One employee is required for every 250 units, therefore for 1,200 units, five employees will be required.

Budgeted labour cost	=	5 × £3,000
	=	£15,000

Production overheads is a fixed cost so remains unchanged.

Budgeted cost for 1,200 units	=	£3,000

General expenses are a semi-variable cost.

			£
At 1,000 units	Fixed element	=	5,000
	Variable element	=	3,000
	Total		8,000

Variable element = £3,000/1,000 units = £3 per unit

			£
At 1,200 units	Fixed element	=	5,000
	Variable element		
	1,200 × £3	=	3,600
			8,600

The flexed budget will appear as follows:

Sales volume 1,200 units	Quarter 4 flexed budget £
Sales revenue	48,000
Materials	(12,000)
Labour	(15,000)
Production overhead	(3,000)
Gross profit	18,000
General expenses	(8,600)
Operating profit	9,400

The flexed budget can then be compared with the actual figures in the form of an operating statement, and the true variances calculated.

Martin Engineering: Quarter 4 Operating statement

Original budget 1,000 units £		Flexed budget 1,200 units £	Actual 1,200 units £	Variance £
40,000	Sales revenue	48,000	45,600	2,400 Adv
(10,000)	Materials	(12,000)	(12,480)	480 Adv
(12,000)	Labour	(15,000)	(13,800)	1,200 Fav
(3,000)	Production overhead	(3,000)	(3,200)	200 Adv
15,000	Gross profit	18,000	16,120	1,880 Adv
(8,000)	General expenses	(8,600)	(9,080)	480 Adv
7,000	Operating profit	9,400	7,040	2,360 Adv

We can now see that there is a significant adverse profit variance, with all the variances other than labour being adverse.

Activity 4: Flexed budget 1

The budget for production supervisors' costs for a period for a business at an activity level of 120,000 units is £12,000. One production supervisor is required for every 50,000 units of production.

Required

If actual production is 180,000 units, what figure would appear in the flexed budget for production supervisors' costs?

£ [ ]

Activity 5: Flexed budget 2

The budgeted production overhead for a business is £15,800 at an activity level of 2,000 units, and £19,950 at an activity level of 3,000 units.

Required

If the actual activity level is 2,600 units, what is the flexed budget figure for production overhead?

The budget allowance is £ [ ] .

Activity 6: Variances – QuikMaid Ltd

QuikMaid Ltd is a specialist retailer that sells a blender machine.

The following is a copy of the original budget and the actual performance of the company's current financial year.

Draft budget and actual results

	Budget		Actual	
Sales volume (units)		400,000		500,000
	£000	£000	£000	£000
Sales revenue		14,000		20,000
Materials	4,800		6,475	
Labour	2,600		3,335	
Warehousing costs	720		800	
Distribution costs	60		90	
Insurance	12		10	
Rent and rates	15		18	
Other administration	28		33	
Depreciation	50		50	
Total		8,285		10,811
Operating profit		5,715		9,189

You are given the following information:

- Materials and labour costs are variable.
- Warehousing costs are semi-variable. The fixed element is budgeted at £40,000.
- Distribution cost is a stepped cost, varying with every 100,000 blenders sold.
- All other costs are fixed.

Required

Complete the monthly operating report below by flexing the budget, calculating all variances and showing whether each variance is favourable or adverse.

Show adverse variances as negative figures using brackets.

	Flexed budget		Actual		Variance	
Sales volume		500,000		500,000		
	£000	£000	£000	£000	£000	F/A
Sales revenue				20,000		
Materials			6,475			
Labour			3,335			
Warehousing costs			800			
Distribution costs			90			
Insurance			10			
Rent and rates			18			
Other administration			33			
Depreciation			50			
Total				10,811		
Operating profit				9,189		

3.4 Limitations of budget flexing

Although it is useful to flex budgets to eliminate volume related variances, the flexed budget is still indirectly based on the assumptions applied when the original budget was drawn up.

These assumptions may not always hold true at flexed volumes and the budget assumptions may need to be revisited when assessing performance against a flexed budget.

Budget flexing, therefore, is not a means of re-budgeting for a new strategy, since this means the underlying assumptions, other than volume, will change.

Problems with budget flexing include the following:

- **Separating mixed costs can be difficult**. Mixed (semi-variable) costs need to be split into fixed and variable elements before the budget can be flexed, and this separation is not always straightforward.
- **The assumptions behind the original fixed budget must be reviewed.** Factors such as limiting constraints, expected inflation, uncertainty about future conditions and anticipated demand may no longer hold true. Flexing a budget without revisiting these assumptions can lead to misleading conclusions.
- **Flexing can create a sense of shifting targets.** By flexing a budget, a manager is effectively saying, 'If I knew then what I know now, this is the budget I would have set'. While useful, this can cause frustration if managers feel that performance is being judged against continually changing benchmarks.

Chapter summary

- In a standard costing system, all output is valued at a standard cost per unit.
- A standard cost card shows full details of the expected cost of producing one unit and provides a benchmark for cost control, budgeting and variance analysis.
- The standards that can be set are a basic standard, current standard, target standard and ideal standard.
- Basic standards usually result in very large variances that don't reflect current conditions. They are not useful for day-to-day control.
- Current standards usually result in small to moderate variances that help management manage costs. They are good for motivating staff.
- Target standards make some allowances for wastage and inefficiency and usually result in moderate adverse variances. They are more motivational for employees than ideal standards.
- Ideal standards usually result in large, frequent variances.
- Standard costing complements budgetary control by providing detailed, unit-level expectations that allow fair comparisons, support flexing, highlight inefficiencies, and strengthen the organisation's ability to monitor and control costs.
- A fixed budget is set in advance of a budgeting period as a pre-determined plan of activity for all areas of a business.
- A flexed budget can be prepared which adjusts the budget to reflect the actual activity level or volume for the period.
- A flexed budget is used in the control aspect of the budgetary system as the actual results are compared to the flexed budget in order to determine any variances.
- In order to flex a budget, a distinction must be drawn between variable costs and fixed costs, and the variable or fixed elements of a semi-variable cost – the variable elements of cost will increase or decrease with changes in activity level, whereas the fixed elements of cost do not vary with changes in activity levels.

Activity answers

Activity 1: Latt

Unit	Quantity (kgs or hours)	Rate £	Unit cost
Material	3	5	15
Labour	2	12	24
Fixed overheads	2	5	10
Total			49

Activity 2: Press Co

(a) The standard quantity of labour per unit is [12] minutes.

(2,400 hrs/12,000 units) × 60

(b) The budgeted quantity of materials needed to produce 15,000 units of C06 is [26,250] kg.

21,000 kg/12,000 units × 15,000 units

(c) The budgeted labour hours to produce 15,000 units of C06 is [3,000] hours.

(12 mins × 15,000 units)/60

(d) The budgeted labour cost to produce 15,000 units of C06 is £ [45,000] .

£36,000/12,000 units × 15,000 units

(e) The budgeted overhead absorption rate per unit is £ [4.50] .

£54,000/12,000 units

Activity 3: Types of standard

The correct answers are:

Statement	True ✓	False ✓
Current or target standards are a better basis for budgeting because they represent the level of productivity which management will wish to plan for.	✓	
Basic standards may provide an incentive to greater efficiency even though the standard cannot be achieved.		✓
Ideal standards usually lead to large adverse variances because they assume perfect efficiency.	✓	
A target standard can motivate employees by encouraging improved efficiency.	✓	

The first statement is true. Current or target standards are realistic and achievable, so they provide a better basis for budgeting and planning productivity.

The second statement is false. Basic standards are outdated and unchanged for long periods; they do not motivate efficiency because they don't reflect achievable performance.

The third statement is true. Ideal standards are unrealistic, so actual performance almost always falls short.

The fourth statement is true. When standards are challenging but realistic, they can drive better performance without being demoralising.

Activity 4: Flexed budget 1

£ 16,000

This is a stepped fixed cost.

120,000 units would require three supervisors, therefore the cost per 50,000 units is £12,000/3 = £4,000.

For 180,000 units four supervisors would be required: 4 × £4,000 = £16,000

Activity 5: Flexed budget 2

The budget allowance is £ 18,290 .

	Units	£
High	3,000	19,950
Low	2,000	15,800
	1,000	4,150

Variable cost per unit = £4,150 / 1,000 = £4.15 per unit

Fixed cost: £19,950 – (3,000 × £4.15) = £7,500

@ 2,600 units:

	£
Total variable cost (£4.15 × 2,600)	10,790
Fixed cost	7,500
Total cost	18,290

Activity 6: Variances – QuikMaid Ltd

	Flexed budget		Actual		Variance	
Sales volume		500,000		500,000		
	£000	£000	£000	£000	£000	F/A
Sales revenue (W1)		17,500		20,000	2,500	F
Materials (W2)	6,000		6,475		(475)	A
Labour (W3)	3,250		3,335		(85)	A
Warehousing costs (W4)	890		800		90	F
Distribution costs (W5)	75		90		(15)	A
Insurance	12		10		2	F
Rent and rates	15		18		(3)	A
Other administration	28		33		(5)	A
Depreciation	50		50		–	
Total		10,320		10,811	(491)	A
Operating profit		7,180		9,189	2,009	F

Workings

1 ***Budgeted selling price per unit***

£14,000,000 / 400,000 = £35

£35 × 500,000 = £17,500,000

2 ***Budgeted cost of materials per unit***

£4,800,000 / 400,000 = £12

£12 × 500,000 = £6,000,000

3 ***Budgeted cost of labour per unit***

£2,600,000 / 400,000 = £6.50

£6.50 × 500,000 = £3,250,000

4 ***Budgeted variable cost of warehousing***

	£
Total cost	720,000
Less fixed cost	(40,000)
Total variable cost	680,000

Variable cost per unit = £680,000 / 400,000 units = £1.70

Actual cost of warehousing:

	£
Variable cost (£1.70 × 500,000)	850,000
Fixed cost	40,000
	890,000

5 ***Budgeted distribution costs per 100,000 blenders***

£60,000 / (400,000 / 100,000) = £15,000

Steps for 500,000 blenders = 500,000 / 100,000 = 5

£15,000 × 5 = £75,000

Test your learning

1 **What is the primary purpose of flexing a budget?**

	✓
To correct errors in the original budget	
To restate costs to reflect the actual level of activity	
To increase the accuracy of profit forecasts	
To remove fixed costs from performance reports	

2 **Ideal standards tend to produce variances that are:**

	✓
Small and stable	
Non-existent	
Large and adverse	
Favourable	

3 **Standard costing supports budgetary control mainly by:**

	✓
Ensuring actual costs always meet standards	
Providing benchmarks for comparing budgeted and actual performance	
Eliminating the need for budgets	
Calculating cash flow forecasts	

4 **Which of the following would not change when a budget is flexed?**

	✓
Direct materials per unit	
Total variable costs	
Total fixed costs	
Revenue per unit	

5 **The main purpose of a standard cost card is to:**

	✓
Record actual costs of production	
Provide information for variance calculations	
Control fixed overhead expenditure	
Allocate overheads to departments	

7 Variance analysis

Learning outcomes

2.2 **Standard costing**

Understand:

- Why variances occur

Be able to:

- Calculate variances for revenue and costs:
  - Sales price
  - Sales volume
  - Total materials variance
  - Material price
  - Material usage
  - Total labour variance
  - Labour rate
  - Labour efficiency
  - Labour idle time
  - Total variable overhead variance
  - Variable overhead price
  - Variable overhead efficiency
  - Total fixed overhead variance
  - Fixed overhead expenditure
  - Fixed overhead volume

Assessment context

Budget flexing and the calculation of the resulting variances could appear as part of the assessment.

Variance analysis will be examined in the assessment. Different assessment variants will test different types of variances, so you need to be comfortable with all the variances covered within the chapter to fully prepare yourself for the assessment.

Business context

A core part of any business is to determine its objectives and come up with a plan of how to achieve these objectives (strategy). Budgeting provides detail of how the business should operate in order to achieve its objectives. A business must then monitor how it is performing against its budget and take actions to ensure its performance is as strong as possible.

Variance calculations are universally performed to enable management to understand which areas of the business are/are not performing well.

Chapter overview

Variance analysis

Variances

- Calculation of variances

Variance analysis

- Calculations
  - 'Should' X
    'Did' (X)
    X
  - **Variable cost variances**
    - Materials → Price, Usage
    - Labour → Rate, Efficiency, Idle Time
    - Variable overhead variances → Expenditure and efficiency
  - **Fixed overhead variances**
    - Under MC → Expenditure only
    - Under AC → Expenditure and volume
  - **Sales variances**
    - Sales price
    - Sales volume

Introduction

As we discussed in Chapter 6, one use of standard costing is to control business operations as it enables an organisation to perform variance analysis. For comparisons to be meaningful, the original budget needs to be amended or 'flexed' to the actual level of activity. The process of comparing a flexed budget to actual results is known as variance analysis.

Variances show the difference between actual results and expected results under the standard. They can either be **favourable** (F) – better than expected – or **adverse** (A) – worse than expected.

Each standard cost is made up of a quantity element and an expenditure element.

- Differences in quantities create efficiency, usage or volume variances.
- Differences in expenditure create rate, price or expenditure variances.

The purpose of calculating variances is to adjust the budget to actual activity levels so that performance can be compared on a like-for-like basis.

1 Variable cost variances

We've already learned how to flex a budget so that we compare actual results with what our costs should have been at the actual level of activity. A flexed budget tells us how big the variance is but not why it happened. To understand the cause of a variance, we break it down using formulae.

The variable cost variances cover direct materials, direct labour and variable overheads. Each of the total variances can be broken down as follows:

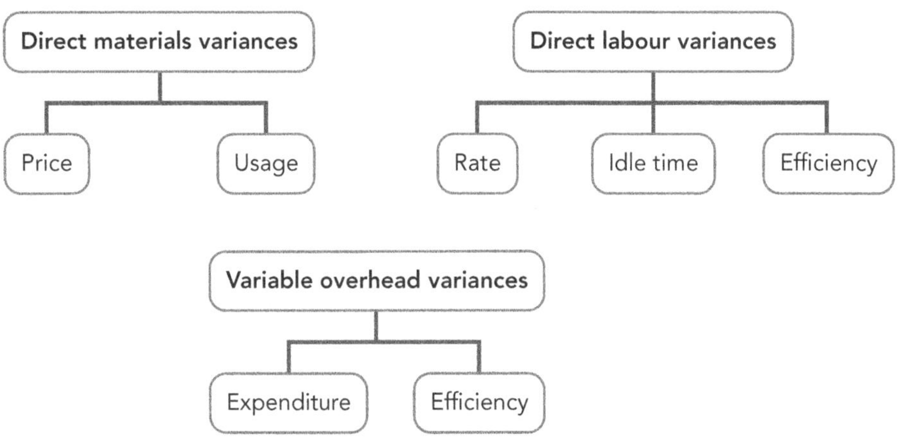

1.1 Materials variances

1.1.1 Total direct materials variance

KEY TERM

> **Total materials variance:** A comparison of the total standard cost of materials for actual production, to the total actual cost of materials.

The total materials cost variance measures the cost of spending more or less on materials for actual production units than the standard allows.

The total direct materials variance is based on the actual number of units produced – the budgeted production units are ignored. Calculating the standard cost of actual production units is known as flexing the budget.

The total direct materials variance can, therefore, be calculated as follows:

Formula to learn

		£
'Should'	**Actual units** should cost (Act units × std kg per unit × std £ per kg)	X
'Did'	Actual materials used did cost	(X)
Total materials variance		X

The total materials variance can then be split into the materials price and materials usage variances.

1.1.2 Materials price variance

KEY TERM

Materials price variance: A comparison of the standard cost of the actual materials purchased, to the actual cost of materials purchased.

The **materials price variance** measures the cost of spending more or less on actual materials purchases than the standard allows.

The materials price variance can be calculated either via a proforma or a formula, as detailed below.

Formula to learn

Proforma method

		£
'Should'	**Actual purchases** should cost (Act kg × std £ per kg)	X
'Did'	Actual purchases did cost	(X)
Materials price variance		X

Formula method

Materials price variance = AQM × (AP – SP)

Where:

AQM is the actual quantity of materials used

AP is the actual price paid per unit of direct materials

SP is the standard price paid per unit of direct materials

1.1.3 Materials usage variance

KEY TERM

Materials usage variance: A comparison of the standard usage of materials for actual production units, to the actual usage of materials for actual production units, valued at standard cost per unit of material.

The **materials usage variance** measures the cost of using more or less materials to produce actual production units than the standard allows.

To calculate the usage variance the actual and standard materials usage for actual production is compared, and the difference is converted into a cost variance by applying the standard price per unit of direct material.

The materials usage variance can be calculated by either using a proforma or formula as detailed below.

Formula to learn

Proforma method

		£
'Should'	**Actual production** should use (Act units × std kg per unit)	X
'Did'	Actual production did use	(X)
		X
× standard price per kg		× $X
Materials usage variance		X

Formula method

Materials usage variance = (AQM – SQM) × SP

Where:

AQM is the actual quantity of materials used

SQM is the standard quantity of materials for the units produced

SP is the standard price per unit of direct materials

The sum of the price and usage variances should equal the total materials cost variance as follows:

	£
Materials price variance	X
Materials usage variance	X
Total materials variance	X

Illustration 1: Direct materials variances

The standard cost card for one of Lawson Ltd's products, the George, is shown below:

	£
Direct materials 4 kg @ £2.00 per kg	8.00
Direct labour 2 hours @ £7.00 per hour	14.00
Fixed overheads 2 hours @ £3.00 per hour	6.00
Total standard absorption cost	28.00

The budgeted level of production for July was 20,000 units but in fact only 18,000 units were produced.

The actual quantity of materials used in July was 68,000 kg. The total cost of the materials was £142,800.

Required

Calculate the following variances:

(a) Direct materials total variance

(b) Direct materials price variance

(c) Direct materials usage variance

Solution

(a) Direct materials total variance

	£
18,000 units should have cost (18000 units × 4 kg × £2.00)	144,000
But did cost	142,800
Total materials variance	1,200 (F)

The actual cost is less than the standard, so the total materials cost variance is favourable.

(b) Direct materials price variance

	£
68,000 kg of materials should have cost (68,000 kg × £2.00)	136,000
But did cost	142,800
Materials price variance	6,800 (A)

The actual price paid for the materials is more than the standard price, so the price variance is adverse.

(c) Direct materials usage variance

	Kg
18,000 units should have used (× 4 kg)	72,000
But did use	68,000
Materials usage variance in kg	4,000 (F)
× Standard price per kg of materials	× £2
Material usage variance in £	£8,000 (F)

The actual quantity of materials used is less than the expected or standard quantity, so the usage variance is favourable.

The materials variances can be reconciled as follows:

	£
Materials price variance	6,800 (A)
Materials usage variance	8,000 (F)
Total materials cost variance	1,200 (F)

Activity 1: News Co

News Co operates a standard costing system. It purchases and uses 53,000 kg of materials at a cost of £2.38 per kg.

The budgeted production was 25,000 units which requires 50,000 kg of materials at a total standard cost of £125,000. The actual production was 27,000 units.

Required

Calculate:

(a) **The total materials variance**

The total materials variance is £ [ ] [▼]

(b) **The materials price variance**

The materials price variance is £ [ ] [▼]

(c) **The material usage variance**

The materials usage variance is £ [ ] [▼]

Picklist

- Adverse
- Favourable

1.2 Labour variances

1.2.1 Total labour cost variances

KEY TERM

Total labour variance: A comparison of the standard labour cost of actual production units to the actual labour cost of actual production units.

The total labour cost variance measures the cost of spending more or less on labour for actual production units than the standard allows.

As with the total direct materials cost variance, the total direct labour cost variance is based on the actual number of units produced, therefore flexing the budget to actual production levels.

The total direct labour variance can be calculated as follows:

Formula to learn

		£
'Should'	**Actual units** should cost (Act units × std hrs per unit × std £ per hour)	X
'Did'	Actual labour used did cost	(X)
Total labour variance		X

The total labour cost variance can then be split into the labour rate, labour efficiency and idle time variances.

1.2.2 Labour rate variance

KEY TERM

> **Labour rate variance:** A comparison of the standard cost of actual hours paid to the actual cost of actual hours paid.

The **labour rate variance** measures the cost of spending more or less on actual labour hours paid than the standard allows.

The labour rate variance can be calculated either via a proforma or a formula, as detailed below.

Formula to learn

Proforma method

		£
'Should'	**Actual hours paid** should cost (Act hrs paid × std £ per hour)	X
'Did'	Actual hours paid did cost	(X)
Labour rate variance		X

Formula method

Direct labour rate variance = AH × (AR – SR)

where

AH is the actual hours worked and paid for

AR is the actual rate paid per direct labour hour

SR is the standard rate per direct labour hour

1.2.3 Labour efficiency variance

KEY TERM

> **Labour efficiency variance:** A comparison of the standard hours worked for actual production units to the actual hours worked for actual production units, valued at standard rate per hour.

The **labour efficiency variance** measures the cost of the workforce working more or less efficiently than the standard allows.

To calculate the efficiency variance, the actual and standard labour hours for actual production is compared, and the difference is converted into a cost variance by applying the standard rate per labour hour.

The labour efficiency variance can be calculated by either using a proforma or formula as detailed below.

Formula to learn

Proforma method

		Hours
'Should'	**Actual production** should take (Act units × std hrs per unit)	X
'Did'	Actual production did take	(X)
		X
× standard rate per hour		× £X
Labour efficiency variance		£X

Formula method

Labour efficiency variance = (AH – SH) × SR

where

AH is the actual hours worked (excluding idle time)

SH is the standard hours of actual units produced

SR is the standard rate of pay per direct labour hour

1.2.4 Idle time variance

KEY TERM

Idle time variance: A comparison of actual hours worked and actual hours paid, valued at the standard rate per labour hour.

The **idle time variance** measures the cost of the workforce being unproductive in the period. When idle time occurs, the labour force is still paid but no actual work is done.

Idle time could occur as a result of machine breakdowns, bottlenecks in production, a shortage of materials, or a shortage of customer orders.

As the workforce is paid for idle time, the number of hours paid is compared to the actual hours worked in production, and the difference is converted into a cost variance by applying the standard rate per labour hour.

Idle time can therefore be calculated as follows:

Formula to learn

	Hours
Hours worked	X
Hours paid	(X)
	X
× standard rate per hour	× £X
Labour idle time variance	£X

The sum of the rate, efficiency and idle time variances should equal the total labour cost variance as follows:

	£
Labour rate variance	X
Labour efficiency variance	X
Idle time variance	X
Total labour cost variance	X

Illustration 2: Direct labour variances

The standard direct labour cost of product X is as follows:

2 hours of labour at £5 per hour = £10 per unit

During the period, 1,500 units of product X were made. The cost of labour was £17,500 for 3,080 hours, however 2,980 hours were worked.

Required

Calculate the following variances:

(a) The direct labour total variance

(b) The direct labour rate variance

(c) The direct labour efficiency variance

(d) The idle time variance

Solution

(a) Direct labour total variance

	£
1,500 units of product X should have cost £10 per unit	15,000
But did cost	17,500
Direct labour total variance	2,500 (A)

Actual cost is greater than standard cost. The variance is therefore adverse.

(b) Direct labour rate variance

	£
3,080 hours should have cost (3,080 hours × £5 per hour)	15,400
But did cost	17,500
Direct labour rate variance	2,100 (A)

Actual cost is greater than standard cost. The rate variance is therefore adverse.

(c) Direct labour efficiency variance

	Hours
1,500 units should take (1,500 units × 2 hours)	3,000
But did take	2,980
Direct labour efficiency variance in hours	20 (F)
× Standard rate per hour	× £5
Direct labour efficiency variance in £	£100 (F)

20 fewer hours were worked to produce 1,500 units, so the variance is favourable.

(d) Idle time variance

	Hours
Hours worked	2,980
Hours paid	3,080
Idle time variance in hours	100 (A)
× Standard rate per hour	× £5
Idle time variance in £	£500 (A)

The variances can be reconciled as follows:

	£
Direct labour rate variance	2,100 (A)
Direct labour efficiency variance	100 (F)
Idle time	500 (A)
Direct labour total cost variance	2,500 (A)

Activity 2: Yard Co

Yard Co, operating a standard costing system, expects to produce 3,000 units of Y using 12,000 hours of labour. The standard cost of labour is £12.50 per hour.

Last month the company actually made 2,195 units. The actual labour cost was £110,750 for the 9,200 hours worked.

Required

Calculate:

(a) The total labour variance

The total labour variance is £ [ ] [▼]

(b) The labour rate variance

The labour rate variance is £ [ ] [▼]

(c) The labour efficiency variance

The labour efficiency variance is £ [ ] [▼]

Picklist

- Adverse
- Favourable

Activity 3: Flight Co

Flight Co expected to produce 200 units of its product. Actual production was 260 units. The standard labour cost per unit was £120 (10 hours at a rate of £12 per hour).

During the period the workforce worked 2,200 hours but were paid for 2,300 hours.

Required

Calculate the idle time variance.

The idle time variance is £[ ] [▼]

Picklist

- Adverse
- Favourable

1.3 Variable overheads variances

1.3.1 Total variable overhead variance

KEY TERM

Total variable overhead variance: A comparison of the standard variable overhead cost for actual production units, to the actual variable overhead cost for actual production units.

The total variable overhead variance measures the cost of spending more or less on variable overhead for actual production units than the standard allows.

The total variable overhead cost variance is calculated as follows:

Formula to learn

		£
'Should'	**Actual units** should cost	X
'Did'	Actual variable overheads did cost	(X)
Total variable overhead variance		X

The total variable overhead variance is then split into variable overhead price (expenditure) and variable overhead efficiency variances.

1.3.2 Variable overhead price variance

KEY TERM

Variable overhead price variance: A comparison of the standard variable overhead cost of actual hours worked, to the actual variable overhead cost of actual hours worked.

The variable overhead price variance measures the cost of spending more or less on variable overheads than the standard allows.

To calculate the variable overhead price variance, it is assumed that the amount of variable overhead incurred varies with the number of direct labour hours actually worked (total direct labour hours less idle time).

The variable overhead price variance is calculated as follows:

Formula to learn

		£
'Should'	**Actual hours worked** should cost (Act hrs worked × std £ per hour)	X
'Did'	Actual hours worked did cost	(X)
Variable overhead price variance		X

This will measure whether the actual hours worked have cost more or less in overhead than expected.

1.3.3 Variable overhead efficiency variance

KEY TERM

Variable overhead efficiency variance: A comparison of the standard hours for actual production units, to the actual hours for actual production units, valued at the standard variable overhead per hour.

The variable overhead efficiency variance is calculated in the same way as the labour efficiency variance, but to convert it into a monetary variance the hourly difference is multiplied by the standard variable overhead rate per hour rather than the standard labour rate per hour.

The variance is calculated as follows:

Formula to learn

		£
'Should'	**Actual production** should take	X
'Did'	Actual production did take	(X)
		X
× standard variable overhead rate per hour		× £X
Variable overhead efficiency variance		£X

Illustration 3: Variable overheads variances

The variable overheads of Glitch Ltd are consumed on a labour hour basis. The standard variable overhead cost of their product, UC, is as follows:

3 hours at £2.30 per hour = £6.90 per unit

During the period, 3,000 units of UC were made. The cost of variable overheads was £18,600 for 9,500 hours worked.

Required

Calculate the following variances:

(a) The variable overheads total variance

(b) The variable overhead price variance

(c) The variable overhead efficiency variance

Solution

(a) **The variable overhead total variance**

	£
3,000 units of product X should have cost £6.90 per unit	20,700
But did cost	18,600
Variable overheads total variance	2,100 (F)

Actual cost is lower than standard cost. The variance is therefore favourable.

(b) **Variable overhead price variance**

	£
9,500 hours should have cost (9,500 hours × £2.30 per hour)	21,850
But did cost	18,600
Variable overhead price variance	3,250 (F)

Actual cost is lower than standard cost. The expenditure variance is therefore favourable.

(c) **Variable overhead efficiency variance**

	Hours
3,000 units should take (3,000 units × 3 hours)	9,000
But did take	9,500
Variable overhead efficiency variance in hours	500 (A)
× Standard rate per hour	× £2.30
Variable overhead efficiency variance in £	£1,150 (A)

500 more hours were worked to produce 3,000 units, so the variance is adverse.

The variances can be reconciled as follows:

	£
Variable overhead price variance	3,250 (F)
Variable overhead efficiency variance	1,150 (A)
Variable overheads total variance	2,100 (F)

Activity 4: Bee Co

Bee Co uses the following standard cost card for product H:

2 hours of labour at £15 per hour = £30 per unit

During the period, 1,000 units of product Z were made in 1,960 hours. The cost of variable production overhead was £30,750.

Required

Calculate:

(a) **The total variable overhead variance**

The total variable overhead variance is £ ______ ▼

(b) **The variable overhead price variance**

The variable overhead price variance is £ ______ ▼

(c) **The variable overhead efficiency variance**

The variable overhead efficiency variance is £ ______ ▼

Picklist

- Adverse
- Favourable

2 Fixed overhead variances (under absorption costing)

As discussed in Chapter 1, under absorption costing all of the production overheads (both fixed and variable) are included in the cost of producing a cost unit. In order to include an estimated amount of production overhead per unit, an overhead absorption rate (OAR) is calculated. To control overheads, the OAR is used with actual production units to calculate over- or under-absorption of overheads.

Over- or under-absorption occurs because:

(a) The overhead incurred cost more or less than expected or;

(b) Greater or fewer units were produced than expected.

For the purposes of variance analysis, any over- or under-absorption is referred to as a fixed overhead variance. To understand the reasons behind the over- or under-absorption, the total fixed overhead variance is broken down as follows:

Total variance (over/under-absorption)

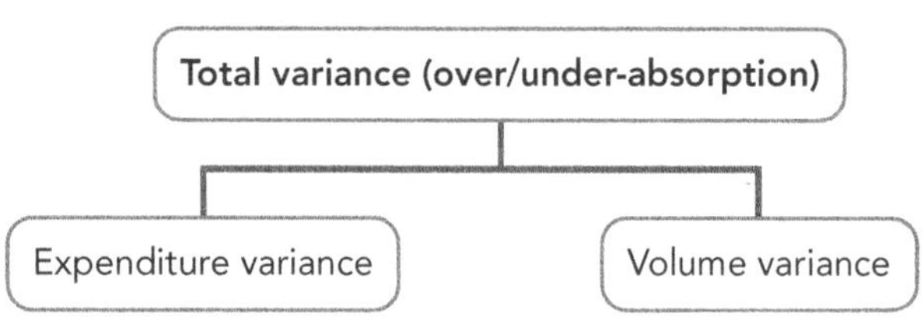

2.1 Fixed overhead expenditure variance

KEY TERM

Fixed overhead expenditure variance: A comparison of budgeted and actual fixed overhead incurred.

The **fixed overhead expenditure variance** measures whether the over- or under-absorption was caused by a difference in the level of spending on fixed overheads.

For example, if actual fixed overhead is higher than budgeted fixed overhead, this indicates that under-absorption has occurred.

The fixed overhead expenditure variance is, therefore, calculated as follows:

Formula to learn

		£
'Should'	Budgeted fixed overhead	X
'Did'	Actual fixed overhead	(X)
Fixed overhead expenditure variance		X

2.2 Fixed overhead volume variance

KEY TERM

Fixed overhead volume variance: A comparison of budgeted and actual units produced, valued at standard OAR per unit.

The **fixed overhead volume variance** measures whether the over- or under-absorption was caused by a difference in production volumes:

- If actual units produced was higher than budgeted units, more units have been produced to spread the fixed cost over. This contributes to over-absorption of overheads and generates a favourable volume variance.
- If actual units produced was lower than budgeted units, then there are fewer units to spread the fixed cost over. This contributes to under-absorption of overheads and generates an adverse volume variance.

The volume variance is calculated as follows:

Formula to learn

		£
'Should'	Budgeted production units	X
'Did'	Actual production units	(X)
		X
Difference valued at standard OAR per unit		£X

The expenditure and volume variances are sub-divisions of the total over- or under-absorption of fixed overheads. The sum of these variances should reconcile back to under- or over-absorption as follows:

	£
Fixed overhead expenditure variance	X
Fixed overhead volume variance	X
Fixed overhead total variance (over- or under-absorption)	X

Illustration 4: Fixed overhead variances

Below is the standard cost card for one of Kettle Ltd's products, T:

	£
Fixed overheads 2 hours @ £3.00 per hour	6.00

Actual production was 18,000 units rather than the budgeted figure of 20,000 units.

The actual fixed overhead incurred in the period was £115,000.

Required

Calculate:

(a) The total fixed overhead cost variance

(b) The fixed overhead expenditure variance

(c) The fixed overhead volume variance

Solution

(a) Fixed overhead cost variance

	£
Fixed overhead expenditure incurred	115,000
Fixed overhead absorbed (18,000 units × £6.00 per unit)	108,000
Total cost variance = Fixed overhead under-absorbed	7,000 (A)

There is under-absorption of overhead and under-absorption is an adverse variance.

(b) Fixed overhead expenditure variance

	£
Budgeted fixed overhead (20,000 units × £6.00)	120,000
Actual fixed overhead	115,000
Fixed overhead expenditure variance	5,000 (F)

As the actual fixed overhead expenditure is less than the budgeted amount, this is a favourable variance.

(c) Fixed overhead volume variance

	Units
Actual production in units	18,000
Budgeted production in units	20,000
Fixed overhead volume variance in units	2,000 (A)
Standard fixed overhead cost **per unit**	£6
Fixed overhead volume variance in £	12,000 (A)

The variance is adverse, as actual production is less than budgeted production.

The variances can be reconciled as follows:

	£
Fixed overhead expenditure	5,000 (F)
Fixed overhead volume	12,000 (A)
Total fixed overhead variance	7,000 (A)

Activity 5: Armour

Armour Ltd has budgeted to make 1,100 units of a product called Soul during the month of April 20X3. The budgeted fixed overhead cost is £33,000 and the standard time to make a unit of Soul is 3 hours.

The actual fixed overhead cost during the month turns out to be £33,980. 1,000 units of Soul were produced.

Required

Calculate the following variances:

(a) Fixed overhead total variance

	£
Amount of overhead absorbed	
Fixed overhead incurred	
Fixed overhead total variance (under absorbed)	▼

(b) Fixed overhead expenditure variance

	£
Budgeted fixed overhead expenditure	
Actual fixed overhead expenditure	
Fixed overhead expenditure variance	▼

(c) Fixed overhead volume variance

Budgeted production	
Actual production	
× standard absorption rate per unit	
Fixed overhead volume variance	
Or	
Budgeted labour hours	
Standard hours produced	
× standard OAR per hour	
Fixed overhead volume variance	▼

Picklist

- (3,980) A
- (£3,000) A
- 980 A
- £1,000 A
- £1,000 F
- £2,000 A
- £2,000 F
- £3,000 F
- £3,980 F
- £5,000 A
- £5,000 F
- £980 F

3 Fixed overheads variances under marginal costing

Under marginal costing, the standard cost card includes only the variable cost of production. The fixed overheads are not included in the cost of the cost units, and are written off as period costs.

As no OAR is calculated under marginal costing, no over- or under-absorption of overhead is incurred. Therefore, the difference in budgeted and actual fixed overhead incurred is due to the difference in the level of spend on fixed overheads. Therefore, the only fixed overhead variance calculated in marginal costing is the fixed overhead expenditure variance.

4 Sales variances

4.1 Sales price variance

KEY TERM

Sales price variance: A comparison of the standard selling price of the actual units sold to the actual sales revenue of actual units sold.

The **sales price variance** measures the effect of selling units for more or less than the standard selling price. Remember an adverse variance will occur if the actual sales price is less than the standard selling price – this is the opposite of cost variances.

The sales price variance can be calculated either via a proforma or a formula, as detailed below.

Formula to learn

Proforma method

		£
'Should'	**Actual units sold** should sell for (Act sales × std selling price per unit)	X
'Did'	Actual units sold did sell for	(X)
Sales price variance		X

Formula method

Sales price variance = AQS × (AP – SP)

where: AQS is the actual quantity of units sold; AP is the actual selling price per unit; SP is the standard price paid per unit.

4.2 Sales volume variance

KEY TERM

Sales volume variance: A comparison of the budgeted units sold, to the actual number of units sold, valued at standard profit per unit (under absorption costing) and the standard contribution per unit (under marginal costing).

Sales volume variance measures the financial impact of selling more or less units than forecast.

To calculate the sales volume variance the actual and budgeted number of units is compared. The difference is multiplied by the standard profit per unit if the company is using absorption costing and the standard contribution per unit if the company is using marginal costing.

The sales volume variance can be calculated by either using a proforma or formula:

Formula to learn

Proforma method

		£
'Should'	**Budgeted sales units**	X
'Did'	Actual sales units	(X)
		X
× standard profit/contribution		× £X
Sales volume variance		£X

Formula method

Sales volume variance = (BSV– ASV) × SP/C

where:

BSV is the budgeted sales volume

ASV is the actual sales volume

SP/C is the standard profit/contribution per unit

Illustration 5: Sales variances

Budgeted information for one of Savan Ltd's products, the Web, is shown below:

	£
Budgeted sales price per unit	8.00
Budgeted profit per unit	3.00
Actual sales price per unit	9.00

The budgeted level of sales for June was 1,500 units but in fact only 1,200 units were sold.

Required

Calculate the following variances:

(a) Sales price variance

(b) Sales volume variance

Solution

(a) Sales price variance

	£
1,200 units should have sold for (1,200 units × £8.00)	9,600
But did sell for (1,200 units × £9.00)	10,800
Sales price variance	1,200 (F)

The actual sales price per unit is higher than the standard selling price, so the sales price variance is favourable.

(b) Sales volume variance

	Units
Budgeted sales volume (should sell)	1,500
But did sell	1,200
Sales volume variance in units	300 (A)
× Standard profit per unit	× £3
Sales volume variance in £	£900 (A)

The actual quantity of units sold is less than expected so the sales volume variance is adverse.

Activity 6: Fly Co

Fly Co operates a standard marginal costing system. It budgeted to sell 2,000 units in August, for £20 each. The standard contribution per unit is £4.

Actual sales were 2,500 units at a slightly lower price of £19 per unit and actual contribution of £3 per unit.

Required

Calculate:

(a) The sales price variance

The sales price variance is £ [ ] [▼]

(b) The sales volume variance

The sales volume variance is £ [ ] [▼]

Picklist

- Adverse
- Favourable

Chapter summary

- For this unit materials, labour, variable overhead, fixed overhead and sales variances must be calculated.
- The total direct materials cost variance can be split into a materials price variance and a materials usage variance.
- The total direct labour cost variance can be split into the labour rate variance, the labour efficiency variance and the idle time variance.
- The total variable overhead variance can be split into an expenditure and an efficiency variance.
- The total fixed overhead cost variance in an absorption costing system is the amount of fixed overhead that has been under- or over-absorbed in the period.
- The total fixed overhead variance can then be analysed into the fixed overhead expenditure variance and fixed overhead volume variance.
- In a standard marginal costing system, there is only one fixed overhead variance, the fixed overhead expenditure variance.
- The sales price variance represents a change in the sales price compared to the standard and the sales volume variance represents a change in the number of units sold compared to the budgeted sales volume.
- The sales volume variance is valued at standard profit under absorption costing and the standard contribution under marginal costing.

Activity answers

Activity 1: News Co

(a) The total materials variance is £ 8,860 [Favourable]

Total material variance

	£
Actual units should cost (27,000 × 2 kg × £2.50)	135,000
Actual material used did cost (53,000 kg × £2.38)	(126,140)
	8,860 F

(b) The materials price variance is £ 6,360 [Favourable]

Material price variance

	£
Actual purchases should cost (53,000 × £2.50)	132,500
Actual purchases did cost (53,000 kg × £2.38)	(126,140)
	6,360 F

(c) The materials usage variance is £ 2,500 [Favourable]

The material usage variance

	£
Actual production should use (27,000 × 2 kg)	54,000
Actual production did use	(53,000)
	1,000 F
@ std cost £2.50	£2,500 F

Activity 2: Yard Co

(a) The total labour variance is £ 1,000 [Adverse]

Total labour variance

	£
Actual units should cost (2,195 × 4 hrs × £12.50)	109,750
Actual labour used did cost	(110,750)
	(1,000) A

(b) The labour rate variance is £ 4,250 [Favourable]

Labour rate variance

	£
Actual hours paid should cost (9,200 × £12.50)	115,500
Actual hours paid did cost	(110,750)
	4,250 F

(c) The labour efficiency variance is £ 5,250 [Adverse]

Labour efficiency variance

	Hours
Actual production should use (2,195 × 4 hrs)	8,780
Actual production did use	(9,200)
	(420) A
@ std cost £12.50	£5,250 A

Activity 3: Flight Co

The idle time variance is £ 1,200 [Adverse]

	Hours
Hours worked	2,200
Hours paid	(2,300)
	(100) A
× £12 per hour	£(1,200) A

Activity 4: Bee Co

(a) The total variable overhead variance is £ 750 [Adverse]

Total variable overhead variance

	£
Actual units should cost (1,000 units × £30)	30,000
Actual units did cost	(30,750)
	750 A

(b) The variable overhead price variance is £ 1,350 [Adverse]

Variable overhead price

	£
Actual hours worked should cost (1,960 hrs × £15)	29,400
Actual hours worked did cost	(30,750)
	1,350 A

(c) The variable overhead efficiency variance is £ 600 Favourable

Variable overhead efficiency

	£
Actual units should take (1,000 units × 2 hrs)	2,000
Actual units did take	(1,960)
	40 F
@ std cost £15	£600 F

Activity 5: Armour

(a)

	£
Amount of overhead absorbed (1,000 units × £30 per unit)	30,000
Fixed overhead incurred	(33,980)
Fixed overhead total variance (under absorbed)	(3,980) A

(b)

	£
Budgeted fixed overhead expenditure	33,000
Actual fixed overhead expenditure	33,980
Fixed overhead expenditure variance	980 A

(c)

Budgeted production	1,100 units
Actual production	1,000 units
	(100) units A
× standard absorption rate per unit	× £30
Fixed overhead volume variance	(£3,000) A
Or	
Budgeted labour hours (3 hrs × 1,100 units)	3,300 hrs
Standard hours produced (3 hrs × 1,000 units)	3,000 hrs
	(300) hrs A
× standard OAR per hour	× £10
Fixed overhead volume variance	(£3,000) A

Activity 6: Fly Co

(a) The sales price variance is £ 2,500 Adverse

	£
2,500 units should sell for (2,500 units × £20)	50,000
2,500 units did sell for (2,500 units × £19)	47,500
	2,500 A

(b) The sales volume variance is £ 2,000 Favourable

Budgeted sales – should sell	2,000 units
Actual sales – did sell	2,500
	500
Valued at standard contribution per unit £4	£2,000 F

Test your learning

1 The following budgeted and actual information is provided by Crispy PLC for their product YG:

	Budget	Actual
Production	1,600	1,800
Materials – kg	11,200	12,000
Materials – £	67,200	70,800
Direct labour – hrs	4,000	5,000
Direct labour – £	27,200	25,000
Total hours paid	4,000	5,500

Required

(a) Using the information in the table above, calculate the following variances:

(i) The total materials cost variance

Total materials cost variance: £ ☐

(ii) The materials price variance

Materials price variance: £ ☐

(iii) The materials usage variance

Materials usage variance: £ ☐

(b) Using the information in the table above, calculate the following variances:

(i) The total labour cost variance

Total labour cost variance £ ☐

(ii) The labour rate variance

Labour rate variance £ ☐

(iii) The labour efficiency variance

Labour efficiency variance £ ☐

2 The table below shows management accounting information for a chocolate manufacturer:

	Budget		Actual	
Units		7,000		6,400
Machine hours		21,000		20,000
		£		£
Materials	5,500 kg	16,500	4,750	13,300
Labour	10,000 hrs	70,000	12,800	76,800
Fixed overheads		52,500		56,000

Fixed overheads are absorbed on the basis of machine hours.

Required

(a) Using the information in the table above, calculate the following:

(i) Standard materials usage for 6,400 units

	kg

(ii) Standard labour hours for 6,400 units

	hrs

(iii) Standard machine hours for 6,400 units

	hrs

(b) Using the information in the above table, calculate the following variances:

(i) Fixed overhead expenditure variance

(ii) Fixed overhead volume variance

8 Interpretation of variances

Learning outcomes

2.1	**Flexed budgets** **Be able to:** Provide potential reasons for variances (either calculated or given)
2.2	**Standard costing** **Understand:** • Why variances occur • Courses of action to be taken to address divergences from standard • The interaction of variances **Be able to:** • Provide potential reasons for variances

Assessment context

Understanding why variances have arisen and the interrelationship of variances is as important as being able to do the calculations. It is important that you are able to consider what could cause the different types of variance.

Business context

Once variances have been calculated, businesses need to understand why those variances have arisen. This will help managers control the operations of the business. Variance reporting is therefore an important part of an organisation's control process – indeed many businesses still use variance reporting as their primary control tool.

Chapter overview

Interpretation of variances

Interpretation

- Consider:
  - Causes of variances
  - Interdependence of variances
  - Courses of action

Introduction

When reporting variances to management, a simple list is a useful starting point. However, management will also need to understand why variances occurred so that control action can be taken to either prevent them happening again, or to achieve similar results in the future.

1 Causes of variances

Having calculated variances, the cause of the variance must be determined before appropriate action can be taken. Assessment questions may need you to consider:

- What has caused the variance to occur; and
- The impact this has had on the performance of the organisation.

The following table may help you to think about some of the operational causes of variances:

Variance	Favourable	Adverse
Material price	• Unforeseen bulk/trade discounts received. This can either be due to a change in supplier, or more units being produced meaning that a bulk discount could be obtained. This is known as generating **economies of scale.** • Negotiating better prices with suppliers. • Cheaper materials used in production. This could have a negative impact on quality.	• A general market price increase and all suppliers have consequently increased their prices. • An unexpected change to a more expensive supplier. • More expensive materials used in production. This could also have a positive impact on the quality of material used.
Material usage	• Material used of higher quality than standard, generating less wastage. • More experienced labour used, meaning fewer mistakes were made and less wastage.	• Excessive waste due to defective material, inexperienced labour or machinery malfunction. • Theft of material, meaning more material was purchased, increasing the usage per unit. • Stricter quality control leading to more rework and more materials being used in production.
Labour rate	• Cheaper, less experienced (or lower skilled) labour was used. This could have an impact on labour hours worked and materials used.	• Use of higher paid workers than standard. This could have a positive impact on labour hours worked and materials used. • A shortage of staff meaning that more expensive, temporary staff were used in the period. • An unexpected increase in the rates of pay for employees.
Idle time	• Possible if idle time was budgeted but less occurred than expected.	The workforce may be unproductive in the period due to: • Machine breakdown • Illness or injury to worker • Materials delivered late

Variance	Favourable	Adverse
Labour efficiency	• Increased worker motivation, meaning the workforce worked quicker on each production unit. • Better quality materials used meaning less rework of production units was required. • Higher skilled staff used who were experienced in production, therefore producing units in fewer hours than expected. • More efficient machinery used making the production process less labour intensive than expected. • Greater production volumes enables staff to find techniques to produce units more quickly. This is known as the **learning effect** and helps to facilitate economies of scale.	• Lack of training making staff inexperienced in the production process, increasing the amount of time spent in production. • Lower skilled staff who were less experienced in production, therefore producing units in more hours than expected. • Inefficient machinery used, meaning that more labour hours were required to meet production requirements. • Lower quality materials used leading to more rework and more time spent in production.
Fixed overhead expenditure	• Unexpected savings in cost, for example a re-negotiation of rent or an unexpected market decrease in the price of utilities. • Change of supplier of the type of service used eg a change in electricity provider.	• An overall market increase in the cost of the service used eg telephone line rental charges.
Fixed overhead volume	• Production or level of activity greater than budgeted, increasing the amount of production units that fixed costs can be spread over (economies of scale have been achieved).	• Production or level of activity less than budgeted, meaning there are fewer production units that fixed overheads can be spread over.

Activity 1: Causes of variances

Answer the following questions using the picklists:

Which of the following situations would probably cause a favourable labour rate variance?

(1) ▼

Which of the following situations would probably cause a favourable materials usage variance?

(2) ▼

Picklist 1

- Higher grade of labour used
- Lower grade of labour used
- Lower grade of material used
- More overtime worked

Picklist 2

- Excessive wastage of materials
- Machine breakdowns
- More experienced staff used
- Stricter quality control

1.1 Interdependence of variances

You may have noticed from the above table that some causes of variances are likely to be connected, eg a lower grade of material can cause a favourable material price variance, but an adverse materials usage variance. This is known as the **interdependence of variances**.

Illustration 1: Interdependence of variances

The following direct cost variances were generated in January for Armada Ltd:

	£
Materials price variance	6,300 (F)
Materials usage variance	6,000 (A)
Labour rate variance	5,040 (A)
Labour efficiency variance	2,400 (F)
Idle time	1,500 (A)
Fixed overhead expenditure variance	3,200 (F)
Fixed overhead volume variance	900 (A)

Upon investigation of the variances, the following is discovered:

- A new supplier was used in the period, which provided materials at a cheaper price than the old supplier.

- More material wastage was reported through the period as some of the materials received onto the production line were defective and had to be replaced.
- The defective material caused problems with production machinery, resulting in increased machinery maintenance and production downtime. However, due to the downtime, the power costs were lower than anticipated.
- To attempt to overcome this downtime, Armada employed a higher grade of labour than normal. These production operatives were highly experienced in the production process, resulting in production that was just below that which was budgeted.

Required

Explain why each variance has occurred.

Solution

The causes of these variances can be explained by referring to the interdependence of the variances.

The materials provided by the new supplier were cheaper than those obtained by the old supplier. This would mean that actual materials purchased would cost less than the standard cost of materials, causing a favourable materials price variance.

However, some material used in production was defective and had to be replaced. This would have caused more material being used to produce each unit than the standard allowed. The result of this is an adverse materials usage variance.

The defective material could also explain the idle time and fixed overhead volume variances. Since production was halted as a result of the machine downtime, this has led to production operatives being unproductive in the period, leading to the idle time variance. This has also led to an adverse fixed overhead volume variance – as workers were unable to produce units, production was just below that which was budgeted.

It is important to note that should more highly skilled workers not have been used, the fixed overhead volume variance could have been even more adverse than the £900 reported.

Due to the defective materials, Armada employed a higher grade of labour than planned. This higher grade of labour was more skilled, so commanded a higher wage than normal labour. This resulted in actual labour cost per hour being more than standard cost per hour, and an adverse labour rate variance.

However, this higher grade of labour was skilled in the production process, and efficiently worked to bring production just below that budgeted. The increased efficiency resulted in each unit being produced more quickly than the standard allowed, causing the favourable labour efficiency variance.

Activity 2: Shoebox Ltd

Shoebox Ltd is a manufacturer of trainers. It operates a standard absorption costing system. It has provided the following operating statement and information relating to its operations during the previous month:

	£
Standard cost of actual production	588,000
Variances	
Material price variance	21,740 (A)
Material usage variance	(11,760) (F)
Labour rate variance	27,930 (A)
Labour efficiency variance	13,230 (A)
Fixed overhead expenditure variance	(2,000) (F)
Fixed overhead volume variance	7,740 (A)
Actual cost of production	644,880

Recent events

Supplier

One of our suppliers went out of business during the month. We had to unexpectedly change to a new supplier who was more expensive, but who provided a higher quality material.

Machinery

A machine on the production line was upgraded during the month. Production was halted for 4 days whilst the machinery was installed. To ensure that sales volumes weren't excessively impacted we paid our staff slightly more per hour than expected, to recover some of the lost production.

Warehouse

During the month our warehouse rent contract was renewed. We unexpectedly managed to negotiate our rent down for the coming year. This was so unexpected that we even estimated a rental increase when we set the budget.

Required

(a) Which of the following variances was caused by buying more expensive material?

	✓
Adverse material price variance	
Favourable material usage variance	
Adverse labour rate variance	
Favourable fixed overhead expenditure variance	

(b) **Which of the following variances was caused by higher quality material?**

	✓
Adverse material price variance	
Favourable material usage variance	
Adverse labour rate variance	
Favourable fixed overhead expenditure variance	

(c) **Which of the following variances was caused by staff being paid more per hour?**

	✓
Adverse material price variance	
Favourable material usage variance	
Adverse labour rate variance	
Favourable fixed overhead expenditure variance	

(d) **The decrease in rent caused which of the following variances?**

	✓
Adverse material price variance	
Favourable material usage variance	
Adverse labour rate variance	
Favourable fixed overhead expenditure variance	

2 Courses of action

Once a variance has been identified and its cause understood, managers must decide on appropriate corrective action. The response depends on the type of variance and the underlying reason for it.

Issue	Possible actions
Pricing	Talk to suppliers and try to agree a better price Look for cheaper alternatives (without hurting quality) Review wage rates or overtime use Check if selling prices or discounts need updating
Material usage	Give extra training to staff about usage Improve quality checks on materials Fix storage or handling problems that cause waste Review whether materials used are suitable for the job
Labour efficiency	Provide training or refreshers Improve supervision or support on the shop floor Update work instructions or processes Check machinery because slow machines = slow workers
Idle time	Improve scheduling so materials/job cards arrive on time Fix or maintain machines more often Review staffing to reduce gaps in cover
Variable overhead variance	Check for overspending on energy or indirect materials Improve how resources (like power or supplies) are used Review supplier contracts
Fixed overheads	Review contracts (rent, utilities, service charges) Make sure budgets are up to date Look for long-term savings or efficiency improvements

Chapter summary

- Each type of variance can have a variety of causes.
- Often the variances are interdependent, meaning that a factor that caused one variance is also the factor that causes other variances.
- Once the cause of the variance has been established, targeted action can be taken (process, people, price or update of standard).

Activity answers

Activity 1: Causes of variances

Which of the following situations would probably cause a favourable labour rate variance?

Lower grade of labour used

Which of the following situations would probably cause a favourable materials usage variance?

More experienced staff used

Activity 2: Shoebox Ltd

(a) The correct answer is:

	✓
Adverse material price variance	✓
Favourable material usage variance	
Adverse labour rate variance	
Favourable fixed overhead expenditure variance	

The new supplier being more expensive has meant that more was paid for materials per kg than was originally planned. This has led to more being spent overall on materials and an adverse materials price variance.

(b) The correct answer is:

	✓
Adverse material price variance	
Favourable material usage variance	✓
Adverse labour rate variance	
Favourable fixed overhead expenditure variance	

The materials from the new supplier were of better quality. This has led to less wastage of material when the trainers were produced, and consequently less material being used overall in production. This has helped to generate a favourable material usage variance.

(c) The correct answer is:

	✓
Adverse material price variance	
Favourable material usage variance	
Adverse labour rate variance	✓
Favourable fixed overhead expenditure variance	

To recover the lost production time staff were paid a slightly higher rate per hour than anticipated. This has led to a higher labour cost per hour than was planned and an adverse labour rate variance.

(d) The correct answer is:

	✓
Adverse material price variance	
Favourable material usage variance	
Adverse labour rate variance	
Favourable fixed overhead expenditure variance	✓

The renegotiation of the warehouse rent downwards has meant that less was spent on rent than was budgeted. This has led to reduced fixed overhead expenditure and therefore a favourable fixed overhead expenditure variance.

Important note: The reduced rent needs to be reflected in future budgets to stop this variance occurring again.

Test your learning

1 **Which situation is most likely to cause a favourable materials price variance?**

	✓
Switching to a higher-quality supplier	
Buying in smaller quantities	
Unexpected bulk discounts from a supplier	
Strict quality control causing more rework	

2 **Buying cheaper materials would most likely lead to:**

	✓
A favourable price variance and a favourable usage variance	
An adverse price variance and a favourable usage variance	
A favourable price variance and an adverse usage variance	
No variances at all	

3 **A favourable labour rate variance may happen because:**

	✓
Higher-skilled workers were used	
Overtime was required	
A shortage led to using temporary staff	
Cheaper labour was used than planned	

4 **Which situation is most likely to cause a favourable fixed overhead expenditure variance?**

	✓
Increased rent	
Unexpected savings on utility costs	
Lower production levels	
More rework than expected	

5 If material usage is higher than expected, managers should:

	✓
Increase selling prices	
Review quality checks and storage/handling processes	
Reduce maintenance	
Increase the overhead absorption rate	

9 Activity-based costing (ABC)

Learning outcomes

2.3 Activity-based costing (ABC)

Understand:

- The circumstances where ABC would be most appropriate
- The benefits of ABC over traditional absorption costing
- Issues surrounding the introduction of ABC
- The potential implications for unit selling prices and profitability where ABC leads to a different unit cost

Be able to:

- Calculate product costs using ABC
- Compare product costs derived under ABC to those under absorption costing

Assessment context

Calculation of various absorption rates using ABC may be required.

Business context

The concepts of ABC were developed in the manufacturing sector of the US during the 1970s and 1980s. Absorption costing has become outdated for many businesses due to the diversity of product ranges and high level of overheads. As such, ABC is becoming a much more appropriate tool for businesses to use when costing their products.

Chapter overview

Activity-based costing

Calculation of cost/unit

- Overheads are grouped into activities (cost pools)
- Identify the item which causes cost to be incurred (cost driver)
- Calculate a cost per unit for each cost driver

$$\frac{\text{Cost pool}}{\text{Cost driver}} = \text{OAR}$$

- Absorb costs into production based on actual usage of cost drivers

Suitability of ABC

- Better analysis of costs leads to better:
  - Cost control
  - Pricing decisions
  - Profitability analysis
- Criticisms:
  - Time consuming
  - Costly
  - Some arbitrary apportionment may still exist
  - Limited benefit if products have similar cost structures

Introduction

Traditional absorption costing uses a single basis for absorbing production overheads into cost units, usually using machine or labour hours, ignoring other reasons why overheads are incurred. Therefore, production overheads are absorbed using one overhead absorption rate (OAR):

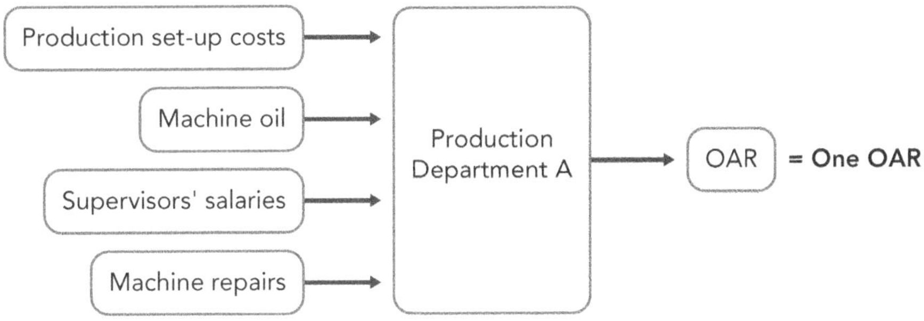

In modern manufacturing organisations, fixed overheads tend to form a large part of product costs over variable costs. Direct labour in particular is nowadays a much less significant part of production. **Activity based costing** (ABC) recognises this, and attempts to charge production costs in a more realistic way.

ABC identifies activities outside of production, and then charges overheads to cost units on the usage of these activities. The activities will vary from business to business, but some examples are:

- Material receipts into stores
- Material requisitions from stores to production
- Repairs and maintenance of production machinery
- Setting up machines for a production run
- Quality control checks

ABC matches overhead costs to individual activities. An OAR is calculated per activity, and these OARs are used to absorb production overheads into production units. As a result, ABC calculates multiple OARs depending on the number of activities that take place in the organisation:

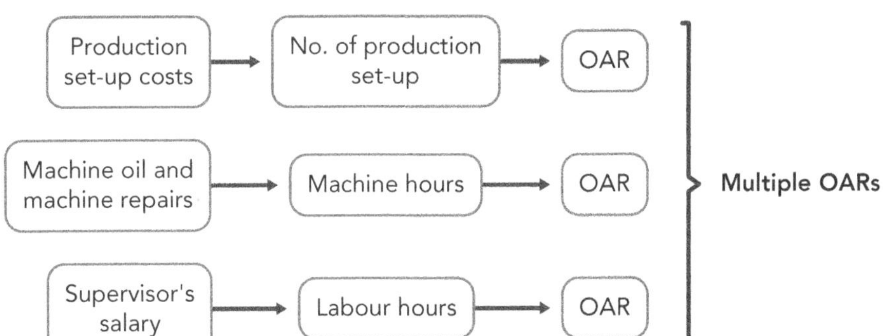

It's important to note that under ABC, a product that is made in small batches will incur more production overhead than a product made in larger batches. This is because it uses up more of certain activities, such as materials requisitions and production set-ups. If a single OAR was used, this additional activity usage would not be reflected, and the OAR is inaccurate as a result.

ABC is therefore beneficial when there are a number of different products being made by the organisation, with considerable differences in the use of activities between the products.

1 Calculation of costs per unit under ABC

1.1 ABC terminology

There is some specific terminology that you need to be comfortable with when using ABC:

KEY TERM

Cost pool: A breakdown of total overheads into different categories depending on the activity that has generated the cost.

Cost driver: A factor that drives a change in the usage of an activity.

An important step in ABC is to match the cost pool (ie the category of cost) to the cost driver (ie the factor that has caused the activity related to the cost pool to change).

1.2 Steps to take to calculate cost per unit under ABC

Step 1 Group total overheads into cost pools according to the nature of the activity that has caused the cost pool to be incurred.

Step 2 Identify what causes each cost pool to change, and match the cause to the cost driver, ie identify a cost driver per cost pool.

Step 3 Calculate an OAR per unit of cost driver for each individual cost pool as follows:

Total cost pool/Total number of cost drivers

Step 4 Absorb total activity costs based on the total usage of cost drivers, as follows:

OAR per unit of cost driver × Total usage of cost driver

Step 5 Calculate activity cost for each cost unit by dividing the total activity cost by the total number of units as follows:

Total activity cost/Total number of units

Assessment focus point

Step (2) requires you to match a cost pool to a cost driver. You will need to make a logical guess in the assessment as to the best cost driver to use for each cost pool, although the vast majority of the time it should be obvious.

Illustration 1: Dodo Ltd

Dodo Ltd manufactures three products, A, B and C. Data for the period just ended is as follows:

	A	B	C
Output (units)	20,000	25,000	2,000
Direct material cost per unit (£)	5.00	10.00	10.00
Direct labour cost per unit (£)	10.00	5.00	5.00
Labour hours per unit	2	1	1
Machine hours per unit	2.5	2	5
Number of component requisitions	1000	800	200

Total production overheads incurred in the period were £150,000, being made up of £55,000 for machinery and £95,000 for component requisitions.

Required

(a) Calculate the overhead absorption rate if overheads are absorbed on the basis of labour hours.

(b) Calculate the total overhead cost for each of the products using ABC principles.

Round each cost driver to two decimal places.

Round the total overhead cost for each product to the nearest whole pound.

(c) Calculate the total cost per unit for each of the products under the two different methods. Round your answer to two decimal places.

Solution

(a)

	A	B	C	Total
Units	20,000	25,000	2,000	
Hrs/unit	2	1	1	
Total hours required	40,000	25,000	2,000	67,000

& £150,000 / 67,000 hours = £2.24 per hour

(b)

	A £	B £	C £	Total £
Machining costs	(£0.50 × 2.5 × 20,000) 25,000	(£0.50 × 2 × 25,000) 25,000	(£0.50 × 5 × 2,000) 5,000	55,000
Components handling	(£47.50 × 1000) 47,500	(£47.50 × 800) 38,000	(£47.50 × 200) 9,500	95,000
Total overhead costs	72,500	63,000	14,500	150,000

Total machine hours = (2.5 × 20,000) + (2 × 25,000) + (5 × 2,000) = 110,000 hours

Therefore £55,000 / 110,000 hours = £0.50 per machine hour

Total component requisitions = 1000 + 800 + 200 = 2000

Therefore £95,000 / 2000 = £47.50 per component requisition

(c) Under labour hours the total unit cost is calculated as follows:

	A £/unit	B £/unit	C £/unit
Direct materials	5.00	10.00	10.00
Direct labour	10.00	5.00	5.00
Production overheads	(£2.24 × 2hrs) 4.48	(2.24 × 1hr) 2.24	(£2.24 × 1hr) 2.24
Total cost	19.48	17.24	17.24

Under ABC the total unit cost is calculated as follows:

	A £/unit	B £/unit	C £/unit
Direct materials	5.00	10.00	10.00
Direct labour	10.00	5.00	5.00
Production overheads	(£72,500 / 20,000) 3.63	(£63,000 / 25,000) 2.52	(£14,500 / 2,000) 7.25
Total cost	18.63	17.52	22.25

Activity 1: Roasted Ltd

Roasted Ltd is a medium-sized coffee manufacturing company that produces two products, ground coffee and coffee beans. The company has invested in new integrated technologies throughout all sections of the business, from the use of robotics in the production line, through to reporting software in the accounting function. A traditional absorption costing method is currently used and it has been suggested that activity based costing maybe more appropriate following the introduction of improved technologies throughout the company. The following information regarding the company has been provided:

	Ground coffee	Coffee beans
Direct materials per unit	£10	£11
Direct labour hours per unit @ £10 per hour	4	6
Forecast production and sales (units)	40,000	30,000
Number of inspections	680	120
IT support (hours)	20,000	4,000

The budgeted costs for the two overhead activities is as follows:

- Inspections £400,000
- IT Support £960,000

Required

(a) Calculate the direct costs and production overheads per unit for ground coffee and coffee beans using the traditional direct labour hours absorption method.

	Ground coffee £	Coffee beans £
Direct costs		
Production overheads		
Total cost		

(b) Calculate the inspections and IT support costs per unit for ground coffee and coffee beans using the ABC method. Enter your answers to two decimal places.

	Ground coffee £	Coffee beans £
Direct costs		
Inspections		
IT support		
Total cost		

(c) **Under ABC, why do the two coffee products end up with almost the same cost per unit?**

	✓
Both products use the same quantity of direct materials	
ABC ignores overheads and uses only direct costs	
ABC allocates overheads using cost drivers that reflect technology-driven activities	
ABC uses labour hours as the main cost driver	

(d) **Why has traditional absorption costing become less appropriate in highly automated production environments?**

	✓
Labour hours increase as automation increases	
Automation reduces the need for overhead allocation	
Overheads are no longer related to labour hours in automated systems	
Automation eliminates direct costs entirely	

2 Advantages and disadvantages of ABC

The use of ABC provides opportunities for:

- **Improved decision making**: ABC provides a more realistic estimate of costs and profits which can be used in performance appraisal, meaning that more relevant decisions can be taken about products. For example, a more accurate decision can be made as to whether that product should continue to be manufactured based on a more realistic view as to whether that product is suitably profitable.
- **Improved cost control and reduction**: Having visibility of the different cost drivers enables managers to understand how costs are being incurred, and improvements can be sought to reduce the usage of those cost drivers. For example, ABC analysis may show that a product may take substantially longer in machine time than other products. Steps can then be taken to improve the production efficiency of the product to reduce machine time.
- **Improved pricing**: Better costing information enables better pricing structures to be established for products to improve their overall profitability or to make the products more competitive. For example, if ABC indicates that a product is using substantially less overheads than under traditional absorption costing, managers may decide to decrease the price of the product, which may attract greater sales volumes.
- **Diversity of overheads**: ABC does not assume that overheads are merely driven by volume, and recognises the complexity and diversity of costs associated with producing different types of product. For example, lower volume products attract a lower absolute amount of fixed

overheads because there are fewer labour or machine hours associated with producing them. However, it could be argued that a higher proportion of overheads should be allocated to lower volume products because they are produced in small batches and so should, for example, incur more of the production line set-up cost.

However, there are some criticisms of ABC:

- **Time and cost**: Breaking down overheads into cost pools and ascertaining cost drivers can be time consuming and expensive. Finance staff will need to spend time analysing overheads and cost drivers, and there may need to be an investment in information systems if the current system is not sophisticated enough to gather the necessary data about an organisation's cost drivers.
- **Standardised products**: ABC has limited benefit in organisations where there is little customisation of products. In these situations products will be manufactured in very similar ways, for example taking similar amounts of machine and quality control time, so each product will incur a similar amount of overhead. The time and effort spent in breaking down overheads and identifying cost drivers can be wasted in these situations.
- **Cost drivers**: In more complex environments it can be difficult to find specific reasons why overheads are incurred making identification of cost drivers difficult. Likewise, it can sometimes be difficult to match a cost pool to a cost driver. There is still some arbitrary apportionment associated with ABC, just as there is with traditional absorption costing.

3 When ABC should be used

- When production overheads are high relative to prime costs (eg service sector)
- When there is diversity of the product range
- When there are considerable differences in the use of resources by products
- When consumption of resources is not driven by volume

Chapter summary

- Activity-based costing (ABC) considers the activities that cause overheads to be incurred and the factors that give rise to these activity costs (cost drivers).
- ABC is a method of absorbing overheads into products on the basis of the amount of each activity that the particular product is expected to use in the period.
- ABC may be more suitable than traditional absorption costing in manufacturing businesses where overhead costs are much larger than direct production costs.

Activity answers

Activity 1: Roasted Ltd

(a)

	Ground coffee £	Coffee beans £
Direct costs	50	71
Production overheads	16	24
Total cost	66	95

(b)

	Ground coffee £	Coffee beans £
Direct costs	50	71
Inspections	8.50	2.00
IT support	20.00	5.33
Total cost	78.50	78.33

(c) The correct answer is:

	✓
Both products use the same quantity of direct materials	
ABC ignores overheads and uses only direct costs	
ABC allocates overheads using cost drivers that reflect technology-driven activities	✓
ABC uses labour hours as the main cost driver	

ABC uses cost drivers based on activities (eg inspections), which better reflect technology-based production.

(d) The correct answer is:

	✓
Labour hours increase as automation increases	
Automation reduces the need for overhead allocation	
Overheads are no longer related to labour hours in automated systems	✓
Automation eliminates direct costs entirely	

As technology increases, labour hours reduce, so allocating overheads based on labour time becomes less representative of the resources consumed.

Test your learning

1 A business produces two products, the LM and the NP. The direct costs of the two products are:

	LM	NP
Direct materials	£2.60	£3.90
Direct labour	£3.50	£2.70

The total overhead cost is made up as follows:

	£
Stores costs	140,000
Production set-up costs	280,000
Quality control inspection costs	180,000
	600,000

The budgeted production is for 50,000 units of LM and 20,000 units of NP.

Each product is expected to make the following use of the service activities:

	LM	NP	Total
Materials requisitions from stores	100	220	320
Production set-ups	80	200	280
Quality control inspections	30	60	90

Required

Complete the following table to show the budgeted cost per unit for each product using activity based costing and how much total budgeted overhead is included in the unit cost for each product.

Product	Budgeted cost per unit £	Budgeted overhead per unit £
LM		
NP		

2 **How does ABC provide better decision-making information compared with traditional absorption costing?**

	✓
It allocates overheads using a single cost driver	
It recognises that different activities generate different overhead costs	
It removes the need to analyse direct costs	
It ensures all products have the same profit margin	

3 **Which of the following is a key benefit of ABC over traditional absorption costing?**

	✓
ABC always uses fewer cost pools than absorption costing	
ABC provides a more accurate cost per unit by linking costs to activities	
ABC reduces the need to record overheads	
ABC eliminates the need for overhead absorption rates	

10 Target costing and life cycle costing

Learning outcomes

2.4	**Target costing** **Understand:** • Principles underpinning target costing • The concept of value analysis • Actions to take to reduce cost gaps **Be able to:** • Calculate target costs • Calculate a cost gap
2.5	**Life cycle costing** **Understand:** • Principles underpinning life cycle costing • How the use of life cycle costing can benefit an organisation • The concepts of economies of scale, mechanisation and the learning effect **Be able to:** • Identify components of the life cycle cost of a product • Calculate the discounted and non-discounted life cycle cost of a product • Interpret the results of calculations of life cycle costs

Assessment context

You may be required to carry out straightforward calculations using target costing and life cycle costing. In assessments, this typically includes identifying a target cost from a given selling price and profit margin, calculating a cost gap, or selecting appropriate actions to close that gap. For life cycle costing, tasks may involve identifying cost components, calculating total life cycle costs (discounted or non-discounted), and interpreting whether a product is financially viable over its full life.

Business context

Modern business is radically different from that of 80 years ago. New techniques have emerged – many coming from Japanese companies such as Toyota – which are more appropriate for today's environment.

Product life cycles are becoming shorter and shorter. Organisations increasingly reassess product life cycle costs and revenues as the time available to sell the product and recover the investment shrinks.

Target costing was developed in Japan in response to the problems of controlling and reducing costs over a product's life cycle.

Technology is also playing an increasing part in the way businesses control their costs.

Chapter overview

Target costing and life cycle costing

Product life cycle

- Development
- Introduction
- Growth
- Maturity
- Decline

Life cycle costing

- Costs a product over its entire life cycle – from design to abandonment
- Stages of product life cycle:
  - Development
  - Introduction
  - Growth
  - Maturity
  - Decline

Target costing

Selling price	X
Less: desired margin	(X)
Target cost	X

Value analysis

- Cost reduction technique
- Aims to reduce:
  - Cost value
- Maintain/improve:
  - Exchange value
  - Use value
  - Esteem value

Introduction

Managing costs effectively is important to an organisation in order to control its profitability. Managers can therefore adopt a range of techniques in order for them to manage costs effectively, in particular:

- Being aware of how costs change within the product life cycle, and ensuring that all costs have been considered in the life cycle of products and services
- Considering cost reductions in products using target costing and value analysis

1 Product life cycle

KEY TERM

Product life cycle: A model to show the different sales and profitability patterns at different stages of a product's life cycle.

A product life cycle consists of different phases or stages in the commercial life of the product. At each stage sales volumes, costs and profitability are different.

1.1 Stages of the product life cycle

The stages of the product life cycle, as identified by Raymond Vernon in 1966, are detailed on the below graph:

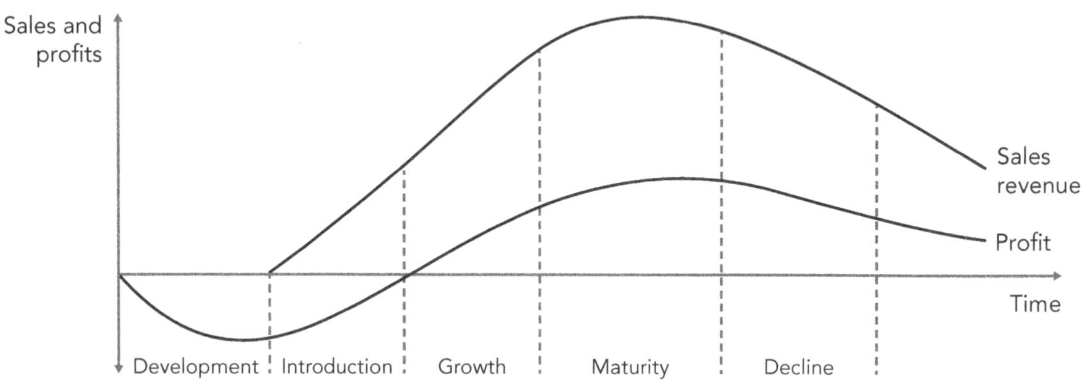

The nature of the market and costs incurred will change as the product progresses through the product life cycle, as demonstrated in the below table:

Stage	Nature of market	Costs
Development	No external market.	High level of capital development costs, eg purchase of non-current assets.
Introduction	Little to no competition. Customers have few alternative products to switch to.	Advertising and promotion and continuing development costs. Direct costs (materials, labour and overheads) start to be incurred.
Growth	Demand for the product increases leading to a rapid increase in sales. New competitors enter the market attracted by the success and profitability of the product.	Fixed promotion cost can remain high to combat the new entrants into the market. Direct material, labour and overheads become biggest proportion of cost as production is increased to satisfy demand.

Stage	Nature of market	Costs
Maturity	Demand peaks then becomes stagnant. New entrants are not evident, but competition is fierce between established, large organisations. Economies of scale are established.	Costs of production are driven down by economies of scale and the learning effect. These are secured as follows: • Mechanisation of the production process, reducing the labour cost of production • Bulk buying discounts due to higher volumes being produced • Staff being more skilled in production producing greater efficiencies. This learning effect reduces labour costs • Fixed production overheads spread over more units Mechanisation generates more fixed production overheads.
Decline	Market saturation reached. Eventual drop in demand. The business will consider whether production of the product should continue.	Production costs reduce. Increased obsolescence cost (eg lost contribution on discounted products, wastage costs of unsold inventory).

It is important to note that the product life cycle varies from industry to industry. For example, a chocolate cake may not ever reach the decline phase unless social tastes for chocolate change. In contrast, a tablet computer can have a very short life cycle due to rapid changes in technology.

1.2 Life cycle costing

KEY TERM

> **Life cycle costing:** Costing of a product throughout all stages of its life cycle, including costs incurred in the development stage and market withdrawal stage.

Traditional costing methods analyse the cost of a product once production of the product has begun. However, the product life cycle demonstrates that product costs are incurred throughout all stages of its life cycle. In particular, costs are incurred in the development stage prior to production commencing, and the decline stage when the product is withdrawn from the market.

Life cycle costing (LCC) recognises that costs are incurred prior and post production, and aims to cost a product, service, customer or project over its entire life cycle. It therefore ensures that all costs are covered by sales revenue to ensure the product is profitable over its entire life cycle.

Examples of costs that life cycle costing aims to include are:

- Design costs
- Prototyping
- Programming
- Process design
- Equipment acquisition

Activity 1: Co X

Co X is in a high-tech industry and is often first to market with new technological advances. It has recently spent £500,000 designing a new product. The new product is expected to have an 18-month life cycle. Co X are expecting to spend £1.1m on advertising immediately after the product's launch.

The anticipated performance of this product is as follows:

	Introduction	Growth	Maturity	Decline
Sales volume (units)	4,000	15,000	30,000	10,000
Per unit (£)				
Selling price	600	550	450	350
Variable cost	250	250	200	150
Overhead	100	100	60	75

Required

Calculate the profitability of the new product and indicate if the new product should go ahead.

	Development	Introduction	Growth	Maturity	Decline	Total
Sales volume (units)		4,000	15,000	30,000	10,000	
	£000	£000	£000	£000		
Revenue						
Variable cost						
Overhead						
Development cost		–	–	–	–	
Advertising cost	–		–	–	–	
Profit						

The new product [▼] be launched.

Picklist

- Should
- Should not

In an LCC exercise, the costs consist of present and future costs. Therefore, in order to arrive at a better picture of life cycle costs, these may be discounted to their present value, and a net present value calculated. Net present value is covered in Chapter 12.

2 Target costing

KEY TERM

Target cost: The desired cost of a product which must be achieved, based on deducting the desired profit from a target selling price.

Traditionally an organisation establishes the cost of producing a product and the profit margin they want to achieve from the product. A mark-up is then applied to the cost to generate the selling price needed to achieve the required profit margin.

Therefore, total cost + required profit = selling price.

In a target costing situation, an organisation may have an idea of the maximum amount customers are willing to pay for a product, and how much profit it wishes to achieve from the product. In these situations, the selling price is set first, followed by the profit margin that the company wishes to achieve.

A **target cost** is then calculated as follows:

Formula to learn

Target cost is calculated as:

	£
Target selling price/market price	X
Less target profit	(X)
Target cost	X

The target cost required is compared to the expected cost of the product. Any difference between the expected cost and the target cost is known as a cost gap, and managers will seek incremental improvements to both product design and production processes to ensure that the target cost is met.

Assessment focus point

Target costing tasks may ask you to calculate target costs using either a profit margin or mark-up. It is important you are comfortable with how to make these calculations before you take the assessment.

A profit margin is where profit is stated as a percentage of sales. For example, if an assessment task states that 'the organisation wishes to achieve a 20% margin on sales', the cost structure would be as follows:

	%
Sales	100
Costs	80
Profit	20

A mark-up is where profit is stated as a percentage of costs. For example, if an assessment task states that 'the organisation wishes to achieve a 30% mark-up on costs' the cost structure would be as follows:

	%
Sales	130
Costs	100
Profit	30

2.1 Fixed costs within the target cost

Some costs may already be fixed. For example, it may not be possible to change the time taken to produce a unit or the hourly rate of pay for employees. These are costs that the company is unlikely to be able to influence in terms of making savings, and therefore they are deducted from the target cost.

Illustration 1: Lata Ltd

Lata Ltd is looking to manufacture a new product, the Boom. The market is very competitive and the company has established that to sell 1,000 units a year it should set the selling price at £24. It wishes to achieve a profit margin of 20%.

Current total production costs are estimated to be £22,000.

Required

(a) Calculate the target cost per unit to achieve a profit margin of 20%.

(b) Indicate whether the new product should be introduced.

(c) Calculate the target cost of materials required to maintain a profit margin of 20%.

Solution

(a) To calculate this, the target profit to be achieved needs to be subtracted from the target selling price of £24.00 as follows:

	£
Selling price	24.00
Profit margin (20%)	(4.80)
Target cost	19.20

(b) To answer this question, total target costs need to be compared to total estimated cost. If there is a cost gap, the product should not be introduced at this current time:

	£
Total target cost (£19.20 × 1,000 units)	19,200
Total estimated cost	22,000
Cost gap	2,800

As there is a cost gap the product should not be launched at this time. Steps need to be taken in order to reduce this cost gap before the product is launched.

We now have some further information to consider:

Market research has estimated that 12,000 units of the Boom could be sold if the selling price was reduced by £2.00 per unit. Lata will consider this reduction if the 20% profit margin can be maintained. However, it is aware it cannot reduce the cost of labour or fixed overheads.

Each Boom requires one hour of labour, at a rate of £12 per hour. In addition, the total fixed production costs have been estimated as £30,000.

(c) To work this out, we need to calculate the total target cost per unit bearing in mind the sales price reduction. We then need to calculate the cost per unit of each of the costs, and deduct these costs from the total target cost per unit, to calculate how much can be spent per unit on materials:

	£
Reduced selling price per unit (£24.00 – £2.00)	22.00
Target profit per unit (22.00 × 0.2)	(4.40)
Target total cost per unit	17.60
Expected labour cost (1 hr × £12)	12.00
Expected fixed cost per unit (£30,000/12,000 units)	2.50
Target material cost per unit (17.60 – 12.00 – 2.50)	3.10

Activity 2: Target costing

A business is deciding whether to introduce a new product:

- It needs to make a net profit margin of 25%.
- Market research suggests that, in total, the business will be able to sell 25,000 units of the product at £10 per unit.
- The total costs that the business expects to incur over the life of the product are shown in the table below:

Research and development £000	Variable manufacturing costs £000	Fixed manufacturing costs £000	End of life costs £000
45	125	15	5

Required

(a) Complete the following table to determine the target cost per unit for the new product (to the nearest penny).

	£
Total anticipated sales revenue	
Target total net profit	
Target total costs	
Target cost per unit	

(b) **Select the correct option for each sentence.**

	Yes ✓	No ✓
Under traditional costing techniques, would the product be launched?		
Under life cycle costing, would the product be launched?		

The market research, mentioned at the start of the task, also indicated that customers would purchase more of the product if its selling price was reduced by £1 per unit. The company would consider making this price reduction if it could sell enough units to maintain a profit margin of 25%.

Required

(c) **Complete the table below. Assume the life cycle costs are expected to be as in (a) and (b) above. Enter your answers in the table below to the nearest penny.**

	£
Reduced selling price per unit	
Target net profit per unit	
Target total cost per unit	
Expected variable manufacturing cost per unit	
Target fixed costs per unit	

2.2 Closing the cost gap

Attempts to reduce the cost gap should focus on reducing the cost without affecting the quality of the product. For example, using standard components or training staff to be more efficient.

Increasing the selling price will not close the cost gap (because increasing the selling price will negatively affect the sales volume).

2.3 Value analysis

KEY TERM

Value analysis: Analysis of every aspect of existing products/services in order to reduce the cost, with no reduction in value to the customer.

Value analysis is a key technique that an organisation can use to close a cost gap.

Value analysis is where every aspect of a product or service is analysed to determine whether it provides value to the customer and whether the same value can be provided in another way at a lower cost. It aims to reduce the cost of a product or service without any reduction in the value to the customer. This analysis is done to products currently in production.

2.4 Value adding and non-value adding activities

Value analysis ensures that only value-adding activities should take place – those activities which create, or enhance, the quality of saleable products. Any other activity is deemed as non-value adding and should be reduced or eliminated. Examples include:

- Reworking of defective products
- Storage of materials
- Costs associated with staff turnover
- Movement costs (if sub-assemblies between production stages)
- Complex mix of components in products

The aim of value analysis is cost reduction. However, care must be taken to ensure short-term cost reduction does not affect long-term profitability. For example, costs could be reduced by cutting back on staff training, but this could lead to inefficiencies, low morale or high labour turnover.

Care also needs to be taken to ensure that the organisation's sustainability and corporate social responsibility is also not negatively impacted.

Chapter summary

- Most products have a limited life cycle which involves the stages of development and launch, growth, maturity and decline. The position of the product within its life cycle will affect sales and profitability patterns and be an important factor in cost management.
- The aim of life cycle costing is to ensure that all the costs of a product (including development costs) are accumulated over the whole of its life cycle, with or without discounting, in order to ensure that all costs are covered by revenue from the product.
- Target costing involves setting a target for the cost of a product or service by deducting the desired profit margin from the market selling price. The target cost represents the maximum amount of cost that the organisation can incur and still make the desired level of profit.
- Value analysis is a method of analysing the constituent elements of a product or service in order to try to reduce the cost with no loss in value to the customer.

Activity answers

Activity 1: Co X

	Development	Introduction	Growth	Maturity	Decline	Total
Sales volume (units)		4,000	15,000	30,000	10,000	
	£000	£000	£000	£000		
Revenue		2,400	8,250	13,500	3,500	27,650
Variable cost		(1,000)	(3,750)	(6,000)	(1,500)	(12,250)
Overhead		(400)	(1,500)	(1,800)	(750)	(4,450)
Development cost	(500)	–	–	–	–	(500)
Advertising cost	–	(1,100)	–	–	–	(1,100)
Profit	(500)	(100)	3,000	5,700	1,250	9,350

The new product should be launched.

This is because the product is anticipated to produce an overall profit.

Activity 2: Target costing

(a)

	£
Total anticipated sales revenue (£10 × 25,000 units)	250,000
Target total net profit (£250,000 × 0.25)	(62,500)
Target total costs	187,500
Target cost per unit (£187,500/25,000 units)	7.50

(b) The correct answers are:

	Yes ✓	No ✓
Under traditional costing techniques, would the product be launched?	✓	
Under life cycle costing, would the product be launched?		✓

Life cycle costing includes all costs generated by a product over its entire life cycle. This includes any costs incurred prior to the product entering production, and any costs incurred to decommission the product at the end of its life. Traditional costing, however, only considers costs incurred in the product's production phase.

The target cost of the product has been calculated as £7.50 per unit, which is higher than the anticipated variable and fixed production cost per unit of £5.60 (£125,000 + £15,000/25,000 units). Under traditional costing techniques the product should be launched.

However once the complete life cycle costs have been considered, the anticipated total cost is £190,000, and the total cost per unit rises to £7.60 (£190,000/25,000 units). This is £2,500 greater than the total target costs required to achieve a profit margin of 25% (or £0.10 more per unit than required). Under life cycle costing the product should not be launched as there is a risk that the target 25% profit margin may not be achieved.

(c)

	£
Reduced selling price per unit (£10 – £1)	9.00
Target net profit per unit (£9 × 0.25)	(2.25)
Target total cost per unit	6.75
Expected variable manufacturing cost per unit (£125,000/25,000 units)	(5.00)
Target fixed costs per unit	1.75

Test your learning

1 **Identify types of cost that could be incurred in each stage of the product life cycle.**

2 Fox Ltd are about to start developing a new product. It is anticipated that it will have a five-year life cycle.

Development costs are expected to be £400,000. It is anticipated that the product will have a five-year life cycle, at the end of which the machinery used to develop the product will be decommissioned at a cost of £60,000.

The expected cash flows from the product are expected to be as follows:

	Introduction	Growth	Maturity	Decline
Sales volume (units)	5,000	13,000	25,000	10,000
Selling price per unit	250	250	200	150
Variable cost per unit	150	130	70	85
Fixed overhead (£000)	800	650	450	460

Required

Calculate the profitability of the new product.

	Development	Introduction	Growth	Maturity	Maturity	Total
Sales volume (units)		5,000	13,000	25,000	10,000	
	£000	£000	£000	£000	£000	£000
Revenue						
Variable cost						
Fixed Overhead						
Development cost						
Scrap cost						
Profit						

3 Jess Co are developing a product, the Catflap. Jess wants to achieve a profit margin of 20% and needs to set the selling price at £90 per unit.

Required

Calculate the target cost per unit.

The target cost per unit is £ [ ]

11 Short-term decision-making techniques

Learning outcomes

1.4	**Budgeting where resource constraints exist** **Understand:** • The principal budget factor • Identify budget limiting factors: market share, access to finance, shortage of production resources, plant capacity, factory space • The concept of scarce resources • The concept of contribution • When contribution should be used as part of the decision-making criteria **Be able to:** • Calculate the maximum level of production where a constraint exists • Calculate the contribution per unit of scarce resources • Calculate the optimum production plan in situations where there is one scarce resource • Calculate total profit or total contribution based on the optimal production plan
3.1	**Comparison of short-and long-term decisions** **Understand:** • The fundamental differences between short-term and long-term decision making: - Time frame - Capital investment - Risk
3.2	**Relevant costing** **Understand:** • How to identify relevant costs • The concept of opportunity costs • Factors to be considered when a business decides to: - Make or buy products - Supply or buy-in services - Continue or discontinue products - Continue or discontinue services **Be able to:** • Calculate relevant costs and revenues

Assessment context

You probably won't be tested on all these concepts in the same assessment – it depends on the variant of the assessment you are allocated as to which one you get.

Business context

The tools demonstrated in this chapter are widely used by businesses. This is to ensure that risk has been adequately assessed, and that the most profitable option is adopted by the organisation.

Chapter overview

Short-term decision-making techniques

- **Contribution**
  - Contribution = selling price – variable costs
  - Used for decision making
- **Short-term decision making vs long-term decision making**
  - Time frame
  - Capital investment
  - Risk
- **Relevant costs**
  - Future
  - Incremental
  - Cash flow
  - Opportunity cost
  - Decisions:
    - Making or buy products
    - Supply or buy-in services
    - Continue or discontinue products
    - Continue or discontinue services
- **Key factor analysis**
  - Scarce resource
  - Contribution per unit of limiting factor

Introduction

This chapter considers useful techniques for making decisions that will affect the business in the next few months (in the short term).

When making short-term decisions profit should not be the basis of the decision made. Profit includes fixed overheads which are likely to still be incurred at the same rate regardless of the decision that is made. Instead **contribution** is the tool that should be used for short-term decision-making purposes.

Relevant costing is used to appraise short-term decisions, such as: make or buy products, supply or buy-in services, continue or discontinue products or services.

Key factor analysis considers situations where only a certain amount of some resource is available in the short term and therefore the management must decide how to allocate it in the most profitable way.

KEY TERM

> **Contribution per unit:** The selling price per unit less all variable costs per unit
>
> **Total contribution:** Total sales revenue less all variable costs

When using contribution as a decision-making tool the following assumptions are made:

(a) Contribution per unit is a constant figure at each level of activity; but

(b) Total contribution increases directly with increases in output and sales.

Fixed costs are different. As the volume of output and sales increases:

(a) Total fixed costs are unchanged; but

(b) The fixed costs per unit fall with increases in output and sales (because the fixed costs are spread over more units).

1 Short-term decision making vs long-term decision making

There are three fundamental differences between short-term and long-term decision making:

- **Time frame** – Short-term decisions are typically considered to be those with a time frame of less than one year. For example, how to make the best use of a scarce resource next month. Whereas long-term decisions are for a year or more. For example, a long-term plan is implemented for the year ahead using an annual budget.
- **Capital investment** – This will often be required to make a long-term decision. For example, new machinery may be required, which will be expected to bring benefits for many years.
- **Risk –** Short-term decision making is generally considered to be less risky than long-term decision making as predictions in the short-term are generally more accurate than the long-term because there is less uncertainty. For example, material prices for next month can be predicted with reasonable certainty in most industries. However, predicting the residual value of an asset is much harder to forecast.

2 Relevant costs

When making short-term decisions contribution should be used.

KEY TERM

> **Relevant costs:** Costs appropriate to a specific management decision.

Relevant costs have the following characteristics:

- **Future** – The cost will be incurred in the future because of the decision being made. Costs that have been made in the past (ie sunk costs), or costs that are committed and have to be paid regardless of the decision being made (ie committed costs) are unaffected by the decision and therefore irrelevant.

- **Incremental** – As a result of the cost being a future cost, it is an incremental cost (ie a cost that is only incurred as a result of the decision being made).
- **Cash flow** – The cost should reflect additional cash spending. Accounting adjustments, such as depreciation, accruals and prepayments, and over- or under-absorption of overhead, are ignored.

2.1 Opportunity cost

KEY TERM

Opportunity cost: The value of a benefit sacrificed when one course of action is chosen in preference to an alternative.

The opportunity cost is represented by the potential benefit foregone from the best rejected course of action. Opportunity costs are relevant for decision making and are likely to arise when there are several possible uses for a scarce resource. For example, if machine time is limited then an organisation may have to stop making some products to make others, the opportunity cost will be the contribution lost from the products it is unable to manufacture.

2.2 Relevant costs in make-or-buy decisions

A company may want to consider whether it is best to manufacture a unit itself or whether it would be better to outsource the production to a sub-contractor. Some examples include:

(a) Whether a company should manufacture its own components or buy the components from an outside supplier

(b) Whether a construction company should do some work with its own employees or whether it should sub-contract the work to another company

(c) Whether a service should be carried out by an internal department or whether an external organisation should be employed

To numerically analyse the make-or-buy decision, the **relevant costs** need to be considered.

In make-or-buy decisions, the following costs would be deemed examples of relevant costs:

(a) All variable costs

(b) Fixed costs that would be avoided if the product was not being made (or service not provided), meaning that the fixed cost is directly attributable to the product (or service). For example, by choosing to buy a component, the rental cost of a machine used to make that component would be saved. (Assuming the total number of components required are bought in.) This would not be the case for factory rent – as there would be no change to the total factory rent.

Illustration 1: Shellfish Co

Shellfish Co makes three components W, X and Y. Costs of these components in the forthcoming year are as follows:

	W	X	Y
Production (units)	1,000	2,000	4,000
Unit marginal costs	**£**	**£**	**£**
Direct materials	4	5	2
Direct labour	8	9	4
Variable production overheads	2	3	1
	14	17	7

The fixed costs for the period are:

	£
W directly attributable fixed costs	1,000
X directly attributable fixed costs	5,000
Y directly attributable fixed costs	6,000
Other fixed costs (committed)	30,000
	42,000

A sub-contractor has offered to supply units of W, X and Y for £12, £21 and £10 respectively.

Required

Should Shellfish make or buy the components?

Solution

Firstly, we need to establish the relevant costs of this decision. The relevant costs are all the variable costs, plus the directly attributable fixed costs for all the products. We can ignore the committed fixed costs as these will need to be incurred regardless of whether the components are made in-house, or bought from the sub-contractor.

The total cost of making the components is:

	W £	X £	Y £
Total variable cost			
£14 × 1,000 units	14,000		
£17 × 2,000 units		34,000	
£7 × 4,000 units			28,000
Directly attributable fixed costs	1,000	5,000	6,000
Total cost of manufacture	15,000	39,000	34,000

Now, compare the total cost of manufacture to the total cost of buying in each product from the sub-contractor:

	W £	X £	Y £
Total sub-contractor cost			
£12 × 1,000 units	12,000		
£21 × 2,000 units		42,000	
£10 × 4,000 units			40,000
Total cost of manufacture	(15,000)	(39,000)	(34,000)
Additional cost of buying in	(3,000)	3,000	6,000

Shellfish would save £3,000 each year by sub-contracting component W, but would be incurring additional costs by sub-contracting components X and Y. Therefore, Shellfish should buy-in component W but keep producing components X and Y in-house.

Activity 1: Dolphin

Dolphin makes three components. Details for the following year are as follows:

	A	J	H
Production (units)	5,000	4,000	3,000
	£	£	£
Direct material/unit	15	6	18
Direct labour/unit	15	20	22
Variable production overheads/unit	5	4	4
Directly attributable fixed costs	2,000	3,000	6,000
Other general fixed costs are £20,000			
A subcontractor has quoted a price per unit of	30	39	50

Required

Indicate whether the components should be made or bought in.

Dolphin should buy in [▼] .

Picklist

- All the components
- None of the components
- Some of the components

2.3 Non-financial considerations in make-or-buy decisions

Advantages of buying in	Disadvantages of buying in
Cost savings due to the flexibility provided by the outsource partner	Control of the operations is lost
Expertise that the organisation may have difficulty accessing themselves	Quality of the product could be impacted as the organisation is reliant on the processes of the outsourced partner
Capital can be released from the department or product to maximise opportunities	The outsourced partner will have other customers to service, so reliability could drop
Resources can be diverted to more value-adding activities	Confidential information will need to be provided to the outsource partner, and there is potential that this could be misappropriated
	Skills are lost in-house, making it difficult to bring operations back in-house if required
	Employees are likely to be made redundant, negatively impacting morale and motivation

3 Shutdown decisions

Shutdown decisions will include the following:

(a) Whether or not to close down a product line, department or stop providing a service, either because it is making losses or because it is too expensive to run

(b) If the decision is to shut down, whether the closure should be permanent or temporary

3.1 Relevant costs in shutdown decisions

The same relevant costing principles need to be applied as per make or buy decisions when numerically evaluating a shutdown position.

Illustration 2: Shutdown decisions

A company manufactures three products – Pawns, Rooks and Bishops. The net profit from these is shown below:

	Pawns £	Rooks £	Bishops £	Total £
Sales	50,000	40,000	60,000	150,000
Variable costs	(30,000)	(25,000)	(35,000)	(90,000)
Contribution	**20,000**	**15,000**	**25,000**	**60,000**
Fixed costs	(17,000)	(18,000)	(20,000)	(55,000)
Profit/loss	**3,000**	**(3,000)**	**5,000**	**5,000**

The company is concerned about the performance of Rooks and is deciding whether it should cease production of them in order to produce a new product, Crowners.

The fixed costs associated with the production of Rooks are £5,000.

The forecasted profit generated by Crowners is shown below:

	Crowners £
Sales	45,000
Variable costs	(33,000)
Contribution	**12,000**
Fixed costs	(8,000)
Profit/loss	**4,000**

Directly attributable fixed costs of Crowners are £6,000.

Required

Identify whether the company should cease the production of Rooks and start selling Crowners.

Solution

If Rooks were to stop being produced, the company would lose the benefit of the contribution generated by Rooks, but would save on the fixed costs:

	£
Loss of contribution	(15,000)
Savings in fixed costs	5,000
Incremental loss	(10,000)

If production stopped on Rooks, the company would see a fall of £10,000 in their profits.

The profit generated by Crowners would be as follows:

	£
Contribution	12,000
Directly attributable fixed costs	(6,000)
Incremental profit	6,000

If production was switched to Crowners, the company would only make £6,000 profit, so the company would suffer an overall drop in profits of £4,000. They should, therefore, keep making Rooks in preference to Crowners.

Activity 2: Duo

Duo Ltd owns two factories, A and B. The forecasts for both factories for the year ending 31 December 20X5 are below:

		A			B	
	£000	£000		£000	£000	
Revenue		2,200			2,850	
Direct materials	(660)			(784)		
Direct labour	(440)			(448)		
Fixed production overheads	(220)			(420)		
Cost of sales		(1,320)			(1,652)	
Gross profit		880	40%		1,198	42%
Sales and distribution costs		(520)			(640)	
Administration costs		(210)			(250)	
Profit from operations		**150**	**6.8%**		**308**	**10.8%**

Other information:

Inventories are of raw materials and will remain unchanged throughout the year.

Sales and distribution costs are variable with turnover from each factory.

Administration costs are fixed.

The Managing Director has proposed closing factory A. The impact to Factory B's results will be as follows:

- Revenue would increase by 40%
- Materials, labour and sales and distribution costs are all variable with sales revenue
- Fixed production overheads will increase by £100,000
- Administration costs will increase by £60,000
- It is forecast that purchasing costs will decrease by 5% as a result of the closure

Required

(a) Prepare a revised statement of profit or loss for factory B, assuming factory A is closed.

	Factory B £000	%
Revenue		
Materials		
Direct labour		
Fixed production overheads		
Cost of sales		
Gross profit		
Sales and distribution costs		
Administration costs		
Profit from operations		%

(b) Indicate whether factory A should be closed.

Factory A [▼] be closed.

Picklist

- Should
- Should not

3.2 Non-financial considerations of shutdown decisions

Shutdown decisions should not be judged purely on financial analysis. Some other factors to consider are:

- **Staff morale** – Staff will either need to be redeployed or made redundant, which negatively impacts morale and motivation.
- **Customers** – Market share could be lost if customers choose to source the discontinued product from a competitor.
- **Suppliers** – Some suppliers may be reliant on the organisation to stay in business. If the organisation chooses to stop making the product this could have severe consequences on these suppliers.

Assessment focus point

Service organisations may also need to evaluate their future options. Supply or buy-in and continue or discontinue decisions will be made by service organisations. The approach taken is the same as for manufacturing organisations in some much that only the relevant costs and revenues should be considered.

4 Key factor analysis

Normally, a business would want to maximise sales volumes to maximise profits. However, the number of units that can be sold is limited by the number of sales units that customers demand. Sales demand therefore limits the amount of sales volumes generated. This is known as a market share constraint.

However, in practice, other production factors could limit the number of units that can be produced and ultimately sold.

KEY TERM

Scarce resource: is defined as a factor which limits the number of units that can be produced and sold. Scarce resources could be:

- Materials available to purchase
- Labour hours available
- Machine hours available
- Plant capacity
- Factory space
- Access to finance

If a scarce resource is limiting activity, the plans of the business must be built around this limiting factor rather than around sales demand. The challenge for management is how to maximise profit when one of these other factors is limited.

As fixed costs will need to be incurred regardless of the amount of units produced, profit is maximised by looking at the contribution each product earns per unit of the scarce production resource – in other words we maximise the contribution per unit of limiting factor.

4.1 Identifying budget limiting factors

It may appear that a business has more than one budget limiting factor, but if we take into consideration maximum sales demand and available resources there will often be only one constraint.

Illustration 3: Baker Co

Baker Co makes three products, X, Y and Z. The costs and selling prices of the three products are:

	X £	Y £	Z £
Direct materials @ £2 per kg	6	10	8
Direct labour @ £12 per hour	24	12	36
Variable overheads	4	2	6
Marginal cost	34	24	50
Fixed cost	8	4	12
Selling price	44	29	65

Sales demand for the coming period is expected to be as follows:

Product X	2,000 units
Product Y	6,000 units
Product Z	3,000 units

The supply of materials is limited to 50,000 kg during the period and the labour hours available are 18,000. Each unit is manufactured on the same set of machines. One unit takes 2 hours to produce. Machine time is limited to 24,000 hours per period.

Required

What is the budget limiting factor for Baker Co?

- **Materials**
- **Labour**
- **Sales demand**
- **Machine time**

Solution

This can be answered be identifying the limiting factor. The following calculations can be done to identify the limiting factor:

	A	B	C	Total required	Total available
Materials					
(3/5/4 kg)	6,000 kg	30,000 kg	12,000 kg	48,000 kg	50,000 kg
Labour					
(2/1/3 hrs)	4,000 hrs	6,000 hrs	9,000 hrs	19,000 hrs	18,000 hrs
Machine time					
(2/2/2 hrs)	4,000 hrs	12,000 hrs	6,000 hrs	22,000 hrs	24,000 hrs

From the above table we can see that labour hours are the limiting factor (18,000 labour hours are available whereas 19,000 hours are required to meet total sales demand).

If there was sufficient material, labour and machine time sales demand would be the limiting factor.

4.2 Optimal production plan

If a business makes more than one product, we need to find the combination of products that makes the most profitable use of the scarce resource. This is known as the optimal production plan.

The approach taken to establish the optimal production plan is to determine the contribution per unit of limiting factor and concentrate on making the product with the highest contribution per unit of limiting factor.

The following steps are used to calculate the optimal production plan:

(a) Identify the limiting factor

(b) Calculate contribution per unit

(c) Calculate contribution per unit of limiting factor by making the following calculation:

Contribution per unit / Limiting factor per unit

(d) Rank products by contribution per unit of limiting factor

(e) Prepare the optimal production plan

Illustration 4: Farnham Engineering 1

Farnham Engineering makes three products, A, B and C. The costs and selling prices of the three products are:

	A £	B £	C £
Direct materials @ £4 per kg	8	16	12
Direct labour @ £11 per hour	11	33	22
Variable overheads	3	9	6
Marginal cost	22	58	40
Fixed cost	2	5	4
Selling price	26	66	47

Sales demand for the coming period is expected to be as follows:

Product A	3,000 units
Product B	7,000 units
Product C	5,000 units

The supply of materials is limited to 50,000 kg during the period and the labour hours available are 28,000.

Required

(a) Calculate the optimal production plan for Farnham Engineering.

(b) Calculate the maximum amount of profit resulting from the optimal production plan.

Solution

(a) This can be done be following the above steps:

Step 1 Identify the limiting factor

The following calculations can be done to identify the limiting factor:

	A	B	C	Total required
Materials				
(2/4/3 kg)	6,000 kg	28,000 kg	15,000 kg	49,000 kg
Labour				
(1/3/2 hrs)	3,000 hrs	21,000 hrs	10,000 hrs	34,000 hrs

From the above table we can see that labour hours are the limiting factor (28,000 labour hours are available whereas 34,000 hours are required to meet total sales demand).

Step 2 Calculate contribution per unit

Using the above table, the contribution per unit of each of products A, B & C is as follows (remember that contribution per unit = selling price – marginal cost):

A: £26 – £22 = £4 per unit

B: £66 – £58 = £8 per unit

C: £47 – £40 = £7 per unit

Remember that since fixed overheads will not be impacted in a short-term change in production units these are ignored when calculating the ultimate production plan.

Step 3 Calculate contribution per unit of limiting factor

As labour hours is the limiting factor, the contribution earned per labour hour needs to be calculated. This will ensure that we are maximising contribution for every labour hour that is worked.

The calculations needed are as follows:

	A	B	C
Contribution	£4	£8	£7
Labour hours per unit	1 hr	3 hrs	2 hrs
Contribution per labour hour:			
£4/1	£4.00		
£8/3		£2.67	
£7/2			£3.50

Step 4 Rank products by contribution per unit of limiting factor

Once the above calculation has been complete, the products are ranked in order of contribution per labour hour. This ensures that production priority is given to the most profitable product.

Product A makes the most contribution per unit of limiting factor (labour hours) and therefore, in order to maximise contribution, we must concentrate first on production of A up to its maximum sales demand. Then we can concentrate on producing C, and finally, if there are any remaining hours available, on B.

Step 5 Calculate the optimal production plan

The optimal production plan can now be calculated as per the below table:

	Units produced	Labour hours required
A	3,000	3,000
C	5,000	10,000
		13,000
B (balance)	5,000 (15,000 hrs/3 hrs per unit)	15,000 (balancing figure)
		28,000

(b) The optimal amount of profit arising from the optimal production plan is calculated by taking the amount of units per product as calculated in step 5 and multiplying it by the budgeted profit per unit. To do this we now need to take account of contribution generated per unit and the fixed costs incurred per unit. The profit can be calculated as follows:

	A	B	C	Total
Contribution	(£4 × 3,000) £12,000	(£8 × 5,000) £40,000	(£7 × 5,000) £35,000	
Fixed costs	(£2 × 3,000) (£6,000)	(£5 × 7,000) (£35,000)	(£4 × 5,000) (£20,000)	
Profit	£6,000	£5,000	£15,000	£26,000

Activity 3: LF

LF is trying to work out its optimal production plan.

Machine time available is 300 hours.

Labour time available is 200 hours.

	A £/unit	B £/unit	C £/unit
Selling price	150	120	100
Variable costs	100	80	70
Fixed costs	20	20	20
Profit	30	20	10
Machine time	5 hrs	2 hrs	1 hr
Labour time	2 hrs	1 hr	0.5 hrs
Demand	50	50	50

Required

(a) Identify the limiting factor.

The limiting factor is [▼].

Picklist

- Labour hours
- Machine hours

(b) Calculate the contribution per unit of limiting factor for each product.

The contribution per limiting factor for:

A is £ [ ]

B is £ [ ]

C is £ [ ]

(c) Calculate the optimal production plan.

The optimum number of units to be produced of:

A is [ ] units

B is [ ] units

C is [ ] units

(d) Calculate the maximum amount of profit resulting from the optimal production plan

The maximum amount of profit generated is £ [ ] .

Chapter summary

- For short-term decision making we concentrate on marginal costing and contribution – total fixed costs are assumed to be constant for the period.
- In a make-or-buy decisions, or supply or buy-in decisions, continue or discontinue products or services, the relevant costs are any variable costs incurred/saved because of the decision and any savings in attributable fixed costs.
- Qualitative aspects of make or buy, shutdown and mechanisation need to be considered alongside the financial analysis.
- Normally output in any period is limited by sales demand. However, occasionally a factor of production such as the availability of material, labour hours or machine hours may be a limiting factor on output and profitability.
- Where there is more than one product and a limiting factor, overall profit is maximised by concentrating production on the products with the highest contribution per limiting factor unit.

Activity answers

Activity 1: Dolphin

Dolphin should buy in | some of the components | .

The company would save £27,000 by buying in A, but would lose a total of £45,000 if they bought in J & H. This is demonstrated in the below table:

	A	J	H
Cost of making			
Direct material/unit	15	6	18
Direct labour/unit	15	20	22
Variable production overheads/unit	5	4	4
Variable cost of making/unit	35	30	44
Production (units)	5,000	4,000	3,000
Total variable production cost	175,000	120,000	132,000
Incremental fixed costs	2,000	3,000	6,000
Total cost of making	177,000	123,000	138,000
Cost of buying			
Cost per unit	30	39	50
Production (units)	5,000	4,000	3,000
Total cost of buying	150,000	156,000	150,000
Total cost of making	(177,000)	(123,000)	(138,000)
Additional cost of buying the units	(27,000)	33,000	12,000
Production (units)	0	4,000	3,000

Activity 2: Duo

(a)

	Factory B £000	%
Revenue (2,850 × 1.4)	3,990.0	
Materials (784 × 1.4 × 0.95)	1,042.7	
Direct labour (448 × 1.4)	627.2	
Fixed production overheads (420 + 100)	520.0	
Cost of sales	2,189.9	
Gross profit	1,800.1	45.1
Sales and distribution costs (640 × 1.4)	896.0	
Administration costs (250 + 60)	310.0	
Profit from operations	594.1	14.9%

(b) Factory A [should] be closed.

This is because the company will be more profitable:

Current profit = 150 + 308 = £458

New profit = £594.1

Activity 3: LF

(a) The limiting factor is [machine hours].

Labour time required = (50 × 2 hrs) + (50 × 1 hrs) + (50 × 0.5 hrs) = 175 hrs

Labour time available = 200 hrs

Machine time required = (50 × 5 hrs) + (50 × 2 hrs) + (50 × 1 hrs) = 400 hrs

Machine time available = 300 hrs

(b) The contribution per limiting factor for:

A is £ [10]

B is £ [20]

C is £ [30]

(c) The optimum number of units to be produced of:

A is [30] units

B is [50] units

C is [50] units

(d) The maximum amount of profit generated is £ [2,000].

Working

	A	B	C
Contribution per unit	£50	£40	£30
Contribution per machine hour	£10	£20	£30
Rank	3rd	2nd	1st

Production schedule	Hrs used
(1) Produce maximum 50 of C	50
(2) Produce maximum 50 of B	100
(3) Produce A with remaining hours	
$\frac{150}{5} = 30 \text{ units}$	150
	300

	A	B	C	Total
Contribution per unit	£50	£40	£30	
Units produced	30	50	50	
Total contribution	£1,500	£2,000	£1,500	
Fixed costs (£20 × 50)	(£1,000)	(£1,000)	(£1,000)	
Total profit	£500	£1,000	£500	£2,000

Test your learning

1 A business produces three products, the production and sales details of which are given below:

	Product		
	R	S	T
Direct materials @ £2 per kg	£16	£12	£10
Direct labour @ £12 per hour	£24	£48	£12
Selling price	£46	£72	£28
Machine hours per unit	6	4	3
Maximum sales demand	10,000 units	20,000 units	5,000 units

During the next period the supply of materials is limited to 250,000 kg, the labour hours available are 120,000 and the machine hours available are also 120,000. Fixed costs are £50,000 per period.

Required

(a) Identify the limiting factor.

The limiting factor of production resources is [▼] .

Picklist

- Labour hours
- Machine hours
- Materials

(b) Calculate the optimal production plan.

Product	Units produced

(c) Calculate the profit earned under the optimal production plan.

The profit that will be earned under this production plan is £ [ ] .

2 A business has two products, X and Y, with the following costs per unit:

	X Cost per unit £	Y Cost per unit £
Direct materials	2.50	3.00
Direct labour	8.00	6.00
Fixed overheads	3.00	1.50

The business could buy in X from an external supplier at a cost of £11 per unit, and it could buy in Y at £10 per unit.

Fixed overheads are not directly attributable and will be incurred regardless of whether the products will be bought in or not.

Required

Which product(s) should be bought in?

The business should buy in [▼].

Picklist

- Both products
- Neither product
- X
- Y

3 Timmy Co is short on labour hours meaning that it can't meet maximum sales demand.

Labour hours available to Timmy Co are 20,000 hours.

Demand for both its products, Badger and Pelican is unlimited. The following information has been provided:

	Badger	Pelican
Sales demand (units)	5,000	10,000
Labour hours per unit (Hrs)	1	2
Contribution per unit (£)	5.00	7.00

Required

What is the optimum number of units of each product for Timmy Co to manufacture?

	Units
Badger	
Pelican	

12 Long-term decision-making techniques

Learning outcomes

3.3 Discount cash flows

Understand:

- The concept of the time value of money
- The benefits of discounted cash flows over non-discounted cash flows

Be able to:

- Calculate discounted cash flow

3.4 Appraisal methods for long-term decisions

Understand:

- Long-term investment appraisal techniques:
  - Net present value (NPV)
  - Internal rate of return (IRR)
  - Accounting rate of return (ARR)
  - Payback (non-discounted and discounted)
- Strengths and weaknesses of each method

Be able to:

- Calculate net present values
- Use the IRR formula
- Calculate the ARR of projects
- Calculate the payback period of projects
- Compare NPV, IRR, ARR and payback period to support decision making

Assessment context

Long-term decision-making techniques will feature in the assessment. For example, in Task 7 you may be asked to make recommendations based on the net present value, internal rate of return, payback period or accounting rate of return calculations.

Business context

Many decisions that the managers of a business will have to make will affect the business over a fairly long time period. In particular the purchase of buildings, machinery or equipment will be expected to bring benefits to the business over a number of future years. The decisions that managers will have to take are:

'Should this capital item, which is often a significant amount of expenditure, be purchased?' and

'Are the future benefits from this current expenditure enough to justify the investment?'

Most businesses use techniques such as payback, net present value or internal rate of return for appraising investments.

Chapter overview

Long-term decision-making techniques

Payback
- Time taken for cash flows of projects to pay back initial investments
- Accept projects with PP < required PP
- Discounted payback period

NPV
- Difference between
  - Sum of discounted cash flows expected from investment
  - Amount initially invested
- Accept all projects with NPV > zero

IRR
- Discount rate that gives NPV of zero
- Accept all projects with IRR greater than the company's cost of capital or minimum acceptable rate of return

ARR
- Return on investment
- Uses profit
- Accept a project with ARR > company's minimum return

Introduction

In the previous chapter we looked at techniques for making short-term decisions about production and sales. In this chapter we will consider longer-term decisions that have to be made, namely investment decisions. This means comparing initial capital expenditure with the future benefits that are to be received from that expenditure. Do the future benefits give a sufficient return on the initial investment?

To determine whether a future investment opportunity (project) is worthwhile, a number of appraisal methods may be used. Your assessment requires knowledge of the following methods:

(a) **Payback period (PP)**

(b) **Net present value (NPV)**

(c) **Internal rate of return (IRR)**

(d) **Accounting rate of return (ARR)**

1 Payback period (PP)

Suppose a large amount of money is to be spent now on a project, such as the purchase of a major non-current asset. Management want to know whether the decision to purchase the non-current asset is a sensible one. One way that they could do this is keeping the length of time over which the benefits from this asset 'pay back' the original cost within acceptable limits. This is what is meant by the payback period.

KEY TERM

Payback period: The time it takes for the cash inflows from a project to repay the initial investment cost.

Illustration 1: Payback

Uckport Industrials is considering investment in new plant for their factory which will cost £250,000 if purchased now, 1 January 20X6. It will provide major cost savings in future production.

The production manager has estimated that the cost savings for each year will be:

	£
20X6	80,000
20X7	80,000
20X8	80,000
20X9	60,000
20Y0	40,000

The payback period can be calculated by considering the cumulative cost savings:

Year	Cost saving £	Cumulative cost savings £
20X6	80,000	80,000
20X7	80,000	160,000
20X8	80,000	240,000
20X9	60,000	300,000

We assume that the cost savings occur evenly throughout the year and we can see that by the end of 20X8 we have almost recovered the cost with cumulative savings of £240,000. In 20X9 the cost savings total £60,000 but in order to pay back the initial cost we only need a further £10,000 of this. Therefore the payback period can be calculated as:

Payback period	=	3 years + (£10,000/£60,000 × 12 months)
	=	3 years and 2 months

1.1 Decision rule

(a) Accept projects with a payback period of less than the company's required payback period.

(b) When deciding between two projects, the one with the shorter payback period is preferred.

Note that payback should not be used on its own to choose between projects. To choose between projects, other techniques would be needed too.

1.2 Advantages of payback period

(a) Quick, simple calculation. The payback period is one of the most widely used methods of project appraisal. It is a fairly simple calculation.

(b) Easily understood concept, especially by non-financial managers.

(c) Considers liquidity, ie cash flow. It considers the **risk** of a business being parted from its money as it is considering the time period between the cash outflow for the initial cost and the cash inflow from income or cost savings.

1.3 Disadvantages of payback period

(a) The maximum period set is arbitrary.

(b) It ignores the timing of flows within the payback period.

(c) It does not take account of all of the cash flows associated with the project, only those up to the end of the payback period, and it does not take any account of how those cash flows occur over the period.

(d) It ignores the **time value of money** (explained later in this chapter).

Assessment focus point

An assessment question may tell you that a business is particularly interested in limiting its risk. If the business is choosing a project based on limiting risk, then it should choose the project with the quickest payback period.

Activity 1: Payback period – Kirby plc

Kirby plc is considering a five-year project that requires an initial cash outlay of £550,000 on equipment. At the end of the project the equipment is expected to have a scrap value of £25,000.

The equipment will produce annual cash operating revenues of £150,000 for five years.

Kirby has a required payback period of five years.

Required

Calculate the payback period of the project and state whether Kirby plc should accept or reject the project on the basis of payback period.

Simple payback = 3 years and 8 months ((100/150) × 12) _ Accept project

Kirby plc should accept the project on the basis of payback period because the payback is less than the required five years.

Year	Simple payback cash flow £	Cumulative cash flow £
0	(550,000)	(550,000)
1	150,000	(400,000)
2	150,000	(250,000)
3	150,000	(100,000)*
4	150,000	50,000
5	175,000	225,000

*Payback between 3 and 4 years

Payback period = [ ] years and [ ] months

Enter A for accept or R for reject: [ ]

1.4 Discounted payback period (DPP)

Payback can be based on discounted cash flows (covered in Section 2), in which case it is called discounted payback. Aside from being based on discounted cash flows, the calculation is the same and most of the advantages and disadvantages remain.

2 Net present value (NPV)

2.1 Time value of money

For long-term decision making an important factor is the time value of money. The time value of money is all to do with our preference to receive money sooner rather than later. If we are offered £100 now or in a year's time then we would prefer to have the money now rather than wait. There are three main reasons for this:

Risk preference	If the money is received now then it is ours and there is no risk that it might not be paid in one year's time
Consumption preference	If the money is received now then we can spend it now rather than having to wait for a year (when it may be worth less in real terms)
Investment preference	If the money is received now then we can invest it and earn interest on it so that in one year's time it is worth more than £100

2.2 Present values

If we are offered £100 now or £100 in one year's time we are not comparing like with like. If the interest rate is, say, 10% per annum then if the £100 were received now it could be invested for a year at 10% interest. After one year the amount that we would have would be:

£100 × 1.10 = £110

We would therefore definitely prefer the £100 now.

We would only be indifferent if we were offered the option of £100 now or £110 in one year's time. By turning it around we can say that the **present value** of £110 in one year's time is £100 now (if the interest rate is 10%) – the equivalent sum now of that future income. We can calculate the present value (PV) as:

$$PV = \frac{£110}{1.10} = £100$$

Let's now suppose that if we had £100 now we would invest it for two years at 10% interest without removing the interest – this is known as **compound interest**.

After one year our investment would be	£100 × 1.10	=	£110
After two years our investment would be	£110 × 1.10	=	£121

This can be simplified to:

Investment after two years	£100 × 1.10 × 1.10	=	£121
OR	£100 × 1.10^2		

We can therefore also say that the present value of £121 arising after two years is £100. This would have been calculated as:

$$\frac{£121}{1.10^2}$$

$$\text{OR } £121 \times \frac{1}{1.10^2}$$

The element that the cash flow is multiplied by, in this case

$$\frac{1}{1.10^2}$$

Or 0.8264

is known as the **discount factor** or the present value factor (PV factor). The 10% interest rate is known as the **cost of capital**.

Let's summarise where we've got to. To calculate the value in today's money of a future cash flow, a discount factor is applied. This can be calculated using the cost of capital and is expressed as a decimal or a percentage. To calculate the present value the cash flow is multiplied by the discount factor. This means that a fair comparison is possible as it gives a value for what the cash flows are worth at time zero, ie now.

2.3 NPV method

The computation of a present value is a discounted cash flow (DCF) technique. We are finding the discounted (present) value of each individual cash flow or annuity.

If we are appraising a project then the technique that we can use is to find the net present value of all of the cash flows of the project. This involves calculating the present value of each individual cash flow and then totalling them all, remembering that the initial cost of the project is a cash outflow and any income or cost savings are cash inflows. The total of the present value of the inflows minus the outflows is the net present value (NPV).

KEY TERM

> **Net present value:** The net total of the discounted cash flows of the project.

(a) Calculate/list the expected cash flows (per year) that result from the investment or decision.

(b) Discount each cash flow at the cost of capital.

(c) Total up the discounted cash flows, adding cash inflows and subtracting cash outflows.

2.4 Purpose of net present value

The purpose of net present value is to establish the maximum amount that an investor would be willing to pay for a given set of future cash flows, given the investor's cost of capital. This takes into account the time value of money.

2.5 Decision rule

If the net present value is a positive figure, a positive NPV, then the project should be accepted as this means that after taking account of the time value of money, the cash inflows from the project exceed the cash outflows. If, however, the net present value is a negative figure, a negative NPV, then the project should be rejected.

It is important to note when making recommendations in the assessment that NPV calculation is the most important factor when assessing projects. If the NPV of a project is negative you would always reject the project even when all other appraisal methods are favourable.

Assessment focus point

An assessment question may ask you whether a project should be accepted or not. You need to remember these rules:

Accept projects with a NPV greater than zero.

In deciding between two projects, accept the one with the higher NPV.

Illustration 2: Net present value

We will return to Uckport Industrials.

Uckport Industrials is considering investment in new plant for their factory that will cost £250,000 if purchased now, 1 January 20X6. It will provide major cost savings in future production.

The production manager has estimated that the cost savings for each calendar year will be:

	£
20X6	80,000
20X7	80,000
20X8	80,000
20X9	60,000
20Y0	40,000

The **discount rate**, or cost of capital to be used, is 10%.

We can now use discounted cash flow (DCF) techniques to determine the net present value of this project. When using DCF techniques we have to be very careful about our assumptions about the timing of cash flows.

We assume that the cost savings all occur on the last day of each year, but the investment occurs immediately, now, which we shall call year 0. Therefore, the timings are:

1 January 20X6	=	Year 0
31 December 20X6	=	Year 1
31 December 20X7	=	Year 2

and so on.

We can now build up the net present value of these cash flows:

Year	Cash flow £	Discount factor @ 10%	Present value £
0	(250,000)	1.0000	(250,000)
1	80,000	0.9091	72,728
2	80,000	0.8264	66,112
3	80,000	0.7513	60,104
4	60,000	0.6830	40,980
5	40,000	0.6209	24,836
NPV			14,760

There are a number of points to note here:

- The initial cost occurs at Year 0 or now, therefore the discount factor is 1.0000 as £250,000 is the present value of the outflow now.
- Although the cost savings are not actual income, they are the saving of an outflow, ie they are reducing the cash costs of the business, and this is why they are treated as cash inflows.
- The initial cost of the machinery is a cash outflow and is therefore traditionally shown in brackets to distinguish it from the cost savings and cash inflows.

The layout above shows clearly how the NPV is arrived at. An alternative layout is as follows:

	Year 0 £000	Year 1 £000	Year 2 £000	Year 3 £000	Year 4 £000	Year 5 £000
Capital expenditure	(250)					
Cash inflows		80	80	80	60	40
Net cash flows	(250)	80	80	80	60	40
PV factors	1.0000	0.9091	0.8264	0.7513	0.6830	0.6209
Discounted cash flows	(250.000)	72.728	66.112	60.104	40.980	24.836
NPV	14.760					

So for Uckport Industrials, at their cost of capital or discount rate of 10% the project cash flows have a positive NPV and therefore the project should be accepted.

Activity 2: NPV – Kirby plc

Kirby plc is considering a five-year project that requires an initial cash outlay of £550,000 on equipment. At the end of the project the equipment is expected to have a scrap value of £25,000.

The equipment will produce annual cash operating revenues of £150,000 for five years.

Kirby has a cost of capital of 10%.

Required

Calculate the NPV of Kirby's project (to two decimal places) and advise Kirby whether to accept or reject the project.

Year	Cash flow £	DF @ 10%	PV £
0		1	
1		0.9091	
2		0.8264	
3		0.7513	
4		0.6830	
5		0.6209	
			NPV =

2.6 Advantages of NPV method

(a) It correctly accounts for the time value of money (discounting of future cash flows gives greater 'weight' to earlier cash flows).

(b) It is based on cash flows which are less subjective than profit.

(c) It is consistent with the objective of maximising shareholders' wealth. Shareholders will benefit if a project with a positive NPV is accepted.

2.7 Disadvantages of NPV method

(a) It can be difficult to identify an appropriate discount rate.

(b) It is a tricky concept. Some managers are unfamiliar with the concept of NPV.

(c) It does not allow for the risk of the project.

2.8 Net present cost

Sometimes there will be no income associated with a decision and projects will have a **net present cost** overall. The net present cost of a project is the sum of the present value of all costs over the period of interest. If a number of options are being considered then the option with the lowest net present cost will be the most favourable financial option.

Activity 3: NPV and payback period

The following are the relevant cash flows of a project.

	0 £000	1 £000	2 £000	3 £000
Capital expense	720			
Indirect labour cost saving		340	348	448
Operating cost saving		264	272	270

Required

Calculate the NPV and payback period using the information below. Work to the nearest whole thousand in the NPV table.

	0 £000	1 £000	2 £000	3 £000
Capital expense				
Indirect labour cost saving				
Operating cost saving				
Net cash flow				
PV factors 14%	1	0.8772	0.7695	0.6750
Discounted				
NPV				

NPV = [ ]

The payback period is [ ] years (to two decimal places).

Assessment focus point

In an assessment task you will be provided with the discount factors, but may be given a choice and be required to select the correct one.

3 Internal rate of return (IRR)

KEY TERM

Internal rate of return: The discount rate which when applied to project cash flows gives a zero net present value

If the internal rate of return of a project is higher than the organisation's cost of capital or higher than its required return from investments, the project should be accepted. If it is lower, then it should be rejected.

Illustration 3: IRR

A project might have the following NPVs at the following discount rates.

Discount rate %	NPV £
5	5,300
10	2,900
15	(1,700)
20	(3,200)

You can see that the NPV changes from a positive value to a negative value somewhere between 10% and 15%. The IRR is the discount rate which gives an NPV of zero. So the IRR is somewhere between 10% and 15%.

It might help you to see this on a graph, but just ignore the graph if it is not helpful for you. The important points to note are:

- The IRR is the discount rate that gives a zero NPV.
- The IRR must be greater than the organisation's cost of capital for the project to be acceptable.

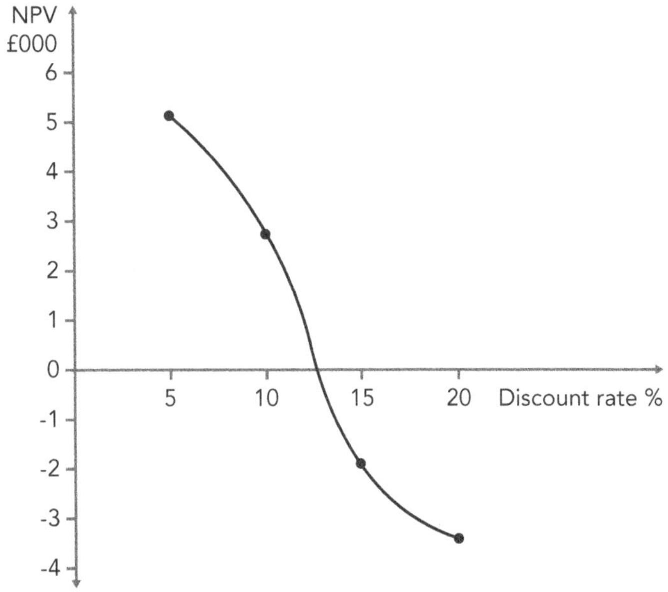

3.1 Method of calculation (linear interpolation)

(a) Take a project and calculate the NPV at two different discount factors.

The approximation is better if the second interest rate used is estimated closer to the IRR, ie if the first NPV is +ve, choose a higher interest rate for the second NPV to bring it as close to zero as possible.

(b) Use the interpolation formula below to calculate the approximate IRR, where a and b represent the chosen discount factors and NPVa and NPVb are their respective NPVs.

Formula to learn

$$IRR = a + \left[\frac{NPVa}{NPVa - NPVb} \times (b-a)\right]$$

Where a and b are the discount rates used.

Note. The formula will work even if both NPVs are +ve or –ve.

Illustration 4: IRR with linear interpolation

A project has the following NPVs at discount rates of 10% and 20%.

Discount rate %	NPV £
9	6,235
11	755
13	–4,430

Use linear interpolation to estimate the IRR.

$$IRR = a + \left[\frac{NPVa}{NPVa - NPVb} \times (b-a)\right]$$

We will use a = 11% and b = 13% (so NPVa = 755 and NPVb = –4,430)

$$IRR = 11 + \left[\frac{755}{755 - -4{,}430} \times (13-11)\right]$$

Look very carefully at NPVa – NPVb. As NPVb = –4,430 we have two minus signs next to each other. Note the rule of maths that says that two minuses make a plus. So we can re-write the formula as:

$$IRR = 11 + \left[\frac{755}{755 + 4{,}430} \times (13-11)\right]$$

$$\therefore IRR = 11 + \left[\frac{755}{5{,}185} \times 2\right]$$

$$\therefore IRR = 11.29\%$$

Activity 4: IRR

The NPV of a project is 1,679 when the cost of capital is 10% and -49 when the cost of capital is 20%.

Required

Calculate the IRR of the project to two decimal places.

The IRR of the project is [ ] %

3.2 Advantages

(a) Results are expressed as a simple percentage and are more easily understood than some other methods.

(b) It does not require an exact cost of capital.

(c) It takes into account the time value of money, unlike other approaches such as payback period.

(d) It indicates how sensitive calculations are to changes in interest rates.

3.3 Disadvantages

(a) It cannot accommodate changing interest rates.

(b) It can sometimes rank projects incorrectly. Projects with unconventional cash flows can produce negative or multiple IRRs.

(c) It is complex to calculate.

4 Accounting rate of return (ARR)

KEY TERM

Accounting rate of return: The actual return a project generates, based on profits, not cash flows.

$$ARR = \frac{\text{Average annual profit}}{\text{Initial investment}} \times 100$$

Or

$$ARR = \frac{\text{Average annual profit}}{\text{Average investment}} \times 100$$

Where average investment =

$$\frac{\text{Initial outlay} + \text{scrap value}}{2}$$

If the ARR of a project is higher than the organisation's required return from investments, the project should be accepted. If it is lower, then it should be rejected.

Illustration 5: ARR

An asset costing £120,000 is to be depreciated over 5 years to a nil residual value. Profits after depreciation are as follows:

Year	1	2	3	4	5
Profits £	12,000	17,000	28,000	37,000	8,000

Required

Calculate the ARR for this project based on:

(a) Average investment; and

(b) Initial investment

Solution

(a) Average investment = (£120,000 + 0) / 2 = £60,000

Average profits = (£12,000 + £17,000 + £28,000 + £37,000 + £8,000) / 5 = £20,400

ARR = (£20,400 / £60,000) × 100% = 34%

(b) Initial investment = £120,000

ARR = (£20,400 / £120,000) × 100% = 17%

Activity 5: ARR – Kirby plc

Kirby plc is considering a five-year project that requires an initial cash outlay of £550,000 on equipment. At the end of the project the equipment is expected to have a scrap value of £25,000.

The equipment will produce annual cash operating revenues of £150,000 for five years.

Kirby has a cost of capital of 10% and requires a return on investments of 15%.

Required

Calculate the ARR of Kirby's project based on average investment (to 2 decimal places) and advise Kirby whether to accept or reject the project.

The ARR of the project is [ ] %

4.1 Advantages of ARR method

(a) It is easy for non-financial managers to understand as it is a quick and simple calculation that involves the familiar concept of a percentage return.

(b) It considers all the project's life.

(c) The percentage measure means that it is easy to compare two investment options even if they are different sizes.

4.2 Disadvantages of ARR method

(a) It is based on accounting profits and not relevant cashflows.

(b) It is a relative measure (ie a percentage) rather than an absolute measure and therefore takes no account of the size of the investment.

(c) Like the payback method, ARR ignores the time value of money.

5 Comparing techniques

Technique	Considers time value of money	Cash flows/profit	Decision rule	Clear decision rule
Payback period	No	Cash flow	Accept projects with PB less than company's target	No
Net present value	Yes	Cash flow	Accept projects with positive net present value	Yes
Internal rate of return	Yes	Cash flow	Accept projects with an IRR greater than the firms cost of capital	No
Accounting rate of return	No	Profit	Accept projects with return greater than company's target	No

Chapter summary

- Long-term decisions are often of the nature of large initial capital expenditure followed by benefits in terms of additional revenue or cost savings.
- The payback period is a method of assessing a project based upon how quickly the inflows from the project repay the initial investment.
- If the payback period for a project is shorter than the organisation's payback period limit then the project will be accepted.
- Discounted payback period can be calculated to take into account the time value of money.
- The net present cost of a project is the sum of the present value of all costs over the period of interest.
- One method of using discounted cash flow techniques for project appraisal is to calculate the net present value of the project cash flows – if the net present value at the organisation's cost of capital is positive then the project should be accepted but if it is negative it should be rejected.
- If the internal rate of return of the project is greater than the organisation's cost of capital the project should be accepted.
- The accounting rate of return is based on accounting profits rather than cashflows.

Activity answers

Activity 1: Payback period – Kirby plc

Payback period = 3 years and 8 months

Enter A for accept or R for reject: A

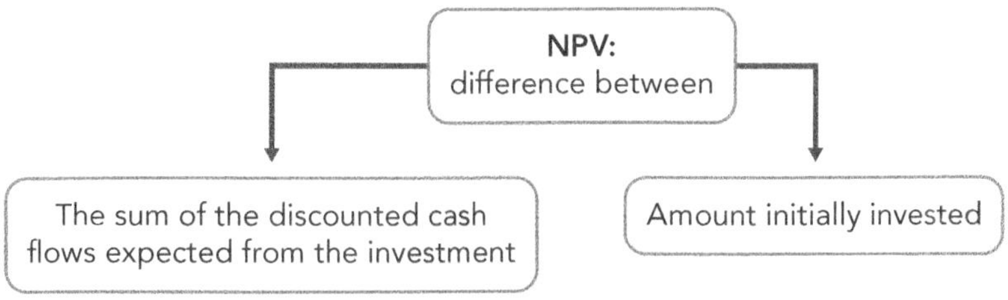

Simple payback = 3 years and 8 months ((100/150) × 12) _ Accept project

Kirby plc should accept the project on the basis of payback period because the payback is less than the required five years.

Year	Simple payback cash flow £	Cumulative cash flow £
0	(550,000)	(550,000)
1	150,000	(400,000)
2	150,000	(250,000)
3	150,000	(100,000)*
4	150,000	50,000
5	175,000	225,000

*Payback between 3 and 4 years

Activity 2: NPV – Kirby plc

Kirby plc should **accept** the project as the NPV is positive.

Year	Cash flow £	DF @ 10%	PV £
0	(550,000)	1	(550,000.00)
1	150,000	0.9091	136,365.00
2	150,000	0.8264	123,960.00
3	150,000	0.7513	112,695.00
4	150,000	0.6830	102,450.00
5	175,000	0.6209	108,657.50
			NPV = £34,127.50

Activity 3: NPV and payback period

	0 £000	1 £000	2 £000	3 £000
Capital expense	(720)			
Indirect labour cost saving		340	348	448
Operating cost saving		264	272	270
Net cash flow	(720)	604	620	718
PV factors 14%	1	0.8772	0.7695	0.6750
Discounted	(720)	530	477	485
NPV	772			

NPV = £772,000

The payback period is 1.19 years (to two decimal places).

Working

Payback period: –720 + 604 = –116

Payback period = 1 + (116/620) = 1.19 years

Activity 4: IRR

The IRR of the project is 19.72 %

$$IRR = a + \left[\frac{NPVa}{NPVa - NPVb} \times (b-a)\right]$$

$$IRR = 10 + \left[\frac{1,679}{1,679 + 49} \times (20-10)\right] = 19.72\%$$

Activity 5: ARR – Kirby plc

The ARR of the project is 15.65 %

ARR = (Average annual accounting profits / investment) × 100%

Average annual profit = £150,000 – £105,000(W) = £45,000

Working

Depreciation = (£550,000 - $25,000) / 5 years = £105,000

ARR based on average investment = (£45,000 / £287,500) × 100% = 15.7% hence project should be accepted as ARR > cost of capital

Test your learning

1 A business is considering investment in new machinery at a cost of £100,000 now, 1 January 20X6. The machinery will be used to make a new product that will provide additional cash inflows as follows:

Year ending	£
31 December 20X6	30,000
31 December 20X7	40,000
31 December 20X8	40,000
31 December 20X9	20,000

The cash inflows occur evenly throughout the year.

Required

What is the payback period?

The payback period is [ ] years and [ ] months.

2 Today's date is 1 January 20X6.

Required

What are the present values of each of the following cash flows?

(i) **A receipt of £3,100 on 31 December 20X7 – discount factor 0.7972**

£ [ ]

(ii) **A payment of £15,000 on 1 January 20X6 – discount factor 1.0000**

£ [ ]

(iii) **A receipt of £1,000 on 31 December 20X6 and 20X7 – discount factors 0.8929 and 0.7972**

£ [ ]

(iv) **A payment of £4,400 on 31 December 20X8 – discount factor 0.8734**

£ [ ]

3 A business is considering investment in new machinery at a cost of £340,000 on 1 April 20X6. This machinery will be used to produce a new product which will give rise to the following net cash inflows:

	£
31 March 20X7	80,000
31 March 20X8	70,000
31 March 20X9	90,000
31 March 20Y0	120,000
31 March 20Y1	60,000

The discount factors to use are 0.9346, 0.8734, 0.8163, 0.7629 and 0.7130.

Required

What is the net present value of this project?

£ [ ]

4 A business is considering investment in new plant and machinery on 1 January 20X6 at a cost of £90,000. The cash cost savings are estimated to be:

	£
31 December 20X6	23,000
31 December 20X7	31,000
31 December 20X8	40,000
31 December 20X9	18,000

The business has a cost of capital of 11%. The discount factors to use are 0.9009, 0.8116, 0.7312 and 0.6587. The business has a payback limit of four years.

Required

(a) What is the net present value of this project? (Round your present values to the nearest whole pound.)

£ [ ]

(b) Advise the business as to whether it should invest in the new plant and machinery and justify your advice.

	✓
Management should accept the project because the net present value is negative	
Management should not accept the project because the net present value is negative	
Management should accept the project because the payback period is less than 4 years	
Management should not accept the project because the payback is less than 4 years	

5 A project has the following NPVs at the following discount rates.

Discount rate %	NPV £
9	22
10	–4

Required

What is the approximate IRR of the project?

	✓
9.15%	
9.85%	
10.15%	
10.85%	

6 A business is considering investment in new machinery at a cost of £200,000 now, 1 June 20X8. The machine is expected to have a useful life of 4 years and will be depreciated using straight line depreciation. The machinery will be used to make a new product that will provide additional cash inflows as follows:

Year ending	£
31 May 20X9	80,000
31 May 20Y0	70,000
31 May 20Y1	70,000
31 May 20Y2	60,000

Required

What is the accounting rate of return (ARR)?

The ARR is [ ] %

13 Liquidity and working capital

Learning outcomes

4.1 Liquidity fundamentals

To understand:

- The importance of cash budgeting in the management of liquidity
- Strengths and weaknesses of cash budgets as a monitoring tool for organisations
- The importance of ensuring organisations can make their financial obligations
- Impacts of not meeting financial obligations
- Signs of overtrading and overcapitalisation
- The difference between liquid and non-liquid assets

4.2 Working capital management

To understand:

The working capital cycle

Be able to calculate:

- Trade receivables (collection period) days = trade receivables/revenue × 365
- Trade payables (payment period) days = trade payables/cost of sales × 365
- Inventory (holding period) days = inventories/cost of sales × 365
- Working capital cycle (days) = inventory days + trade receivable days - trade payable days

Assessment context

You need to understand the terminology in this chapter so that you can identify key liquidity and working capital concepts. You also need to be able to calculate a range measures including receivables days, payables days, inventory days and the working capital cycle.

You should also be able to recognise signs of liquidity issues such as overtrading or overcapitalisation and understand the importance of organisations maintaining sufficient liquidity to meet their financial obligations.

Business context

If a successful business expands too quickly, it can sometimes end up with cash flow problems. This is because expanding costs money initially (investing in inventory, and trade receivables for example) before returns are made later.

Chapter overview

Liquidity and working capital

Liquidity

The availability of cash or other assets which can easily be turned into cash

The working capital cycle

The working capital cycle

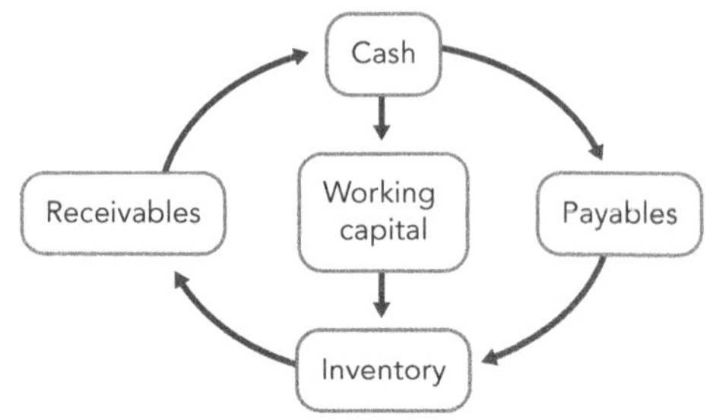

Working capital

- Overtrading
  - When a business tries to do too much with too little capital
- Over-capitalisation
  - When a business has too much cash
- **Inventory holding period**

  $$\frac{\text{Inventory}}{\text{Cost of sales}} \times 365 \text{ days}$$
- **Receivables days**

  $$\frac{\text{Receivables}}{\text{Revenue}} \times 365 \text{ days}$$
- **Payable days**

  $$\frac{\text{Payables}}{\text{Cost of sales}} \times 365 \text{ days}$$
  - Working capital cycle = Inventory days + receivable days – payable days

Introduction

In this chapter, we consider the importance of profitability and liquidity to the success of a business and how the working capital cycle plays a part in the liquidity of the business. In the following chapters, we will look at how the business can deal with a deficit or a surplus in their anticipated cash requirements.

1 What is liquidity?

KEY TERM

> **Cash:** Ready money, most easily thought of as banknotes and coins, and money in a current bank account. A business may be profitable but if it is unable to pay its bills, it will fail.
>
> **Liquidity:** The ease and speed with which an investment can be converted into cash.

Liquidity refers to how easily and quickly a business can access cash to meet its short-term obligations. A liquid business is able to pay suppliers on time, cover day-to-day operating costs such as wages and utilities, and meet any other immediate cash commitments. Adequate liquidity is therefore essential for financial stability and is often a key factor in whether a business succeeds or fails.

A company's liquidity depends on the cash it holds and on assets that can be readily converted into cash, such as trade receivables or inventory. This means liquidity is not just about the amount of cash in the bank, but also about the overall availability of liquid assets that can be turned into cash quickly when needed.

Liquid assets include:

- Cash (the most liquid)
- Short-term investments which can easily be sold and converted into cash (ie those for which there is a ready market, such as listed shares)
- Fixed-term deposits with a bank or building society – for example, six-month deposits with a bank
- Trade receivables

Liquidity is a measure of how safe the business is in terms of its cash availability. Even if a business is profitable, it must also have enough cash to pay amounts due when they become payable. Strong liquidity is therefore essential to the financial health and stability of the business.

Not all assets are equally liquid. Some can be converted into cash quickly, while others take longer. For example, inventories of finished goods in a retail or manufacturing business may be sold relatively quickly and are therefore more liquid. However, raw materials and components are less liquid because they must first pass through the production process before they can be sold. The degree of liquidity depends on how fast inventory is turned over and how long the production cycle takes.

Cash is the most liquid of assets and is part of the **working capital** (covered in Section 3) of the business.

Liquidity is also influenced by how quickly the business collects cash from trade receivables and how long it takes to pay its trade payables. Faster collection and slower payment (within agreed terms) both strengthen the liquidity position, helping the business maintain sufficient cash to operate smoothly.

Non-current assets are **not** liquid assets. A company can sell off non-current assets, but unless they are no longer needed, or are worn out and about to be replaced, they are necessary to continue the company's operations. Selling non-current assets is certainly not a long-term solution to a company's cash needs, and so although there may be an occasional non-current asset item which is about to be sold off, probably because it is going to be replaced, it is safe to disregard non-current assets when measuring a company's liquidity.

In summary, **liquid assets** are current asset items that will, or could soon, be converted into cash, and cash itself. Two common definitions of liquid assets are **all current assets** or **all current assets with the exception of inventories**.

The main source of liquid assets for a trading company is **sales**. A company can obtain cash from sources other than sales, such as the issue of shares for cash, a new loan or the sale of non-current assets. But a company cannot rely on these at all times and in general, obtaining liquid funds depends on making sales and profits.

Activity 1: Liquid and non-liquid assets

Identify examples of liquid and non-liquid assets from the following by selecting the correct option.

	Liquid assets ✓	Non-liquid assets ✓
Notes and coins		
Receivables		
Property		
Raw materials inventory		
Bank balance		
Short-term investments		

2 Meeting financial obligations

A key aspect of managing liquidity is ensuring that an organisation can meet its financial obligations as they fall due. Financial obligations include payments such as wages, supplier invoices, rent, interest, tax liabilities and loan repayments. Being able to make these payments on time is essential for maintaining trust, stability, and good relationships with stakeholders.

If an organisation does not manage its liquidity effectively and fails to meet its obligations, the consequences can be serious and far-reaching.

2.1 Why it is important to meet financial obligations

Maintaining supplier relationships

Paying suppliers on time ensures continued access to goods and services. Late payments can damage relationships, lead to stricter credit terms, reduction in discounts received or even cause suppliers to stop trading with the organisation.

Protecting the organisation's creditworthiness

Consistently meeting payment deadlines supports a positive credit rating. This makes it easier and cheaper to access finance such as bank loans or overdrafts in the future.

Ensuring smooth operations

If wages, utilities or essential operating costs are not paid on time, operations can be disrupted. For example, delayed wage payments may affect staff morale, and unpaid utility bills may lead to service interruptions.

Avoiding penalties and legal consequences

Late payment of taxes, loan instalments or contractual amounts may result in fines, interest charges, or legal action. These additional costs worsen the liquidity situation.

Maintaining stakeholder confidence

Reliable financial behaviour reassures employees, lenders, investors and customers that the organisation is stable and well managed.

2.2 Impacts of not meeting financial obligations

Failing to meet obligations is often a sign of poor liquidity and can trigger a downward spiral of financial difficulty.

Additional interest and penalty charges

Late payments often attract extra costs, making the cash shortage even worse.

Loss of credit terms

Suppliers may shorten credit periods or require payment in advance, increasing pressure on cash flow.

Damage to reputation and relationships

Repeated late payments weaken trust with suppliers, staff, lenders and other partners. This may reduce support at a time when the organisation needs it most.

Interruptions to operations

Suppliers may stop delivering goods, utilities may be restricted or employees may lose confidence in receiving pay on time, all leading to operational disruption.

Increased borrowing costs

Banks may see the organisation as higher risk, tighten lending conditions or refuse additional finance.

Risk of insolvency

Persistent failure to meet obligations may lead to serious cash flow problems. If liabilities cannot be paid when due, the business risks insolvency and potential closure.

Activity 2: Meeting financial obligations

Are the following statements true or false?

	True ✓	False ✓
A business that consistently pays its suppliers late may lose access to favourable credit terms		
Failing to meet financial obligations has no effect on a business's ability to obtain future loans		
Paying wages late can affect operations because employees may become less reliable or leave the business		
A business with poor liquidity may still meet all its obligations on time without any negative consequences		
If a business repeatedly pays its tax liabilities late, this can result in financial penalties and further cash flow pressure		

3 Working capital management

KEY TERM

Working capital: Working capital is the value of current assets less the value of current liabilities.

Current assets: Cash, inventory, receivables.

Current liabilities: Payables, loans falling due within one year, overdraft.

The two main objectives of working capital management are:

However, these objectives can conflict with each other. Increasing profitability often involves reducing the amount of money tied up in working capital (for example, by holding lower inventory levels), while maintaining strong liquidity may require holding higher levels of current assets or keeping more cash available.

Management therefore needs to strike an appropriate balance. They must carefully assess how much to invest in working capital and understand how this affects both profitability and the organisation's liquidity position. One way of viewing this balance is through the **working capital cycle** (also known as the **cash operating cycle**), which shows how long it takes for cash invested in operations to be converted back into cash.

Working capital cycle

The working capital cycle is the period of time between the **outflow** of cash to pay for raw materials and the **inflow** of cash from customers.

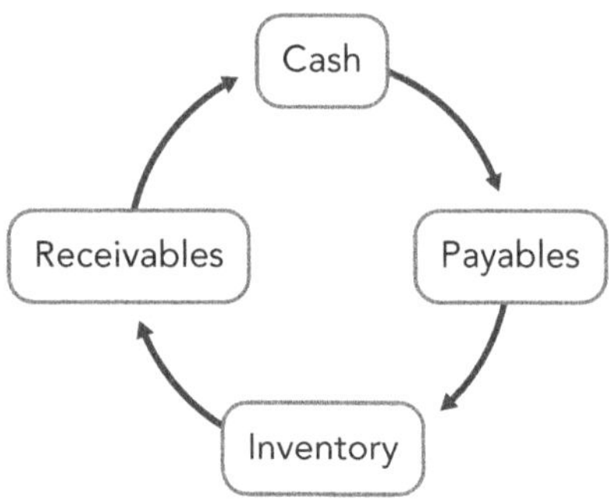

The optimal length of the cycle depends on the industry.

3.1 Calculating the working capital cycle

Formula to learn

Trade receivables collection period	$\frac{\text{Receivables}}{\text{Revenue}}$	× 365	=	days
Inventory holding period	$\frac{\text{Inventory}}{\text{Cost of sales}}$	× 365	=	days
Less: Trade payables payment period	$\frac{\text{Payables}}{\text{Cost of sales}}$	× 365	=	days
	Working capital cycle =			

KEY TERM

Cash operating cycle/Working capital cycle: The period of time between cash being paid for raw materials and cash being received from customers for good sold.

Inventory holding period: The amount of time that inventory is being held by a business.

Trade payables' payment period: The amount of time it takes for a business to pay its trade payables.

Trade receivables' collection period: The amount of time that it takes for trade receivables to pay the amounts they owe.

Illustration 1: Working capital cycle

Set out below are the statement of profit or loss and statement of financial position for Hampton Manufacturing Ltd:

Hampton Manufacturing Ltd

Statement of profit or loss for the year ended 30 September 20X8

	£
Revenue	1,350,400
Cost of sales	837,200
Gross profit	513,200
Less expenses	274,000
Profit from operations	239,200

Statement of financial position as at 30 September 20X8

	£	£
Non-current assets		2,428,300
Current assets:		
– Inventory	156,300	
– Trade receivables	225,000	
– Cash and cash equivalents	10,200	
	391,500	
Trade payables	(169,800)	
Net current assets		221,700
		2,650,000
Equity		2,000,000
Retained earnings		650,000
		2,650,000

We will now calculate the individual working capital ratios.

Inventory holding period days $= \frac{\text{Inventory}}{\text{Cost of sales}} \times 365$

$= \frac{£156{,}300}{£837{,}200} \times 365$

= 68 days

Trade receivables' collection period days $= \frac{\text{Trade receivables}}{\text{Revenue}} \times 365$

$$= \frac{£225,000}{£1,350,400} \times 365$$

= 61 days

Trade payables' payment period days $= \frac{\text{Trade payables}}{\text{Cost of sales}} \times 365$

$$= \frac{£169,800}{£837,200} \times 365$$

= 74 days

Using ratios in this way to assess the working capital cycle has certain limitations:

- To increase the **profits** of a business
- To provide sufficient **liquidity** to meet short-term obligations as they fall due
- Figures extracted from the statement of financial position are a snapshot of a single point in time and may not be representative of the normal level of investment in working capital eg due to seasonal fluctuations. Also, the working capital needs of a business will fluctuate with changes in the level or nature of its business activities.
- The appropriate level of working capital will vary from business to business, eg a retailer making mainly cash sales would be expected to have a low trade receivables balance, whereas a manufacturer of aeroplanes would have a high working capital requirement because of the length of the production period.

Nevertheless, considering the working capital cycle is a useful starting point in the management of cash.

For Hampton, the length of the working capital cycle is as follows:

	Days
Inventory holding period	68
Trade receivables' collection period	61
Less trade payables' payment period	(74)
Working capital cycle	55

Therefore, 55 days elapses between Hampton paying for its raw materials and then getting cash in from the customer who has purchased the goods that these materials have been made into.

Activity 3: Working capital cycle

The table below gives information extracted from the annual accounts of Management Co for the past year.

Management Co – Extracts from annual accounts

	Year 1 £
Inventory	270,000
Cost of sales	756,000
Sales	864,000
Receivables	172,800
Payables	86,400

Required

Calculate the length of the working capital cycle (assuming 365 days in the year) to two decimal places.

Trade receivables collection period	$\frac{\text{Receivables}}{\text{Revenue}}$	× 365	= days
Inventory holding period	$\frac{\text{Inventory}}{\text{Cost of sales}}$	× 365	= days
Trade payables payment period	$\frac{\text{Payables}}{\text{Cost of sales}}$	× 365	= (days)
	Working capital cycle =		

By comparing the working capital cycle from one period to the next, or one company to another, it should be possible to identify potential problems.

A **lengthening** of the working capital cycle, with more inventory and receivables or fewer payables, will **slow down** cash receipts.

A **shorter** working capital cycle, with less inventory and receivables or more payables, will **speed up** a company's cash receipts and should improve its cash balances.

Is there an **optimum cash cycle length**? The answer will depend upon the following:

- Whether the cash cycle is too long, and investment in working capital should be reduced by shortening the cycle; or
- Whether the cash cycle is too short and becoming unsustainable, indicating a need at some time in the future for an increase in working capital investment.

4 Overtrading and over-capitalisation

Effective working capital management requires a balance between liquidity and profitability. When this balance is not maintained, organisations may experience problems such as **overtrading** or **overcapitalisation**. These issues sit at opposite ends of the working-capital spectrum and understanding the difference between them is essential for assessing a business's financial health.

KEY TERM

Overtrading: Occurs when a business tries to do too much too quickly without having enough working capital to support that growth.

A business that is overtrading is attempting to trade at a level beyond what its current resources (especially cash) can sustain.

Indicators of overtrading:

- Rapid rise in sales revenue
- Rising payables days because the business cannot pay suppliers on time
- Falling **cash balances** and increasing use of overdraft
- Inventory shortages or rushed ordering
- Rapid increase in volume of current assets

A key problem is that a business could easily run into liquidity problems ie not have enough capital to provide the cash to pay its debts as they fall due.

Possible actions to reduce the risk of overtrading include:

- Effective debt management and credit control
- Improving inventory control
- Making maximum use of supplier credit lines
- Focusing on cash management
- Maintaining tight control of costs
- Leasing non-current assets (rather than outright purchase)
- Capital injections or the reduction of dividends/drawings

KEY TERM

Over-capitalisation: Occurs when a business has excessive working capital and hence is inefficient and less profitable (customers taking too long to pay, too much inventory, insufficient credit from suppliers).

Indicators of overcapitalisation:

- Excessive **cash** balances that are not being used productively
- High **inventory levels**, with stock turning over slowly
- Long **receivables days**, suggesting overly generous credit terms
- Low **payables days**, meaning the business pays suppliers too quickly
- Overall working capital levels higher than necessary

Why overcapitalisation is a problem

- Too much money is tied up in assets that are not generating returns
- Profitability is reduced because funds are not being used efficiently
- Inventory may become obsolete or deteriorate
- Opportunity cost: the business misses chances to invest cash more effectively

Overcapitalisation is therefore a profitability issue driven by **too much funding, not enough activity.**

Understanding the difference between overtrading and overcapitalisation helps managers diagnose working capital problems correctly.

- If liquidity is tight because the business is growing too fast - **overtrading**
- If profitability is weak because too much cash is tied up unnecessarily - **overcapitalisation**

Recognising which issue is present allows management to take the right corrective action, whether that is raising finance to support growth or tightening working capital controls to release cash.

Activity 4: Overtrading and overcapitalisation

Are the following statements true or false?

	True ✓	False ✓
A business with overcapitalisation is likely to have too much money tied up in inventory or receivables		
Overtrading usually results in high cash balances and low payables days		
Overcapitalisation generally leads to reduced profitability because assets are not being used efficiently		
A business with poor liquidity may still meet all its obligations on time without any negative consequences		
Overtrading is primarily a profitability problem, while overcapitalisation is primarily a liquidity problem		

5 Cash budgeting and liquidity

As we saw in Chapter 5, a **cash budget** is a plan that estimates all expected cash inflows (such as receipts from customers) and cash outflows (such as payments to suppliers, wages, and loan repayments) over a specific period. It shows **when** cash will come in and **when** cash will be needed.

5.1 Why cash budgets matter for liquidity

They identify future cash shortages or surpluses

A cash budget highlights months where cash may be tight or where spare cash may exist. This allows managers to take action in advance, such as arranging short-term finance, delaying non-essential spending, or investing excess cash.

They help ensure liabilities are paid on time

Cash budgets help the organisation schedule payments for:

- suppliers
- wages
- taxes
- loan instalments

By showing when cash will be available, they help avoid missed payments, bank charges and damage to supplier relationships.

They support planning and decision-making

Managers use cash budgets to plan:

- inventory purchases
- staffing and wage payments
- credit terms offered to customers
- timing of capital expenditure

Understanding future cash needs helps avoid liquidity crises and ensures decisions are grounded in financial reality.

They support overall cash-flow control

Once the period begins, managers can compare the **budgeted** cash flows with **actual** cash flows to spot:

- overspending
- slow-paying customers
- areas where operations are using more cash than expected

This helps the business take corrective action quickly.

They help identify overtrading risk

Rapid growth may require more cash than the business has available. Cash budgets show whether cash inflows are likely to fall behind the increased outflows associated with expansion.

They support communication with lenders and investors

Banks and lenders often require cash flow forecasts. A well-prepared cash budget reassures them that the business understands and can manage its liquidity.

5.2 Strengths of cash budgets

- **Early warning system** Shows upcoming cash shortages before they occur.
- **Supports good financial control** Variance analysis (budget vs actual) highlights overspending, inefficiencies, or late-paying customers.
- **Improves decision-making** Helps managers refine spending plans, credit policies and scheduling decisions based on real data.
- **Prevents overtrading** Reveals when growth is outpacing available working capital.
- **Useful for lenders and stakeholders** Demonstrates that cash flow is understood and monitored.

5.3 Weaknesses of cash budgets

- **Reliance on estimates** If forecasts are inaccurate, the cash budget becomes less useful.
- **Can quickly become outdated** Changes in sales, costs or payment timings mean the budget needs frequent updating.
- **Cannot guarantee payments will be on time** Customers may still pay later than expected.
- **May encourage short-term focus** Managers may delay beneficial long-term investment to 'stay within budget'.
- **Requires time and effort** Preparing, updating and reviewing cash budgets can be resource-intensive.

Chapter summary

- Liquidity is the ability of a business to meet its payments, as and when they are due.
- The most liquid asset of all is cash but other major assets which can be converted into cash may include bank deposits, investments, inventory and trade receivables.
- Working capital is made up of inventory, trade receivables and trade payables and the working capital cycle is an important indicator of the liquidity of a business.
- A business can try to reduce its working capital cycle by making changes to its working capital policies.
- Overtrading and over-capitalisation can both be detected by considering the working capital ratios and the working capital cycle. Overtrading is a liquidity problem and overcapitalisation is a profitability problem.
- A cash budget is a key tool for managing liquidity. Without effective cash budgeting, even profitable businesses can experience serious cash flow problems.

Activity answers

Activity 1: Liquid and non-liquid assets

The correct answers are:

	Liquid assets ✓	Non-liquid assets ✓
Notes and coins	✓	
Receivables	✓	
Property		✓
Raw materials inventory		✓
Bank balance	✓	
Short-term investments	✓	

The liquidity of receivables and inventory is variable; they cannot always be converted quickly to cash.

Activity 2: Meeting financial obligations

The correct answers are:

	True ✓	False ✓
A business that consistently pays its suppliers late may lose access to favourable credit terms	✓	
Failing to meet financial obligations has no effect on a business's ability to obtain future loans		✓
Paying wages late can affect operations because employees may become less reliable or leave the business	✓	
A business with poor liquidity may still meet all its obligations on time without any negative consequences		✓
If a business repeatedly pays its tax liabilities late, this can result in financial penalties and further cash flow pressure	✓	

1 is true. Late payments damage supplier relationships, often leading to shorter credit periods or stricter terms.

2 is false. Lenders assess payment history when deciding creditworthiness. Late payments reduce trust and may lead to higher borrowing costs or refusal of credit.

3 is true. Late wage payments undermine staff confidence and can cause operational disruption.

4 is false. A business with poor liquidity might still meet its obligations for a while, but this is rarely sustainable. Poor liquidity usually leads to cash shortages, increasing the risk of late payments, penalties, damaged relationships, and operational problems.

5 is true. Late tax payments usually incur fines and interest charges, worsening liquidity problems.

Activity 3: Working capital cycle

Average collection period	$\frac{172,800}{864,000}$	× 365	= 73.00 days
Inventory days	$\frac{270,000}{756,000}$	× 365	= 130.36 days
Average payables period	$\frac{86,400}{756,000}$	× 365	= 41.71 days
	Cash operating cycle =		161.65 days

Activity 4: Overtrading and overcapitalisation

The correct answers are:

	True ✓	False ✓
A business with overcapitalisation is likely to have too much money tied up in inventory or receivables	✓	
Overtrading usually results in high cash balances and low payables days		✓
Overcapitalisation generally leads to reduced profitability because assets are not being used efficiently	✓	
A business with poor liquidity may still meet all its obligations on time without any negative consequences		✓
Overtrading is primarily a profitability problem, while overcapitalisation is primarily a liquidity problem		✓

1 is true. Overcapitalisation involves excessive investment in current assets relative to activity levels.

2 is false. Overtrading causes cash shortages, rising overdrafts and **longer** payables days (because suppliers are paid late).

3 is true. Too much working capital reduces return on investment and lowers profitability.

4 is false. Poor liquidity usually leads to cash shortages, increasing the risk of late payments, penalties, damaged relationships, and operational problems.

5 is false. It's the opposite:

- Overtrading = liquidity problem
- Overcapitalisation = profitability problem

Test your learning

1 A business had sales of £790,000 during the year and cost of sales of £593,000. Inventory at the year end was valued at £68,000, trade receivables were £102,000 and trade payables were £57,000.

Required

What is the working capital cycle of the business?

	✓
30 days	
40 days	
54 days	
124 days	

2 A business has a working capital cycle of 35 days. Its inventory holding period is 21 days and its trade receivables' collection period is 60 days.

Required

What is the trade payables' payment period?

	✓
25 days	
39 days	
46 days	
56 days	

3 **Select the three most liquid assets that the majority of businesses are likely to have from the list below.**

The three most liquid assets that the majority of businesses have are:

- ▼
- ▼
- ▼

Picklist

- Bank current account
- Bank deposit account
- Business computers
- Business head office
- Cash in hand
- Fleet of cars used in the business
- Inventory of finished goods
- Inventory of raw materials
- Investment in shares

- Trade receivables

4 **Which one of the following might be associated with a lengthening working capital cycle?**

	✓
Longer inventory holding period	
Taking longer to pay suppliers	
Lower investment in working capital	
Improved debt collection	

5 **A business has high levels of current assets but only small amounts of trade payables. What is this an example of? (Tick the appropriate answer.)**

	✓
Overtrading	
Over-capitalisation	

6 **Which of the following is most likely to indicate that a business is overtrading?**

	✓
Increasing cash balances and low reliance on overdraft facilities	
Falling sales volumes and rising inventory levels	
Rapid sales growth combined with rising payables days and a worsening cash position	
High levels of working capital relative to the scale of operations	

14 Financing options

Learning outcomes

4.3 **Financing options**

To understand:

- The financing options available:
  - Bank loans
  - Bank overdrafts
  - Directors' loans
  - Mortgages
  - Shares
- The advantages and disadvantages of each alternative financing option
- The typical terms and conditions of financing options
- The impact on gearing and liquidity of financing options

Be able to:

- Calculate interest charges
- Calculate the total cost of financing
- Identify the most appropriate financing option

Assessment context

You need to be able to identify the main features of various types of financing options, as listed in the assessment criteria above, and identify the best financing option.

Business context

A business can raise finance from a range of sources and each financing option has differing terms and conditions. Organisations may have established regulations, policies and guidelines governing how finance can be raised.

Chapter overview

Financing options

Cash shortages

- Overdrafts
  - High interest rates
  - Repayable on demand
  - Short term
- Loans
  - Lower interest rates
  - Negotiable repayments
  - Useful for capital purchases
  - Loan to value
- Directors' loans
  - Quick to arrange
  - Flexible repayments
  - Uses directors' own funds
- Mortgages
  - Long-term finance
  - Secured on property
  - Lower interest rates
- Shares
  - Long-term finance
  - No compulsory repayments
  - Dilutes ownership

Impact on gearing and liquidity

- Gearing:
  - Debt ↑ → Gearing ↑
  - Equity (shares) ↑ → Gearing ↓
- Liquidity:
  - Overdrafts improve liquidity
  - Loans/mortgages reduce liquidity

Introduction

A cash budget is a useful method of determining whether it is likely that the business will have enough cash to keep going. If a **cash deficit** is forecast in the cash budget, then management will want to find suitable financing options to cover this deficit. In this chapter, we look at some of the financing options available to businesses to cover cash shortages. The chapter also looks at financial **gearing**.

1 Cash shortages

The cash budget enables a business to anticipate future cash shortages. Management can then arrange suitable financing options to cover the cash shortages. For example, finance can be raised from banks in the form of **overdrafts** and **loans**.

There are a number of reasons why a business may need additional finance. A company must match the situation with an appropriate financing option.

Why we need additional finance	Appropriate ways of meeting these needs
• Short-term deficit eg as support for working capital	• Overdraft • Short-term loan • Trade credit
• Long-term deficit eg for the purchase of non-current assets	• Debt via long-term loan or mortgage • Equity share capital • Issue of preference shares

For the purposes of this syllabus, it is important that you appreciate:

- The various forms of finance that are available to deal with a cash deficit
- How to determine the most appropriate type of finance for the particular purpose

1.1 Overdraft versus bank loans

Ideally, short-term cash shortages for working capital should be financed using short-term capital such as overdrafts or short-term bank loans.

Bank loans can have different types of repayment schedule, namely:

- **Bullet repayment**
- **Balloon repayment**
- **Amortising repayment**

KEY TERM

Bullet repayment: In a bullet repayment the amount borrowed is paid back at the end of the loan; only interest is paid during the loan period.

Balloon repayment: In a balloon repayment during the term of the loan, small amounts of the amount borrowed are repaid along with loan interest, but the majority of the amount borrowed is repaid at the end of the term.

Amortising repayment: In an amortising repayment the amount borrowed and interest are paid off over the term of the loan.

Banks usually ask for security so they have an asset they can take and sell if the borrower does not repay the loan (known as defaulting on a repayment). This can be in the form of:

- A fixed charge
- A floating charge
- A personal guarantee

KEY TERM

Fixed charge: A fixed charge is a named asset which the bank can insist is sold to repay the debt.

Floating charge: A floating charge is a class of assets the bank can insist is sold to repay the debt (for example: non-current assets, or receivables).

Personal guarantee: A personal guarantee is where a named individual becomes personally liable in the event the original borrower defaults.

An overdraft is generally a short-term source of finance. If, however, an element of the overdraft is being used into the longer term, this element is known as a '**hardcore overdraft**'.

Banks can also impose conditions on the loan, known as covenants. These might restrict the business from taking out further loans or require it to keep its existing borrowing at a sensible level.

KEY TERM

Loan: An amount of money advanced by a bank to its customer.

Loan principal: The fixed amount of capital borrowed.

Overdraft: The amount by which a customer's bank account is in debt.

Overdraft facility: The amount of potential overdraft that a bank allows a customer.

Hardcore overdraft: An overdraft which has effectively become a permanent part of the capital of the business.

Covenants: Obligations or restrictions placed on the business by the loan provider.

Bank loan features

- A loan is for a fixed amount, for an agreed period of time, with repayments set out in advance.
- It will normally be taken out with formal documentation.

Advantages	Disadvantages
• Both the business (customer) and the bank know the repayment schedule and interest cost in advance, which helps with budgeting. • The business does not risk the bank reducing or withdrawing the facility early. • A loan provides certainty over medium-term finance.	• Regular repayments must be made, which can put pressure on cash flow. • The loan usually requires security, meaning business or personal assets are at risk if repayments are not made. • Interest must be paid for the full term of the loan, even if the business no longer needs the funds. • Less flexible than an overdraft – the amount and repayment schedule are fixed. • Early repayment may result in charges, depending on the loan agreement.

Overdraft facility features

- Allows the customer to borrow on a current account up to an agreed limit.
- Interest is charged only on the amount actually overdrawn, usually at a variable rate
- Overdrafts are normally reviewed each year
- They are often secured by a business charge or personal guarantee
- Although repayable 'on demand', in practice banks rarely demand full repayment without warning

Advantages	Disadvantages
• Interest is only charged when the account is overdrawn. • The facility is flexible and can be adjusted or reviewed regularly. • It can act as short-term or medium-term finance if renewed annually.	• Interest rates are usually higher than for bank loans. • The overdraft is **repayable on demand**, meaning the bank can reduce or remove the facility with little notice. • Because interest is variable, the cost can increase if bank base rates rise. • Charges may apply even if the overdraft is not used (eg arrangement or renewal fees). • Long-term reliance on an overdraft can indicate poor cash-flow management and may concern lenders.

2 Interest

Interest rates may be **variable** or **fixed**, and their calculation can be on a **simple interest** ('flat rate interest') basis (ie interest is charged on the full loan principal at the start of the loan), or on a **compound interest** basis (ie interest is charged on the loan principal, plus unpaid accumulated interest).

KEY TERM

Simple interest/Flat rate interest: Interest is charged on the full loan principal at the start of the loan. Also known as flat rate interest.

Compound interest: Interest is charged on the loan principal plus unpaid accumulated interest.

Fixed rate interest: An agreed fixed rate of interest for the term of the loan.

Variable rate interest: Interest on a loan which changes every time the bank changes its base rate.

Assessment focus point

In the assessment, you may be required to calculate an interest rate if simple flat rate interest is to be applied monthly or daily.

You should also be aware of the term 'annual percentage rate' (APR). If a compound interest rate is given as a percentage per week or per month, the APR is the equivalent interest rate for a whole year, ie the compound annual rate.

Illustration 1: Comparing loans

A company needs a £15,000 loan for 2 years and has been offered the following options, both of which are to be repaid in 2 equal annual instalments:

Option 1: Flat rate of 7% – annual repayments of £8,550 on the last day of each year

Option 2: APR of 9% – annual repayments of £8,527 on the last day of each year

Required

Which loan should it accept if it wants to minimise its interest payments?

Solution

On the face of it, Option 1 looks cheaper at 7% but it is incorrect to compare flat rate with APR.

To decide which is cheapest, the repayment schedules, rather than the interest rates, need to be compared:

	Total repayment	Capital	Interest
Option 1	(2 × 8,550) = £17,100	£15,000	£2,100
Option 2	(2 × 8,527) = £17,054	£15,000	£2,054

Option 2 is cheaper because in total the interest paid is only £2,054, compared to £2,100.

Note. Under Option 1, the company does pay 7% interest for the first year but the annual equivalent rate for the second year is much higher. The first loan repayment of £8,550 at the end of the first year consists of £7,500 capital and £1,050 interest. In year two, the capital outstanding at the start of the year is only £7,500, so the interest paid in year two of £1,050 equates to an annual equivalent rate of 14% (1,050/7,500).

Activity 1: Simple flat interest rates

A business has agreed with its bank to borrow £72,000 in order to purchase a machine. The loan is to be repaid in 36 equal monthly instalments of £2,540.

Required

Assuming simple flat rate interest, calculate:

- **The total interest cost**
- **The simple annual interest rate**

	Workings	£
Total repayments		
Total interest cost		
Interest cost p.a.		
Simple annual interest rate (%)		

Illustration 2: Overdraft interest over several years

A bank agrees to an overdraft of £100,000 for a year for a company to buy some machinery. There is an annual arrangement fee of 2% on the overdraft and annual interest of 9%. The company is confident that the bank will renew the overdraft each year and it intends to repay the amount over a period of 5 years.

Required

What is the total cost of the overdraft?

Solution

Arrangement fee

The annual arrangement fee of 2% will have to be paid every time the overdraft is renewed. The assumption is that the company will continue to ask for a £100,000 overdraft facility, even if it chooses not to use it. Therefore, the cost for 5 years will be:

£100,000 × 2% × 5 years = £10,000

Interest

The interest can either be calculated for the year based on the balance at the start of the year, or it can be calculated based on the average balance.

Based on the balance at the start of the year, assuming that the company pays the £100,000 off over 5 years (ie reduces by £20,000 a year):

	£
Year 1 £100,000 × 9% =	9,000
Year 2 £80,000 × 9% =	7,200
Year 3 £60,000 × 9%=	5,400
Year 4 £40,000 × 9% =	3,600
Year 5 £20,000 × 9% =	1,800
Total interest	27,000

Total cost of the overdraft = £10,000 + £27,000 + £100,000 = £137,000

Interest

Based on the average balance throughout each year, assuming that the company pays the £100,000 off over 5 years (ie reduces by £20,000 a year):

	£
Year 1 £90,000 × 9% =	8,100
Year 2 £70,000 × 9% =	6,300
Year 3 £50,000 × 9% =	4,500
Year 4 £30,000 × 9% =	2,700
Year 5 £10,000 × 9% =	900
Total interest	22,500

Total cost of the overdraft = £10,000 + £22,500 + £100,000 = £132,500

3 Loan-to-value (LTV)

KEY TERM

Loan-to-value ratio: The interest rate will also be dependent on the loan-to-value ratio when the loan is for the purchase of an asset.

You may have seen this in the personal mortgage market, where a higher interest applies at higher loan-to-value ratios. If the company takes out a loan for 90% of the asset value, the interest rate is likely to be higher than a loan for 70% of the asset value.

This is because at a lower loan-to-value ratio, the risk to the lender of the borrower defaulting and being unable to recover their loan is also lower.

4 Directors' loans

A director's loan is money that a director lends to, or borrows from, their own company. In the context of business financing, the term usually refers to a director providing funds to the company to help with cash shortages. This is a flexible source of finance for small companies, particularly those owned and managed by one or two directors.

KEY TERM

Director's loan: Money a director lends to the company, or withdraws from the company, outside of normal salary or dividends. When used as finance, it refers to funds the director puts into the business.

4.1 Features of a director's loan

- A director may temporarily lend personal funds to the company to help with short-term cash needs.
- The amount and timing of repayments are usually flexible and agreed informally.
- Interest may be paid to the director, but this must be agreed and recorded by the company.
- Directors' loans must be recorded properly in the accounting records, usually through a directors' loan account.
- In limited companies, the loan ranks behind secured lenders if the company fails, unless the director has taken formal security.
- For tax purposes, any interest charged must be at a reasonable commercial rate.

4.2 Advantages of a director's loan

- Quick and easy to arrange, as no bank approval or formal application is required.
- A useful source of funding when the company needs cash urgently or cannot obtain a bank loan.
- Repayment terms are flexible and can be adapted to the business's cash flow.
- Interest, if charged, may be cheaper than commercial borrowing.
- Shows commitment from the director, which can be viewed positively by other stakeholders.

4.3 Disadvantages of a director's loan

- The director's personal funds are at risk if the company cannot repay the loan.
- Over-reliance on directors' loans may mask underlying cash flow problems in the business.
- If interest is charged above or below market rates, there may be tax implications.
- Lack of formal structure may lead to disagreements if there is more than one director.
- In insolvency, the director may rank behind secured creditors, making repayment less certain.

5 Mortgages

A mortgage is a type of long-term loan used to finance the purchase of property, such as a business premises or land. Like other loans, the borrower repays the amount borrowed (the loan principal) plus interest over an agreed period. A key feature of a mortgage is that it is secured on the property being purchased. This means that if the borrower does not repay the loan, the bank has the right to sell the property and use the proceeds to repay the outstanding amount.

KEY TERM

> **Mortgage:** A long-term loan secured on property, typically repaid over many years. If the borrower defaults, the lender may sell the property to recover the debt.

5.1 Features of a mortgage

- A mortgage is a long-term loan, often lasting 10–25 years.
- It is normally used to buy business property or land.
- The loan is secured on the property, giving the lender legal rights if repayments are not made.
- Interest may be charged at a fixed rate, a variable rate, or a mixture of both over the life of the mortgage.
- Repayments are usually made monthly and include both interest and capital (an amortising repayment), although interest-only mortgages also exist.
- A formal mortgage agreement sets out the terms, including the interest rate, repayment structure, and any covenants.
- Early repayment may result in additional charges, depending on the terms of the mortgage agreement.

5.2 Advantages of a mortgage

- Mortgages provide a business with access to substantial long-term finance for purchasing premises.
- Because the loan is secured on the property, interest rates are generally lower than for unsecured borrowing.
- Repayments can be structured over a long time, making monthly payments more manageable.
- Owning property may reduce long-term rental costs and provide the business with an asset that may increase in value.

5.3 Disadvantages of a mortgage

- The property is at risk if the business cannot maintain repayments.
- Interest costs can be high over the long life of the mortgage.
- A variable-rate mortgage exposes the business to the risk of interest rate rises.
- The mortgage ties up the property as security, meaning it cannot easily be sold without repaying the loan.

Illustration 3: Monthly repayment and arrangement fee

A business is considering taking out a mortgage of £360,000. The bank charges an arrangement fee of 1.5%, which is added to the amount borrowed. The mortgage is repayable over 20 years in equal monthly instalments and carries a flat interest rate of 5.2% per year.

Required

Calculate the monthly repayment on the mortgage.

Solution

Step 1 Add the arrangement fee to the loan

Arrangement fee = 1.5% × £360,000 = £5,400

Total amount borrowed = £360,000 + £5,400 = £365,400

Step 2 Calculate total interest (flat-rate method)

Flat-rate interest = £365,400 × 5.2% × 20 years = £365,400 × 0.052 × 20 = £380,016

Step 3 Calculate total repayment

Total repayment = Principal + interest = £365,400 + £380,016 = £745,416

Step 4 Calculate monthly repayment

Number of months = 20 × 12 = 240

Monthly repayment = £745,416 ÷ 240 = £3,105.90

Activity 2: Mortgage or director's loan

A company is considering taking out a mortgage of £420,000 to purchase a small warehouse. The bank charges an arrangement fee of 1.2%, which will be added to the amount borrowed. The mortgage will be repaid over 20 years in equal monthly instalments using a flat interest rate of 4.9%.

Required

(a) Calculate the monthly repayment. Enter your answer to two decimal places.

£ [ ]

The company is also considering an alternative source of finance: a director's loan of £420,000 at 4% interest, repayable interest-only for the first year.

Required

(b) Calculate the total interest payable in the first year under the director's loan. Enter your answer to the nearest whole number.

£ [ ]

---

6 Shares (also known as equity finance)

A company can raise long-term finance by issuing new shares. Investors who buy the shares become part-owners of the company and may receive dividends if the company makes sufficient profits. Unlike loan finance, share capital does not have to be repaid.

Ordinary shares have a nominal or 'face' value, typically £1 or 50p. This value times the number of shares issued is shown as **share capital** in the statement of financial position.

KEY TERM

> **Shares:** Units of ownership in a company. Shareholders may receive dividends and have voting rights, depending on the type of shares issued.

6.1 Features of share finance

- Shares are issued to raise long-term finance for the business.
- Investors who buy the shares become part-owners of the company.
- Share capital does not need to be repaid by the business.
- Dividends may be paid if profits allow, but they are not compulsory.
- Issuing new shares reduces (dilutes) the ownership share of existing shareholders.
- Shares can be issued to the public (listed companies) or privately (small companies).

6.2 Advantages of issuing shares

- No legal obligation to repay the capital raised.
- No compulsory interest payments – dividends are paid only when affordable.
- Can raise large amounts of long-term finance.
- Improves the company's gearing position by increasing equity.

6.3 Disadvantages of issuing shares

- Dilution of ownership and control for existing shareholders.
- Raising new share capital can be costly (administration, legal costs).
- Having more shareholders increases the pressure for regular reporting and dividends.
- Not always practical for small companies without access to external investors.

Activity 3: Choosing finance

A company wants to raise £300,000 to expand its production facility. The directors do not want to increase the business's level of debt because interest payments are already high.

Required

Which source of finance would be most appropriate?

	✓
Long term bank loan	
Mortgage	
Issue of new shares	
Overdraft	

7 Risk and the cost of finance

Different sources of finance carry different levels of risk for a business. When choosing between options such as loans, overdrafts, mortgages, directors' loans and shares, management needs to consider both the **cost** and the **risk** of each option.

7.1 Cost of finance

The cost of finance is the amount the business must pay for using borrowed money or raising capital. This may include:

- Interest charges (loans, overdrafts, mortgages, directors' loans)
- Arrangement fees (loans, mortgages, overdrafts)
- Dividends (shares – but only if profits allow)

The chapter has already covered how to calculate:

- simple flat-rate interest
- total repayment costs
- monthly instalments
- alternative-option comparisons

These help the business identify the **cheapest** option.

7.2 Risk of finance

Financing decisions also affect the risk the business faces.

(a) **Financial risk**

Financial risk increases when a business takes on more debt, because:

- Interest must be paid even if profits are low.
- Loans and mortgages must be repaid on agreed dates.
- The business may risk breaching covenants.

Sources that increase risk the most:

- Long-term loans
- Mortgages
- High overdraft dependence

Sources that reduce risk:

- Shares (no compulsory repayments)
- Directors' loans (flexible and often easier to renegotiate)

(b) **Impact on gearing**

Gearing measures the proportion of long-term debt compared to equity.

- Using more loans or mortgages increases gearing.
- Issuing shares reduces gearing, because equity increases.
- Overdrafts are excluded from gearing in this assessment.

A business with high gearing is considered riskier because it has more compulsory repayments.

(c) **Liquidity risk**

Liquidity risk is the risk the business cannot meet its day-to-day cash obligations.

Impact of financing options:

- Overdrafts improve liquidity, as they provide short-term cash.
- Loans and mortgages reduce liquidity, because of regular repayment commitments.
- Shares have no repayment schedule, so they create no pressure on liquidity.
- Directors' loans can improve liquidity, especially if repayment can be delayed.

Summary

When selecting a financing option, businesses should consider:

- **Cost:** interest, fees, repayments
- **Financial risk:** level of debt and fixed repayment obligations
- **Gearing:** how the option affects the long-term debt ratio
- **Liquidity:** ability to meet short-term cash needs

This helps identify not only the **cheapest** option but also the **safest** and most suitable for the business's circumstances.

Chapter summary

- Businesses may face short-term or long-term cash shortages. The appropriate source of finance depends on the purpose and duration of the cash need.
- The main financing options covered in this chapter are bank loans, bank overdrafts, directors' loans, mortgages and shares.
- Bank loans provide medium- to long-term finance with fixed or variable interest and set repayment schedules.
- Bank overdrafts offer flexible short-term finance up to an agreed limit. Interest is charged only on the amount overdrawn, but rates are normally higher than for bank loans.
- Directors' loans allow directors to lend their own funds to the business. These loans can be arranged quickly and repaid flexibly, but the director's personal funds are at risk.
- Mortgages are long-term loans secured on property. They typically carry lower interest rates because of the security offered and are repaid over many years in regular instalments.
- Shares provide long-term finance without creating debt or mandatory repayments. Dividends are paid only when the business can afford them, but issuing new shares dilutes existing ownership.
- Each source of finance has its own advantages and disadvantages, including impacts on cost, flexibility, security requirements and control of the business.
- Interest charges and total repayment costs can be calculated to compare financing options and identify the most cost-effective choice.
- Financing choices also affect risk and liquidity.
- Taking on more debt increases financial risk because interest and repayments are compulsory.
- Loans and mortgages increase gearing, while issuing shares reduces it.
- Overdrafts can improve short-term liquidity, while long-term loans reduce liquidity due to fixed repayment commitments.
- Selecting the most appropriate financing option involves considering the purpose of the finance, the cost and risk of each option, and the effect on the business's gearing and liquidity Selecting the most appropriate financing option involves considering the purpose of the finance, the cost and risk of each option, and the effect on the business's gearing and liquidity.

Activity answers

Activity 1: Simple flat interest rates

	Workings	£
Total repayments	36 × £2,540	91,440
Total interest cost	£91,440 – £72,000	19,440
Interest cost p.a.	£19,440 / 3 years	6,480
Simple annual interest rate (%)	£6,480 / £72,000	9%

Activity 2: Mortgage or director's loan

(a) Add arrangement fee 1.2% × £420,000 = £5,040

Total borrowed = £420,000 + £5,040 = £425,040

Flat-rate interest = £425,040 × 0.049 × 20 = £416,539.20

Total repayment £425,040 + £416,539.20 = £841,579.20

Monthly repayment £841,579.20 ÷ 240 = £3,506.58

(b) £420,000 × 4% = £16,800

Activity 3: Choosing finance

The correct answer is:

	✓
Long term bank loan	
Mortgage	
Issue of new shares	✓
Overdraft	

Issuing new shares raises finance without increasing debt or interest costs.

Test your learning

1 **Which of the following is a typical feature of a bank loan?**

	✓
Repayments are usually made on a fixed schedule	
Interest is charged only on the amount used	
The borrowing limit can be changed daily	
The loan is normally repayable on demand	

2 **Which statement best describes a mortgage?**

	✓
A short-term loan sometimes used for working capital	
A long-term loan secured on property	
An borrowing facility with a fixed limit agreed with the bank	
A loan that is normally expected to be repaid within a year	

3 **Which of the following is an advantage of raising finance through issuing shares?**

	✓
Regular interest payments are compulsory	
Dividends are paid only if the business can afford them	
Issuing shares increases the business's gearing	
The company must repay the capital at the end of the term	

4 Compare overdraft finance with that of a loan.

Required

Which of the following would be advantages of overdraft finance for a company seeking short-term finance?

Tick the appropriate boxes.

	✓
Floating charge required	
Interest charged only on amount of facility used	
Repayable on demand	

5 A Ltd is considering the purchase of shares in B Ltd which will require external finance and will be held for a number of years.

Required

What would be the most appropriate source of finance for this purchase?

	✓
Overdraft finance	
Loan finance	

6 **How can a company reduce its level of gearing?**

	✓
Repaying borrowings from operating funds	
Improved working capital management to repay borrowings	
Increasing equity through issuing shares	
Obtaining a loan	

15 Investment options

Learning outcomes

4.4	**Investment options**
	To understand:
	• The investment options available:
	  - Bank deposit accounts
	  - Bonds
	  - Property
	  - Shares
	• The advantages and disadvantages of each investment option
	• The typical terms and conditions of investment options
	• The relationship between risk, reward and liquidity
	• The portfolio effect of diversifying investments
	To be able to:
	• Calculate the return on investment
	• Calculate the yield
	• Identify the most appropriate investment option

Assessment context

You need to be able to identify the features of different types of investments and recommend an option to invest surplus funds, bearing in mind the three key factors of risk, return and liquidity.

Business context

An organisation needs to be able to utilise cash surpluses in the most appropriate manner to ensure it receives maximum return for the tolerable risk.

Chapter overview

Investment options

Treasury function

- Liquidity management
- Investment of funds

Investments

- Deposit accounts
- Government securities (gilts)
- Local authority stocks
- Shares
- Property

Diversification

- Spreading risk across investments
- Portfolio effect

Introduction

In a similar way to selecting suitable finance for dealing with cash shortages, organisations also need to utilise **cash surpluses** in the most appropriate manner, in order to ensure that they maximise **return** for the tolerable level of **risk**. Surplus funds should not sit idle because they could be earning a return for the organisation.

Businesses invest surplus funds in order to:

- Earn income through interest, dividends or capital growth
- Maintain the value of money against inflation
- Make efficient use of resources

1 Treasury function

In larger organisations, there is likely to be a separate treasury function which is responsible for dealing with liquidity management and the investment of funds.

There are three main factors that should be considered when determining how to invest any surplus funds.

1.1 Risk

When cash is invested there are two main risks. There is the risk that the value of the investment will fall, which is the **capital risk**.

There is also the risk that the return from the investment will be lower than expected due to changes in market rates of return.

KEY TERM

Risk: The chance of making a loss.

Capital risk: The risk that the value of an investment will fall.

1.2 Reward (sometimes called return)

The return on an investment has two potential aspects – the **income return** and the **capital return**.

Most investments will pay some form of interest or dividend which is the income return. However, many investments will also tend to fluctuate in value over time and this gives the capital return (or capital loss).

The general relationship between risk and return with investments is that the higher the risk, the higher the expected return.

KEY TERM

Return: Any income and/or capital gain on an investment.

Income return: Interest or dividend received.

Capital return: The increase/decrease in market value of an investment.

1.3 Liquidity

KEY TERM

Liquidity: is the term used for the ease and speed with which an investment can be converted into cash.

1.4 Relationship between risk, return and liquidity

When a cash surplus is to be invested, the aim will be to earn a good return but without incurring excessive risk of loss and also ensuring that the investment can be realised within the timescale in which the cash is required.

Illustration 1: Risk, return and liquidity

The glass division of SC Fuel and Glass has £60,000 to invest for the next month until the money is needed to pay the quarterly sales tax (VAT) bill. It could be paid into an interest-bearing deposit account at the bank where it will earn 0.5% interest for the month. Alternatively, it could be used to buy shares in another company.

If it is paid into the deposit account then the money bears virtually no risk at all (provided that the bank is creditworthy). One month later, the money will be withdrawn and will total:

£60,000 + (60,000 × 0.005) = £60,300

The business has made a profit or return of £300 and the money is available to pay the sales tax bill.

If the shares were purchased, then it is possible that they would have increased in value to, say, £66,000 in one month's time, meaning that the glass division has earned a profit of £6,000. However, it is also possible, due to the risk of investment in shares, that the shares might have fallen in value to £55,000. This would mean that not only has the glass division made a loss of £5,000 but also the full amount of cash is not available to meet the sales tax bill.

2 Types of investments

There are many ways in which surplus funds can be invested. However, we can identify two main types:

(a) **Cash based investments**:

Bank or building society accounts – Surplus funds can be deposited in a bank or building society account. If the cash is definitely not required in the near future, then it could be invested in a deposit account for a fixed term of up to three months at a variable rate of interest which is linked to money market rates. This will give a higher rate of return.

Money market accounts – These are similar in principle to a bank deposit account. Here funds are deposited with a bank or other financial institution for a fixed period of time and cannot be accessed until the term has ended. Terms range from overnight to 12 months.

(b) **Securities** – A certificate giving evidence of a debt or equity obligation. These include property, shares and bonds.

Investing is often done via a **financial intermediary**, which brings together investors and users of finance. Key options are discussed in more detail below.

KEY TERM

Financial intermediary: An institution bringing together providers and users of finance.

2.1 Bank or building society deposit accounts

One of the safest forms of investment for surplus cash is to pay it into a high street bank or building society deposit account. Retail banks and building societies offer a wide range of such accounts, although the interest rate, particularly for small sums, is generally quite low. Online accounts tend to attract a higher interest rate.

There are higher interest deposit accounts for larger amounts, for example provided that there is always a balance of, say, £10,000 in the account. Access to the cash is usually immediate and therefore useful if cash requirements are not known for certain.

If the cash is definitely not required in the near future, then it could be invested in a deposit account for a fixed term of up to three months at a variable rate of interest which is linked to money market rates. This will give a higher rate of return.

2.2 Money market accounts

These are similar in principle to bank deposit accounts. Here, funds are deposited with a bank or other financial institution for a fixed period of time and cannot be accessed until the term has ended. Terms range from overnight to 12 months. Money market accounts pays a higher interest than a regular savings account but often come with restrictions, such as a minimum balance requirement and limited withdrawals, that make them less flexible.

2.3 Securities

2.3.1 Gilt-edged securities

Gilts are a type of bond.

KEY TERM

Gilt-edged securities: Gilt-edged securities or **gilts** are marketable UK government securities. They are fixed interest securities and they form the major part of the fixed interest market. The interest rate on a gilt is also known as a **coupon rate**.

Coupon rate: The yearly amount of interest that will be paid on the face value of a security.

Gilts are classified according to their redemption dates as follows:

- Shorts – lives up to 5 years, eg Treasury 5% 2028
- Mediums – lives from 5 to 15 years, eg Treasury 5% 2038
- Longs – lives of more than 15 years, eg Treasury 4% 2060
- Undated stocks – no redemption date
- Index-linked stocks, eg Treasury IL 2.5% 2024

KEY TERM

Treasury bill: A government short-term debt, maturing in less than one year, and generally issued at a discount.

Treasury bills are issued weekly by the government to finance short-term cash deficiencies in the government's expenditure programme. The holder is paid the full value of the bill on maturity. Since they are negotiable, they can be resold, if required, before their maturity date.

Treasury bills do not pay interest, but the purchase price of a Treasury bill is less than its face value, the amount that the government will eventually pay on maturity. There is thus an implied rate of interest in the price at which the bills are traded.

2.3.2 Local authority stocks

In a similar way to government securities, there are a large number of marketable local authority securities which are available for investment purposes. However, local authority stocks are not considered to be quite as secure as central government stocks and the market is not so large, which means that local authority stocks have a slightly higher yield than government stocks to compensate. (Local authority stocks are a type of bond.)

KEY TERM

Local authority stocks: A type of bond issued by UK local government bodies (such as councils) to raise money for public projects. It pays a fixed rate of interest and has a set redemption date when the original amount is repaid.

2.3.3 Bonds

KEY TERM

Bond: A term given to any interest-paying security, whether it be issued by the government, a company, a bank or other institution. (Gilts are therefore UK government bonds.) Businesses also issue bonds. They are usually for the long term, and usually pay a fixed rate of interest. They may or may not be secured.

2.3.4 Interest yield

KEY TERM

Interest yield: The earnings from an investment over a period of time, normally a year.

Formula to learn

The interest yield is calculated as follows:

$$\text{Annual interest yield(\%)} = \frac{\text{Annual interest}}{\text{Market value}} \times 100$$

Illustration 2: Interest yield

A company has purchased 6% loan stock with a redemption date in 2030. The cost of the loan stock was £125 per £100 of stock.

Required

What is the current interest yield?

Solution

Interest received = £100 × 6% = £6

Cost of loan stock = £125

Interest yield = (£6 /£125) × 100% = 4.8%

2.3.5 Return on investment (ROI)

Return on investment measures the gain made on an investment compared to the original amount invested. It is expressed as a percentage.

Formula to learn

ROI = [(Gain from investment - Cost of investment) / Cost of investment] × 100

Illustration 3: Return on investment

A business invests £2,000 in a short-term deposit. At the end of the term, it receives £2,080 back.

Required

What is the return on investment?

Solution

ROI = (2,080 - 2,000) / 2,000 × 100 = 4%

2.3.6 Shares (also called equity)

KEY TERM

Equity: An equity investment is generally the purchase of shares in another company.

Often this takes place through a stock market. Income is from dividend payments and capital gains on the increase in the share value.

Formula to learn

The dividend yield from an equity investment can be calculated as follows:

$$\frac{\text{Annual dividend}}{\text{Current share price}} \times 100$$

Dividend yield shows the dividend payments made to shareholders; however, it is common practice for companies not to pay out all their earnings as dividends and to retain some profit for reinvestment into the business. These earnings that are retained may be used to purchase non-current assets or to provide a cushion of cash for any lean times ahead.

Some investors prefer to use an alternative measurement so that all earnings are included in their yield calculation. This is called the earnings yield.

Formula to learn

The earnings yield from an equity investment can be calculated as follows:

$$\frac{\text{Annual earnings}}{\text{Current share price}} \times 100$$

A **backward calculation** can also be completed. If an investor is looking for an 8% earnings yield on their investment and current annual earnings are £0.50 per share the investor may only be willing to pay £6.25 per each share purchased. To meet the 8% earnings yield required the backward calculation would be (£0.50/0.08) × 100 = £6.25.

Both the dividend yield and earnings yield are useful to investors as they enable comparisons between companies and also the return from available current interest rates.

Investments in companies that are traded on a stock exchange are very easily sold, so these are a relatively liquid form of investment. However, unless the investment is a speculative one, in anticipation of a rapid increase in the company's value, investments in equity are normally held for longer periods.

Illustration 4: Calculating dividend per share and dividend yield

The directors of Linton plc have approved a total dividend payment of £540,000 for the year.

The company's share capital is £1,800,000, and each share has:

- a nominal value of £3.00
- a current market value of £12.50

Required

Calculate the total number of shares, dividend payable per share and dividend yield.

Solution

Total number of shares = Share capital / Nominal value per share

= £1,800,000 / £3 = 600,000 shares

Dividend per share = Total dividend paid / Number of shares

= £540,000 / 600,000 = £0.90 per share

Dividend yield = Annual dividend per share / Current share price × 100

= £0.90 / £12.50 × 100 = 7.2%

A dividend yield of 7.2% means that, based on the current market value, shareholders receive a 7.2% return in the form of dividend income.

2.3.7 Property

Investing in property is generally a very safe investment. However, the costs of maintaining and generating an income from property are higher than for other forms of investment.

These are generally long-term investments due to the costs and time associated with purchasing and selling property.

Activity 1: Returns from shares

Marlow Engineering Ltd has £40,000 of surplus cash that it is considering investing in shares of two different companies: Alpha plc and Beacon Ltd. The finance manager wants to compare the potential income and yield from each investment.

Information about the shares is shown below:

Company	Current share price	Last annual dividend per share
Alpha plc	£8.00	£0.40
Beacon Ltd	£5.00	£0.20

Required

(a) Calculate how many shares Marlow Engineering Ltd could buy in either Alpha or Beacon:

Alpha plc [ ] **shares**

Beacon Ltd [ ] **shares**

(b) Calculate the total annual dividend income from each investment.

Annual dividend from Alpha £ [ ]

Annual dividend from Beacon £ [ ]

(c) Calculate the dividend yield.

Alpha: [ ] **%**

Beacon: [ ] **%**

If the market value of Alpha's shares (1) ▼ , the dividend yield will (2) ▼ .

Picklist 1

- Falls
- Rises

Picklist 2

- Decrease
- Increase

3 Diversification

Holding more than one different investment always carries less risk than holding only one. If only one investment is held, the investor could lose a significant amount if that investment performs badly. The extent to which risk can be reduced will depend on the relationship between the returns on the different investments.

If one investment performs poorly, another may perform better, helping to balance the overall return. This is known as the **portfolio effect**, and is the key reason diversification reduces risk.

A business should aim to create a diversified portfolio of investments, with a suitable spread of risk and return based on its objectives and risk appetite.

The diagram below shows how marketable UK securities can be ranked in order of increasing risk and increasing expected return.

KEY TERM

> **Diversification:** The process of reducing risk by increasing the number of separate investments in a portfolio.

A business should aim to create a diversified portfolio of investments, with a spread of risk and return. Marketable UK securities can be ranked in order of increasing risk and increasing expected return.

Government securities
Local authority stocks
Other 'public' corporation stocks
Company loan stocks
Other secured loans
Unsecured loans
Convertible loan stocks
Preference shares
Equities

Low risk
↓
High risk

Activity 2: Evaluating investment options

A company has an investment policy which specifies the following:

- Investments must be medium-low risk.
- The maximum to be invested in a single investment is £50,000.
- The minimum required return is 3% pa
- An investment must be convertible into cash within one month.

The company has £100,000 to invest and is considering the following options.

Option 1:

Minimum investment £60,000, interest rate 3.9% pa, 30-day notice period, the majority of the investment is held in treasury stock, with a small amount in shares of FTSE 100 quoted companies.

Option 2:

No minimum investment, interest rate 3% p.a., investment in gilts.

Option 3:

Minimum investment £50,000, bank deposit account, interest rate 3.5% pa, 30-day notice period.

Option 4:

No minimum investment, investment in portfolio of shares in quoted companies, interest rate 4.5% pa, and no notice period.

Required

(a) Complete the table below to assess whether the investment options comply with the company's investment policy:

Investment policy criteria	Risk	Within investment limit	Annual return	Liquidity acceptable (1 month conversion)
	High/Med/Low	Yes/No	%	Yes/No
Option 1				
Option 2				
Option 3				
Option 4				

(b) Complete the gap fills to recommend an appropriate investment strategy for the company, showing the investments in order of preference.

	Recommended option	Amount invested	Total return
	(insert number)	£	£
Preferred option			
Next best option			
Total			

(c) Overall, the company will earn a [ ] % return on its investment.

Chapter summary

- Organisations that identify a cash surplus should normally invest it to earn additional income for the business. Decisions about how to invest must always consider risk, return and liquidity.
- Larger organisations may have a dedicated treasury function responsible for managing cash and selecting appropriate short-term and long-term investments. All investment decisions must balance potential reward with the level of risk and the need for access to cash when required.
- There are several types of investment suitable for surplus funds. These include bank deposit accounts, bonds, shares and property. Each option offers different levels of risk, return and liquidity, and each has advantages and disadvantages that must be taken into account.
- For some investments, such as shares and bonds, measures such as return on investment and yield can be calculated to assess the income generated relative to the cost or value of the investment.
- Diversification can help reduce overall risk by spreading funds across a range of different investments. If one investment performs poorly, others may perform better, helping to smooth overall returns.

Activity answers

Activity 1: Returns from shares

(a) Total funds available = £40,000.

Alpha share price = £8.00. £40,000 / £8.00 = 5,000 shares

Beacon share price = £5.00. £40,000 / £5.00 = 8,000 shares

(b) Alpha: Dividend per share × number of shares held = £0.40 × 5,000 = £2,000

Beacon: Dividend per share × number of shares held = £0.20 × 8,000 = £1,600

(c) Yield = Annual dividend / current share price × 100

Alpha yield: £0.40 /£8.00 × 100 = 5%

Beacon yield: £0.20 /£5.00 × 100 = 4%

(d) If the market value of Alpha's shares [rises], the dividend yield will [decrease].

Because dividend is unchanged but the denominator (share price) increases.

Activity 2: Evaluating investment options

(a)

Investment policy criteria	Risk	Within investment limit	Annual return	Liquidity acceptable (1 month conversion)
	High/Med/Low	Yes/No	%	Yes/No
Option 1	Medium	No	3.9%	Yes
Option 2	Low	Yes	3.0%	Yes
Option 3	Low	Yes	3.5%	Yes
Option 4	High	Yes	4.5%	Yes

As gilts are readily marketable securities, they should be convertible into cash within one month.

(b)

	Recommended option	Amount invested	Total return
	(insert number)	£	£
Preferred option	3	50,000	1,750
Next best option	2	50,000	1,500
Total		100,000	3,250

(c) Overall, the company will earn a [3.25] % return on its investment.

Working

3,250/100,000 = 3.25%

Test your learning

1 **Use the picklist to complete the following sentence:**

A dividend from an investment is an example of [▼] return and an increase in the value of an investment is an example of [▼] return.

Picklist

- Capital
- Revenue

2 Government securities are also known as gilt-edged securities. They offer a variable interest rate and are deemed low risk.

Required

True or false?

	✓
True	
False	

3 **If there is a general rise in interest rates, what effect is this likely to have on the price of gilt-edged securities?**

Tick the correct answer.

	✓
Increase	
Decrease	

4 **What is the main purpose of diversification?**

	✓
To increase administration costs	
To reduce overall investment risk	
To guarantee a higher return	
To improve short-term liquidity	

5 A bank pays interest of £500 every six months on a £50,000 term deposit but there is a penalty of 1% capital invested if the deposit is cashed in before the end of two years.

Required

What rate of return will a business earn if it cashes in the deposit after holding it for just over 12 months?

[ ] %

6 A business invests £5,000 in a fixed-term deposit. At maturity, the investment is worth £5,150.

Required

Calculate the return on investment (ROI) (to the nearest whole percentage).

[ ] %

7 A company's shares have a market value of £4.00 each. Last year it paid a dividend of £0.16 per share.

Required

Calculate the dividend yield as a percentage (to nearest whole percent).

[ ] %

Test your learning answers

Chapter 1

1 The correct answer is:

	✓
True	✓
False	

10,000 units: Cost per unit £43,600/10,000 = £4.36

12,000 units: Cost per unit £52,320/12,000 = £4.36

As the cost per unit is the same at each level of production this would appear to be a purely variable cost.

2

Activity level	Total fixed cost £	Fixed cost per unit £
3,000 units	64,000	21.33
10,000 units	64,000	6.40
16,000 units	64,000	4.00

Working

3,000 units: £64,000/3,000 = £21.33

10,000 units: £64,000/10,000 = £6.40

16,000 units: £64,000/16,000 = £4.00

3 **The full production cost per month is**

£ 70,000

Working

	Production cost £
Direct material costs (£5 × 3,500)	17,500
Direct labour costs (£10 × 3,500)	35,000
Variable cost	52,500
Rent	10,000
Supervisor cost	7,500
Full production cost	70,000

4 (a) **The variable element of the production cost is**

£ 3 per unit

The fixed element of the production cost is

£ 169,000

Working

		£
Highest level	126,000	547,000
Lowest level	101,000	472,000
Increase	25,000	75,000

$$\text{Variable rate} = \frac{£75{,}000}{25{,}000} = £3 \text{ per unit}$$

Using highest level:

	£
Variable cost 126,000 × £3	378,000
Fixed costs (balancing figure)	169,000
Total cost	547,000

(b)

Level of production	Production cost £
120,000 units	529,000
150,000 units	619,000

Working

120,000 units	£
Variable cost 120,000 × £3	360,000
Fixed cost	169,000
Total forecast cost	529,000

150,000 units	£
Variable cost 150,000 × £3	450,000
Fixed cost	169,000
Total forecast cost	619,000

5 **(a)** The correct answer is:

	✓
£62.50	
£20.00	✓
£15.00	
£100.00	

Working

$$\text{Department P1} = \frac{£50,000}{2,500\text{h}}$$
$$= £20 \text{ per direct labour hour}$$

(b) The correct answer is:

	✓
£62.50	
£20.00	
£15.00	✓
£100.00	

Working

$$\text{Department P2} = \frac{£60,000}{4,000\text{h}}$$
$$= £15 \text{ per machine hour}$$

6 **(a)**

Department	Overhead absorption rate
X	£2.60 per machine hour
Y	£3.17 per direct labour hour

Working

$$X = \frac{£260,000}{100,000}$$
$$= £2.60 \text{ per machine hour}$$

As X is a highly mechanised department, most of the overhead will relate to the machinery therefore machine hours have been used to absorb the overhead.

$$Y = \frac{£380,000}{120,000}$$
$$= £3.17 \text{ per direct labour hour}$$

As Y is a highly labour-intensive department, most of the overhead will relate to the hours that are worked by the labour force therefore labour hours are used to absorb the overhead.

(b) £ 25.68

Working

		£
Product A – department X overhead	£2.60 × 5 =	13.00
Product A – department Y overhead	£3.17 × 4 =	12.68
		25.68

7

Method of costing	Budgeted cost £
Absorption costing	59.70

Working

Absorption costing – unit cost

	£
Direct materials	12.50
Direct labour	
Assembly (4 × £8.40)	33.60
Finishing (1 × £6.60)	6.60
Assembly overheads (£336,000/60,000)	5.60
Finishing overheads (£84,000/60,000)	1.40
	59.70

Chapter 2

1

	Actual £	Three-month moving average £
July	397,500	
August	403,800	400,300
September	399,600	402,900
October	405,300	403,667
November	406,100	406,633
December	408,500	407,500
January	407,900	408,933
February	410,400	411,433
March	416,000	413,167
April	413,100	415,533
May	417,500	417,467
June	421,800	

2

		Actual	Four-quarter moving average	Centred moving average = TREND	Seasonal variations
		£	£	£	£
20X5	Quarter 1	383,600			
	Quarter 2	387,600			
			365,400		
	Quarter 3	361,800		365,688	–3,888
			365,975		
	Quarter 4	328,600		366,575	–37,975
			367,175		
20X6	Quarter 1	385,900		366,013	+19,887
			364,850		
	Quarter 2	392,400		366,125	+26,275
			367,400		
	Quarter 3	352,500		368,225	–15,725
			369,050		
	Quarter 4	338,800		371,288	–32,488
			373,525		
20X7	Quarter 1	392,500		375,575	+16,925
			377,625		
	Quarter 2	410,300		378,325	+31,975
			379,025		
	Quarter 3	368,900		379,750	–10,850
			380,475		
	Quarter 4	344,400		382,388	–37,988
			384,300		
20X8	Quarter 1	398,300			
	Quarter 2	425,600			

3 y = 5,000 + 10x

Production cost of 1,400 units = £19,000

Working

£15,000 = a + (1,000 × b)

£25,000 = a + (2,000 × b)

£(25,000 – 15,000) = (a + (2,000 × b)) – (a + (1,000 × b))

£10,000 = a + 2,000b – a – 1,000b

£10,000 = 1,000 × b

b = £10,000/1,000 = £10

£15,000 = a + (1,000 × 10)

a = £15,000 – £10,000

a = £5,000

so the regression line is y = 5,000 + 10b

Production cost of 1,400 units = 5,000 + (10 × 1,400) = £19,000

4

	Production Units	Costs £
January	5,400	17,320
February	5,600	17,480
March	5,700	17,560
April	6,000	17,800
May	5,500	17,400
June	6,100	17,880

Working

Store costs

		£
January	13,000 + (0.8 × 5,400)	17,320
February	13,000 + (0.8 × 5,600)	17,480
March	13,000 + (0.8 × 5,700)	17,560
April	13,000 + (0.8 × 6,000)	17,800
May	13,000 + (0.8 × 5,500)	17,400
June	13,000 + (0.8 × 6,100)	17,880

5

	Value of x	Trend	Seasonal variation	Forecast sales
Quarter 1 20X9	13	2,785	–200	2,585
Quarter 2 20X9	14	2,830	+500	3,330
Quarter 3 20X9	15	2,875	+350	3,225
Quarter 4 20X9	16	2,920	–650	2,270

Working

Value of × for Quarter 1, 20X9

Quarter 1 20X6 = 1

Add 3 years of 4 quarters = 12

13

Trend for Quarter 1, 20X9: 2,200 + (45 × 13) = 2,785

Trend for Quarter 2, 20X9: 2,200 + (45 × 14) = 2,830

Trend for Quarter 3, 20X9: 2,200 + (45 × 15) = 2,875

Trend for Quarter 4, 20X9: 2,200 + (45 × 16) = 2,920

Chapter 3

1 The correct answer is:

	✓
To record past financial performance	
To plan future financial activity and support decision making	✓
To comply with statutory reporting requirements	
To calculate tax liabilities	

Budgets exist to plan future activity, set targets and support decision-making – not to record past results, meet statutory requirements, or calculate tax.

2 The correct answer is:

	✓
True	✓
False	

Top-down is faster but can reduce commitment because managers don't participate in setting targets.

3 The draft budget is ready for review: The budget committee

The managing director needs help in interpreting the draft budget: The budget accountant

4 Helps eliminate outdated assumptions: Zero-based budget

Saves time where activity is stable: Incremental budget

Keeps forecasts up-to-date: Rolling budget

5 The correct answer is:

	✓
The organisation has stable operations year-to-year	
The organisation wants to challenge existing spending patterns	✓
The organisation wants a quick, low effort budget	
Market conditions are highly predictable	

Zero-based budgeting suits situations where an organisation wants to challenge existing operations and spending.

Chapter 4

1 12,500 units

Closing inventory = 15,000 × 20% = 3,000 units

Production units = Sales units - opening inventory + closing inventory

= 12,000 - 2,500 + 3,000 = 12,500

2

	Period 1 Units	Period 2 Units	Period 3 Units
Opening inventory	1,140	1,200	1,350
Production (bal fig)	3,860	4,150	4,410
Units required	5,000	5,350	5,760
Sales	3,800	4,000	4,500
Closing inventory	1,200	1,350	1,260
Units required	5,000	5,350	5,760

Working

Closing inventory

Period 1	4,000 units × 30%	=	1,200 units
Period 2	4,500 units × 30%	=	1,350 units
Period 3	4,200 units × 30%	=	1,260 units

3 The production budget for the quarter is 43,334 units.

The labour usage budget for the quarter is 151,669 hours.

Working

Production budget

	Units
Sales quantity	42,000
Less opening inventory	(7,000)
Add closing inventory	8,334
Production quantity	43,334

Labour usage budget

Hours required	Hours
43,334 × 3.5	151,669

4

Overhead cost	Quarter 2 £	Quarter 3 £
Light and heat	76,896	85,680
Maintenance	82,090	90,325
Leasing	15,600	20,400
Rent and rates	21,000	21,000

Working

Overhead budget

	Quarter 2 £	Quarter 3 £
Light and heat		
16,020 × £4.80	76,896	
17,850 × £4.80		85,680
Maintenance (W)		
(16,020 × £4.50) + £10,000	82,090	
(17,850 × £4.50) + £10,000		90,325
Leasing	15,600	20,400
Rent and rates £84,000/4	21,000	21,000

Maintenance department costs working

	Activity level Units	Cost £
	13,000	68,500
	17,000	86,500
Increase	4,000	18,000

Variable element	=	£18,000/4,000 units
	=	£4.50 per unit

Fixed element

	£
Variable element 13,000 units × £4.50	58,500
Fixed element (bal fig)	10,000
Total cost	68,500

5 Production budget? 255 units

Materials usage budget? 1,785 kg costing £ 89,250

Labour cost budget? £ 25,570

Production = sales + closing inventory – opening inventory

	Units	Units
Budgeted sales		280
Opening inventory	(30)	
Closing inventory	5	
Decrease in inventory		(25)
Budgeted production		255

Material usage

Budgeted production	255 units
× usage per unit	× 7 kg
Total budgeted usage in kg	1,785 kg
× budgeted cost per kg	× £50
Total budgeted usage in £	£89,250

Labour cost budget – Grade O

Budgeted production	255 units
× hrs per unit	× 2 hrs
Total budgeted labour hrs	510 hrs
× budgeted cost per hr	× £15
Budgeted labour cost	£7,650

Labour cost budget – Grade R

Budgeted production	255 units
× hrs per unit	× 3 hrs
Total budgeted labour hrs	765 hrs

Note that the budgeted labour cost is not dependent on the hours worked.

Budgeted labour cost = 16 × £280 × 4 weeks = £17,920

Total labour cost budget in £ = £ (17,920 + 7,650) = £25,570

6 The purchases budget (in kg) for Period 1 is 27,009 kg

		Kg	Kg
Material issued to production	(J: 450 × 25 kg)		11,250
	(K: 710 × 40 kg)		28,400
			39,650
Opening inventory		(40,000)	
Closing inventory		27,359	
Decrease in inventory			(12,641)
Purchases			27,009

7 Budgeted labour hours: 4,460 hours

Cost of labour budget for Period 7: £ 44,812.50

Hours

Labour hours required for production of X (W1)	2,100
Labour hours required for production of Y (W2)	2,360
Total labour hours required	4,460
Basic hours available (W3)	4,375
Overtime hours	85

Budget

	£
Basic wages during Period 7 (W4)	43,750.00
Overtime (W5)	1,062.50
	44,812.50

Workings

1 Labour hours required = 420 units × 5 hours per unit = 2,100 hrs

2 Labour hours required = 590 units × 4 hours per unit = 2,360 hrs

3 Basic hours available = 35 hours × 5 weeks × 25 employees = 4,375 hrs

4 Basic wages = £10 × 4,375 hours (from (a)) = £43,750

5 Overtime = overtime hours × £ (10 × 125%) per overtime hour = 85 hrs (from (a)) × £12.50 = £1,062.50

Chapter 5

1

Forecast cash receipts

	January £	February £	March £
Budgeted cash receipts from sales	695,500	677,000	683,000

Working

		January £	February £	March £
Cash sales (10% of sales figure)		70,000	73,000	76,000
Credit sales	40% × 720,000	288,000		
	40% × 700,000		280,000	
	40% × 730,000			292,000
	45% × 750,000	337,500		
	45% × 720,000		324,000	
	45% × 700,000			315,000
		695,500	677,000	683,000

2

	January £	February £	March £
Budgeted payments	560,340	538,275	529,560

Working

Purchases

	October £	November £	December £	January £	February £
75% of sales	592,500	562,500	540,000	525,000	547,500

Cash payments

	January £	February £	March £
October purchases			
592,500 × 15%	88,875		
November purchases			
562,500 × 65%	365,625		
562,500 × 15%		84,375	
December purchases			
540,000 × 20% × 98%	105,840		
540,000 × 65%		351,000	
540,000 × 15%			81,000
January purchases			
525,000 × 20% × 98%		102,900	
525,000 × 65%			341,250
February purchases			
547,500 × 20% × 98%			107,310
	560,340	538,275	529,560

3

Cash budget for the quarter ending 31 December

	October £	November £	December £
Cash receipts			
Sales proceeds from equipment	0	4,000	0
Cash payments			
Wages	42,000	42,000	42,000
General overheads (W1)	25,000	29,800	31,000
New equipment	0	40,000	0

Working

General overheads

	October £	November £	December £
September overheads			
(30,000 – 5,000) × 20%	5,000		
October overheads			
(30,000 – 5,000) × 80%	20,000		
(30,000 – 5,000) × 20%		5,000	
November overheads			
(36,000 – 5,000) × 80%		24,800	
(36,000 – 5,000) × 20%			6,200
December overheads			
(36,000 – 5,000) × 80%			24,800
	25,000	29,800	31,000

4 The correct answer is:

	✓
£58,000	
£154,000	
£212,000	
£270,000	✓

Proceeds = carrying amount + profits = £212,000 + £58,000 = £270,000.

Chapter 6

1 The correct answer is:

	✓
To correct errors in the original budget	
To restate costs to reflect the actual level of activity	✓
To increase the accuracy of profit forecasts	
To remove fixed costs from performance reports	

A flexed budget adjusts variable elements so that they reflect the actual output achieved. This creates a fair comparison between what costs should have been and what they actually were.

2 The correct answer is:

	✓
Small and stable	
Non-existent	
Large and adverse	✓
Favourable	

Because ideal standards are nearly impossible to achieve, actual results usually fall short, resulting in large adverse variances.

3 The correct answer is:

	✓
Ensuring actual costs always meet standards	
Providing benchmarks for comparing budgeted and actual performance	✓
Eliminating the need for budgets	
Calculating cash flow forecasts	

Standard costing supplies the expected cost per unit, enabling meaningful comparisons between actual and planned performance.

4 The correct answer is:

	✓
Direct materials per unit	
Total variable costs	
Total fixed costs	✓
Revenue per unit	

Fixed costs do not depend on production volume in the short term, so these remain unchanged when a budget is flexed.

5 The correct answer is:

	✓
Record actual costs of production	
Provide information for variance calculations	✓
Control fixed overhead expenditure	
Allocate overheads to departments	

Standard cost cards provide the benchmark figures against which actual costs can later be compared, forming the basis for variance analysis.

Chapter 7

1 (a) (i) Total materials cost variance: £ 4,800 (F)

Total materials cost variance

	£
Standard cost of actual production	
1,800 units should have cost (× 7 kg × £6.00)	75,600
But did cost	70,800
	4,800 (F)

(ii) Materials price variance: £ 1,200 (F)

Materials price variance

	£
12,000 kg should have cost (× £6.00)	72,000
But did cost	70,800
	1,200 (F)

(iii) Materials usage variance: £ 3,600 (F)

Materials usage variance

1,800 units should have used (× 7 kg)	12,600
But did use	12,000
Variance in kg	600 (F)
× standard price per kg	× £6
Material usage variance in £	3,600 (F)

(b) (i) Total labour cost variance £ 5,600 (F)

Total labour cost variance

	£
Standard cost of actual production	
1,800 units should have cost (× £17)	30,600
But did cost	25,000
	5,600 (F)

(ii) Labour rate variance £ 9,000 (F)

Labour rate variance

Actual hours at standard rate	
5,000 hrs should cost (× £6.80)	34,000
But did cost	25,000
	9,000 (F)

(iii) Labour efficiency variance £ 3,400 (A)

Labour efficiency variance

Standard hours for actual production at standard rate	
1,800 units should have taken (× 2.5 hrs)	4,500
But did take	5,000
	500 (A)
× standard rate per hour	× £6.80
	3,400 (A)

2 (a) (i) 5,029 kg

Standard materials usage for 6,400 units:

6,400 units × 5,500 kg / 7,000 units = 5,029 kg

(ii) 9,143 hrs

Standard labour hours for 6,400 units:

6,400 units × 10,000 hrs / 7,000 units = 9,143 hrs

(iii) 19,200 hrs

Standard machine hours for 6,400 units:

6,400 units × 21,000 hrs / 7,000 units = 19,200 hrs

(b) (i) 3,500 (A)

Fixed overhead expenditure variance

	£
Budgeted fixed overhead	52,500
Actual fixed overhead expenditure	56,000
Fixed overhead expenditure variance	3,500 (A)

(ii) 4,500 (A)

Fixed overhead volume variance

	Units
Budgeted output	7,000
Actual output	6,400
Volume variance in units	600 (A)
Standard fixed overhead cost per unit	£7.50
Fixed overhead volume variance in £	4,500 Adv

Chapter 8

1 The correct answer is:

	✓
Switching to a higher-quality supplier	
Buying in smaller quantities	
Unexpected bulk discounts from a supplier	✓
Strict quality control causing more rework	

Bulk or trade discounts reduce the actual price per kg below the standard price, creating a favourable price variance. Higher quality usually costs more (A), and smaller orders (B) tend to lose discounts.

2 The correct answer is:

	✓
A favourable price variance and a favourable usage variance	
An adverse price variance and a favourable usage variance	
A favourable price variance and an adverse usage variance	✓
No variances at all	

Buying cheaper materials reduces price (favourable) but often increases waste or rework, pushing **usage** adverse. That's the classic price–usage trade-off.

3 The correct answer is:

	✓
Higher-skilled workers were used	
Overtime was required	
A shortage led to using temporary staff	
Cheaper labour was used than planned	✓

Paying cheaper labour than standard drops the actual hourly rate, giving a favourable labour rate variance. Using higher-skilled or overtime/temporary staff (A–C) generally raises the hourly rate (adverse).

4 The correct answer is:

	✓
Increased rent	
Unexpected savings on utility costs	✓
Lower production levels	
More rework than expected	

Unexpected savings on utilities (or a rent reduction) reduce actual fixed overhead spend below budget, giving a favourable expenditure variance.

5 The correct answer is:

	✓
Increase selling prices	
Review quality checks and storage/handling processes	✓
Reduce maintenance	
Increase the overhead absorption rate	

Excess usage points to waste or handling/quality issues; the direct fixes are better quality checks and improved storage/handling. Changing selling prices or OAR doesn't treat the root cause.

Chapter 9

1

Product	Budgeted cost per unit £	Budgeted overhead per unit £
LM	9.78	3.68
NP	27.41	20.81

Working

(1) Stores cost	=	$\frac{£140,000}{320}$
	=	£437.50 per materials requisition
(1) Production set-up costs	=	$\frac{£280,000}{280}$
	=	£1,000 per set-up
(1) Quality control costs	=	$\frac{£180,000}{90}$

	=	£2,000 per inspection

Product costs		LM £	NP £
Direct materials	50,000 × £2.60	130,000	
	20,000 × £3.90		78,000
Direct labour	50,000 × £3.50	175,000	
	20,000 × £2.70		54,000
Stores costs	100 × £437.50	43,750	
	220 × £437.50		96,250
Production set-up costs	80 × £1,000	80,000	
	200 × £1,000		200,000
Quality control costs	30 × £2,000	60,000	
	60 × £2,000		120,000
Total cost		488,750	548,250
Cost per unit		488,750	548,250
		50,000	20,000
		= £9.78	= £27.41

Analysis of total unit cost

Direct costs	(2.60 + 3.50)	6.10	
	(3.90 + 2.70)		6.60
Overheads	$\frac{(43,750 + 80,000 + 60,000)}{50,000}$	3.68	
	$\frac{(96,250 + 200,000 + 120,000)}{20,000}$		20.81
		9.78	27.41

2 The correct answer is:

	✓
It allocates overheads using a single cost driver	
It recognises that different activities generate different overhead costs	✓
It removes the need to analyse direct costs	
It ensures all products have the same profit margin	

Because ABC identifies multiple activities and cost drivers, it highlights how different products consume resources differently.

3 The correct answer is:

	✓
ABC always uses fewer cost pools than absorption costing	
ABC provides a more accurate cost per unit by linking costs to activities	✓
ABC reduces the need to record overheads	
ABC eliminates the need for overhead absorption rates	

ABC improves accuracy by assigning overheads based on activities that drive the costs.

Chapter 10

1 **Development** – Fixed research and development costs

Introductory – Continuing research and development costs, fixed advertising expenditure, low level direct materials and labour costs

Growth – Continuing advertising and promotion expenditure, high level of direct materials and labour costs, high fixed and variable production overheads

Maturity – Lower level of direct materials and labour costs due to economies of scale, higher level of production overheads due to mechanisation

Decline – Low level of direct materials and labour, production overheads low, decommissioning and opportunity costs high due to wastage of obsolete stock

2

	Development	Introduction	Growth	Maturity	Maturity	Total
Sales volume (units)		5,000	13,000	25,000	10,000	
	£000	**£000**	**£000**	**£000**	**£000**	**£000**
Revenue		£250 × 5 1,250	£250 × 13 3,250	£200 × 25 5,000	£150 × 10 1,500	11,000
Variable cost		£150 × 5 (750)	£130 × 13 (1,690)	£70 × 25 (1,750)	£85 × 10 (850)	(5,040)
Fixed Overhead		(800)	(650)	(450)	(460)	(2,360)
Development cost	(400)					(400)
Scrap cost					(60)	(60)
Profit	(400)	(300)	910	2,800	130	3,140

3 The target cost per unit is £ 72

	£
Target selling price	90

	£
Target profit margin (90 × 20%)	(18)
Target cost	72

Chapter 11

1 (a) The limiting factor of production resources is machine hours.

Working

Resource requirements for maximum demand

	R	S	T	Total
Materials	80,000 kg	120,000 kg	25,000 kg	225,000 kg
Labour hours	20,000 hours	80,000 hours	5,000 hours	105,000 hours
Machine hours	60,000 hours	80,000 hours	15,000 hours	155,000 hours

The limiting factor is machine hours.

(b)

Product	Units produced
S	20,000
T	5,000
R	4,166

Working

Contribution per machine hour

	R	S	T
Contribution	£6	£12	£6
Machine hours	6	4	3
Contribution/machine hour	£1.00	£3.00	£2.00
Ranking	3	1	2

Production plan

Product	Units produced	Machine hours used
S	20,000	80,000
T	5,000	15,000

Product	Units produced	Machine hours used
R (balance 25,000/6 = 4,166.67 = 4,166 complete units)	4,166	24,996
		119,996

(c) The profit that will be earned under this production plan is £ 244,996 .

Working

Product contribution

	£
R (4,166 × £6)	24,996
S (20,000 × £12)	240,000
T (5,000 × £6)	30,000
Total contribution	294,996
Less fixed costs	(50,000)
Profit	244,996

2 The business should buy in neither product .

	X £	Y £
Direct materials	2.50	3.00
Direct labour	8.00	6.00
Variable cost of production	10.50	9.00
External price	11.00	10.00

On the basis of costs alone, neither product should be purchased externally as they are cheaper to make.

3

	Units
Badger	20,000
Pelican	0

Since demand for both products is unlimited Timmy Co should manufacture as many of the product which makes the best use of the scarce resource, labour, which in this case is the Badger.

There are 20,000 labour hours available and each unit of Badger uses I hour, which means 20,000 units can be made.

	Badger	Pelican
Sales demand (units)	5,000	10,000
Labour hours per unit (Hrs)	1	2
Contribution per unit (£)	5.00	7.00
Contribution per labour hour (£)	5.00	3.50
Rank to manufacture	1	2

Chapter 12

1 The payback period is 2 years and 9 months.

Time	Cash flows £	Cumulative cash flows £
31 Dec X6	30,000	30,000
31 Dec X7	40,000	70,000
31 Dec X8	40,000	110,000
31 Dec X9	20,000	130,000

The initial cost of the investment is fully covered after three years; however, as the cash inflows occur evenly throughout the year, this can be calculated more accurately.

2 years + £30,000/£40,000 × 12 months = 2 years and 9 months

2

(i) £ 2,471.32

£3,100 × 0.7972 = £2,471.32

(ii) £ 15,000.00

£15,000 × 1.0000 = £15,000.00

(iii) £ 1,690.10

£1,000 × 1.6901 (add discount factors to arrive at cumulative discount factor for an annuity cash flow) = £1,690.10

(iv) £ 3,842.96

£4,400 × 0.8734 = £3,842.96

3 £ 3,701

Year	Cash flows	Discount factor@ 7%	Present value
	£		£
0	(340,000)	1.0000	(340,000)
1	80,000	0.9346	74,768
2	70,000	0.8734	61,138
3	90,000	0.8163	73,467
4	120,000	0.7629	91,548
5	60,000	0.7130	42,780
Net present value			3,701

4 **(a)** £ 3,014

Year	Cash flows	Discount factor@ 11%	Present value
	£		£
0	(90,000)	1.0000	(90,000)
1	23,000	0.9009	20,721
2	31,000	0.8116	25,160
3	40,000	0.7312	29,248
4	18,000	0.6587	11,857
Net present values			(3,014)

(b) The correct answer is:

	✓
Management should accept the project because the net present value is negative	
Management should not accept the project because the net present value is negative	✓
Management should accept the project because the payback period is less than 4 years	
Management should not accept the project because the payback is less than 4 years	

As the investment in the new plant and machinery has a negative net present value at the cost of capital of 11% then the investment should not take place.

5 The correct answer is:

	✓
9.15%	
9.85%	✓
10.15%	
10.85%	

$$IRR = a + \left[\frac{NPVa}{NPVa - NPVb} \times (b-a)\right]$$

$$IRR = 9 + \left[\frac{22}{22 - -4} \times (10-9)\right]$$

$$IRR = 9 + \left[\frac{22}{22 + 4} \times 1\right]$$

$$\therefore IRR = 9 + \left[\frac{22}{26}\right]$$

$$\therefore IRR = 9.85\%$$

6 The ARR is 10 %

Time	Cash flows £	Depreciation £	Profit £
31 May X9	80,000	50,000	30,000
31 May Y0	70,000	50,000	20,000
31 May Y1	70,000	50,000	20,000
31 May Y2	60,000	50,000	10,000
Total			80,000

Average annual profit = 80,000/4 = 20,000

Investment = 200,000

ARR = Average annual profit/investment × 100

ARR = (20,000/200,000) × 100% = 10%

Chapter 13

1 The correct answer is:

	✓
30 days	
40 days	
54 days	✓
124 days	

Working

	Days
Inventory holding period = $\frac{£68,000}{£593,000} \times 365$	42
Trade receivables' collection = $\frac{£102,000}{£790,000} \times 365$	47
Trade payables' payment = $\frac{£57,000}{£593,000} \times 365$	(35)
Cash operating cycle	54

2 The correct answer is:

	✓
25 days	
39 days	
46 days	✓
56 days	

Working

	Days
Inventory holding period	21
Plus trade receivables' collection period	60
Less trade payables' payment period	(X)
Cash operating cycle	35

The trade payables' payment period in days is: 21 + 60 – 35 = 46 days.

3 The three most liquid assets that the majority of businesses have are:

- Cash in hand

- Bank current account
- Bank deposit account

4 The correct answer is:

	✓
Longer inventory holding period	✓
Taking longer to pay suppliers	
Lower investment in working capital	
Improved debt collection	

5 The correct answer is:

	✓
Overtrading	
Over-capitalisation	✓

6 The correct answer is:

	✓
Increasing cash balances and low reliance on overdraft facilities	
Falling sales volumes and rising inventory levels	
Rapid sales growth combined with rising payables days and a worsening cash position	✓
High levels of working capital relative to the scale of operations	

Overtrading occurs when a business expands too quickly without enough working capital to support that growth. Typical symptoms include:

- rapid increase in sales
- cash shortages
- rising payables days (suppliers being paid late)
- reliance on overdrafts or short-term finance

Chapter 14

1 The correct answer is:

	✓
Repayments are usually made on a fixed schedule	✓
Interest is charged only on the amount used	
The borrowing limit can be changed daily	
The loan is normally repayable on demand	

2 The correct answer is:

	✓
A short-term loan sometimes used for working capital	
A long-term loan secured on property	✓
An borrowing facility with a fixed limit agreed with the bank	
A loan that is normally expected to be repaid within a year	

3 The correct answer is:

	✓
Regular interest payments are compulsory	
Dividends are paid only if the business can afford them	✓
Issuing shares increases the business's gearing	
The company must repay the capital at the end of the term	

4 The correct answer is:

	✓
Floating charge required	
Interest charged only on amount of facility used	✓
Repayable on demand	

5 The correct answer is:

	✓
Overdraft finance	
Loan finance	✓

A medium-term loan from a bank would probably be the most appropriate source of finance for the purchase of the shares in B Ltd. Provided that the intention is to keep the shares for some time and therefore to benefit from income from those shares in that period, then the loan would match the timescale of the investment in the company and the income could be used to service the loan.

6 The correct answers are:

	✓
Repaying borrowings from operating funds	✓
Improved working capital management to repay borrowings	✓
Increasing equity through issuing shares	✓
Obtaining a loan	

If a company is to lower its capital gearing, it needs either to increase the value of its equity or to decrease the size of its borrowings.

Reduction of borrowing could be achieved by:

- Repaying borrowings from operating funds (if growth is high and cash resources allow)
- Using leases to convert owned assets into operating leases or sale and leaseback of assets, in order to release cash to redeem borrowings
- Improved working capital management to repay borrowings, through reducing inventory and receivables, and increasing credit from suppliers
- Increasing equity through issuing shares, either through a rights issue or placement of shares with financial institutions

---

Chapter 15

1 A dividend from an investment is an example of [revenue] return and an increase in the value of an investment is an example of [capital] return.

2 The correct answer is:

	✓
True	
False	✓

Government securities are also known as gilts and they are considered low risk; however, the interest on gilts is fixed interest.

3 The correct answer is:

	✓
Increase	
Decrease	✓

4 The correct answers are:

	✓
To increase administration costs	
To reduce overall investment risk	✓
To guarantee a higher return	
To improve short-term liquidity	✓

Diversification spreads investments so poor performance in one area is balanced by good performance in another.

5 | 1 | %

Working

In the first year, the deposit will pay two lots of interest:

£500 × 2 = £1,000.

However, there is a penalty for cashing in the deposit early of 1% × 50,000 = £500.

So, overall the business earns £500/£50,000 = 1%.

6 | 3 | %

ROI = Gain/Cost × 100%

= 150/5,000 × 100% = 3%

7 | 4 | %

Dividend per share/Share price × 100 = £0.16 / £4.00 × 100 = 4%

Glossary

Chapter 1: Costing techniques

Absorption costing: A method whereby all production costs are included in the costing of a cost unit, both variable and fixed, direct and indirect. This method of costing distinguishes between production and non-production costs.

Activity-based costing: A method of absorption costing which uses more sophisticated methods of allocating overheads to cost units. This method is covered later in this Course Book.

Contribution: The amount of money generated by a cost unit to contribute towards fixed costs incurred in a period in order to make a profit.

Direct costs: Costs which can be specifically identified with, and allocated to, a single cost unit.

Fixed costs: Those costs that will not vary with output. These are often referred to as fixed overheads (eg rent and rates).

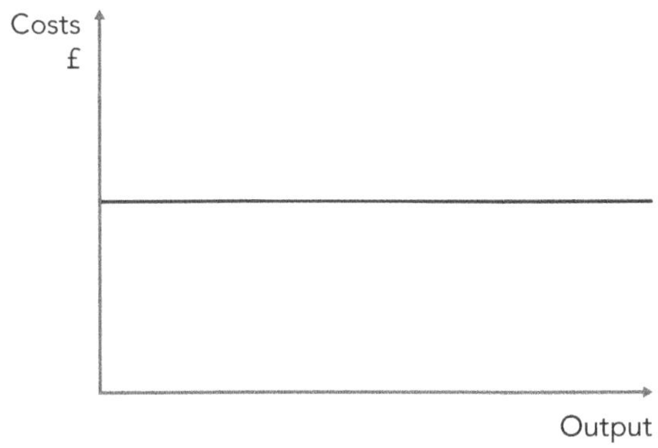

Indirect costs: Incurred in the course of making a product/service, but which cannot be identified with a particular cost unit.

Marginal costing: Under this method only the variable costs of production are included in the cost per unit. The fixed overheads are treated as period costs and not as part of the cost unit. Instead, the fixed overheads are charged to the statement of profit or loss as an expense for the period.

Overhead absorption rate: An estimated amount of fixed overhead which can be used to calculate the overhead cost incurred to produce one cost unit.

Prime costs: Total of all direct costs in manufacturing a product/providing a service.

Semi-variable costs: Those costs which are part fixed and part variable and are therefore partly affected by changes in the level of activity (eg telephone bill, where there is a fixed line rental charge and a charge per call made).

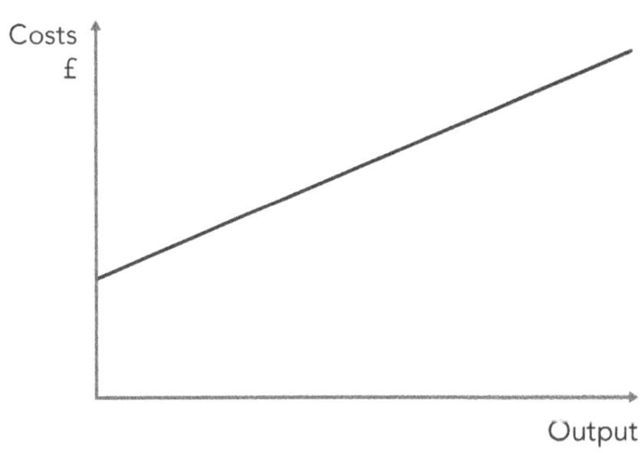

Stepped costs: Costs that remain fixed for a certain level of output and then increase until a further level of output is reached. They then become fixed again until output levels reach another point, then increase again (eg supervisors' costs where a supervisor is required for every 20 members of staff and rent, which may increase with the addition of new facilities or space).

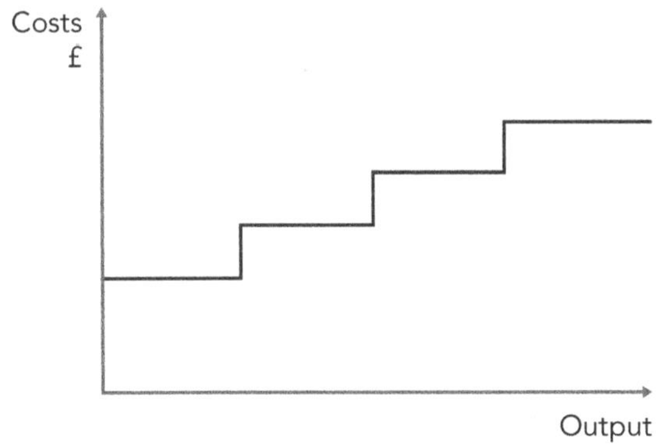

Variable costs: Those costs that vary, ie rise and fall, with output (eg materials and labour costs vary with the number of units produced).

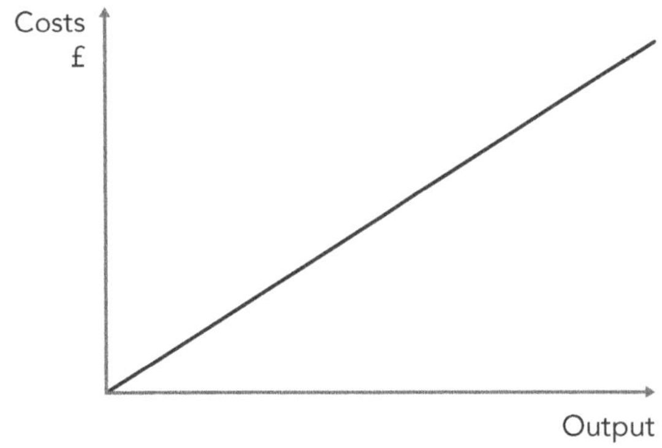

Chapter 2: Forecasting techniques

Extrapolation: Forecasts data outside of the historical data range.

Interpolation: Forecasts data within the historical data range.

Linear regression: A technique for forecasting costs or sales using the equation of a straight line.

Seasonal variation (SV): The regular short-term fluctuations in recorded values due to circumstances that affect results at different times of the year, on different days of the week or at different times of the day.

Time series: A series of figures or values recorded over time.

Trend: The underlying movement over time in the values of the data recorded.

Chapter 3: Budgetary control systems

Bottom-up budgeting: A budgeting system in which operational managers have a degree of input into the budget. It is a form of negotiated budgeting in which operational and senior management negotiate the final budget.

Budget accountant: An accountant who helps the budget committee in the preparation of budgets.

Budget committee: A committee of senior executives who oversee the preparation of budgets.

Budget holder: A member of staff, usually a manager, who is responsible for the budget for a particular area of the business.

Budget manual: A set of instructions as to how the budget is to be prepared.

Budgetary slack: An extra amount of cost built into a budget, by budget holders, in order to make the targets easier to meet.

External data: Data collected from sources outside the business.

Fixed budgets: Budgets that are set in advance of a period and their purpose is to provide a single achievable target for the entire organisation to work towards. This target level of activity means that all areas of the business will be co-ordinated towards achieving this goal.

Flexed budgets: Budgets that are prepared at the actual activity level that was achieved during the period, in order to show what the standard costs should have been at that particular activity.

Flexible budgets: Budgets which, by recognising different cost behaviours, are designed to change as the volume of activity changes.

Goal congruence: Where the goals of individual functions or departments are consistent with the overall goals and strategy of the organisation.

Incremental budgeting: A method of budgeting whereby the previous budget is adjusted for changes in prices and activity levels.

Internal data: Data collected from inside the business such as internal documents or sources.

Rolling budgets: Are continually updated in order to project a continual amount of time into the future.

Top-down budgeting: A budgeting system in which the budget is set and imposed by senior management.

Zero-based budgeting: A method of budgeting whereby the budget for each cost centre is looked at from scratch for each period.

Chapter 4: Preparing operating budgets

Principal budget factor: This is the resource or condition that restricts the activities of an organisation and therefore limits what can be included in the budget.

Chapter 5: Preparing cash budgets

Cash budgets: Methods of determining the expected net cash flow for a future period, and the expected cash balance at the end of that future period.

Inflation: Increase in prices of goods and services over time.

Irrecoverable debt: Invoiced amounts that it is considered will never be received in cash.

Lagged payment: If cash is paid at a later time to the recording of the purchase or expense, it is a lagged payment.

Lagged receipt: If cash is received at a later time to when the sale was recorded, there is a lagged receipt.

Chapter 6: Standard costing and flexed budgets

Basic standards: Standards that have been unaltered over a long period of time.

Current standards: Standards based on current working conditions.

Fixed budgets: Budgets that are set in advance of a period and their purpose is to provide a single achievable target for the entire organisation to work towards. This target level of activity means that all areas of the business will be co-ordinated towards achieving this goal.

Flexed budgets: Budgets that are adjusted to reflect the actual activity level that was achieved during the period, showing what costs and revenues should have been at that particular activity level using standard rates.

Flexible budgets: Budgets which, by recognising different cost behaviours, are designed to change as the volume of activity changes.

Ideal standards: Standards set on the basis that perfect working conditions apply at all times.

Standard cost card: Shows full details of the standard cost of each product.

Standard cost: An estimated unit cost.

Standard costing: A control technique which compares standard costs and revenues with actual results to obtain variances which are used to improve performance.

Target (or attainable) standards: Standards that incorporate some improvement but allow for some inefficiency.

Chapter 7: Variance analysis

Fixed overhead expenditure variance: A comparison of budgeted and actual fixed overhead incurred.

Fixed overhead volume variance: A comparison of budgeted and actual units produced, valued at standard OAR per unit.

Idle time variance: A comparison of actual hours worked and actual hours paid, valued at the standard rate per labour hour.

Labour efficiency variance: A comparison of the standard hours worked for actual production units to the actual hours worked for actual production units, valued at standard rate per hour.

Labour rate variance: A comparison of the standard cost of actual hours paid to the actual cost of actual hours paid.

Materials price variance: A comparison of the standard cost of the actual materials purchased, to the actual cost of materials purchased.

Materials usage variance: A comparison of the standard usage of materials for actual production units, to the actual usage of materials for actual production units, valued at standard cost per unit of material.

Sales price variance: A comparison of the standard selling price of the actual units sold to the actual sales revenue of actual units sold.

Sales volume variance: A comparison of the budgeted units sold, to the actual number of units sold, valued at standard profit per unit (under absorption costing) and the standard contribution per unit (under marginal costing).

Total labour variance: A comparison of the standard labour cost of actual production units to the actual labour cost of actual production units.

Total materials variance: A comparison of the total standard cost of materials for actual production, to the total actual cost of materials.

Total variable overhead variance: A comparison of the standard variable overhead cost for actual production units, to the actual variable overhead cost for actual production units.

Variable overhead efficiency variance: A comparison of the standard hours for actual production units, to the actual hours for actual production units, valued at the standard variable overhead per hour.

Variable overhead price variance: A comparison of the standard variable overhead cost of actual hours worked, to the actual variable overhead cost of actual hours worked.

Chapter 9: Activity-based costing (ABC)

Cost driver: A factor that drives a change in the usage of an activity.

Cost pool: A breakdown of total overheads into different categories depending on the activity that has generated the cost.

Chapter 10: Target costing and life cycle costing

Life cycle costing: Costing of a product throughout all stages of its life cycle, including costs incurred in the development stage and market withdrawal stage.

Product life cycle: A model to show the different sales and profitability patterns at different stages of a product's life cycle.

Target cost: The desired cost of a product which must be achieved, based on deducting the desired profit from a target selling price.

Value analysis: Analysis of every aspect of existing products/services in order to reduce the cost, with no reduction in value to the customer.

Chapter 11: Short-term decision-making techniques

Contribution per unit: The selling price per unit less all variable costs per unit

Opportunity cost: The value of a benefit sacrificed when one course of action is chosen in preference to an alternative.

Relevant costs: Costs appropriate to a specific management decision.

Scarce resource: is defined as a factor which limits the number of units that can be produced and sold. Scarce resources could be:

- Materials available to purchase
- Labour hours available
- Machine hours available
- Plant capacity
- Factory space
- Access to finance

Total contribution: Total sales revenue less all variable costs

---

Chapter 12: Long-term decision-making techniques

Accounting rate of return: The actual return a project generates, based on profits, not cash flows.

Internal rate of return: The discount rate which when applied to project cash flows gives a zero net present value

Net present value: The net total of the discounted cash flows of the project.

Payback period: The time it takes for the cash inflows from a project to repay the initial investment cost.

Chapter 13: Liquidity and working capital

Cash operating cycle/Working capital cycle: The period of time between cash being paid for raw materials and cash being received from customers for good sold.

Cash: Ready money, most easily thought of as banknotes and coins, and money in a current bank account. A business may be profitable but if it is unable to pay its bills, it will fail.

Current assets: Cash, inventory, receivables.

Current liabilities: Payables, loans falling due within one year, overdraft.

Inventory holding period: The amount of time that inventory is being held by a business.

Liquidity: The ease and speed with which an investment can be converted into cash.

Over-capitalisation: Occurs when a business has excessive working capital and hence is inefficient and less profitable (customers taking too long to pay, too much inventory, insufficient credit from suppliers).

Overtrading: Occurs when a business tries to do too much too quickly without having enough working capital to support that growth.

Trade payables' payment period: The amount of time it takes for a business to pay its trade payables.

Trade receivables' collection period: The amount of time that it takes for trade receivables to pay the amounts they owe.

Working capital: Working capital is the value of current assets less the value of current liabilities.

Chapter 14: Financing options

Amortising repayment: In an amortising repayment the amount borrowed and interest are paid off over the term of the loan.

Balloon repayment: In a balloon repayment during the term of the loan, small amounts of the amount borrowed are repaid along with loan interest, but the majority of the amount borrowed is repaid at the end of the term.

Bullet repayment: In a bullet repayment the amount borrowed is paid back at the end of the loan; only interest is paid during the loan period.

Compound interest: Interest is charged on the loan principal plus unpaid accumulated interest.

Covenants: Obligations or restrictions placed on the business by the loan provider.

Director's loan: Money a director lends to the company, or withdraws from the company, outside of normal salary or dividends. When used as finance, it refers to funds the director puts into the business.

Fixed charge: A fixed charge is a named asset which the bank can insist is sold to repay the debt.

Fixed rate interest: An agreed fixed rate of interest for the term of the loan.

Floating charge: A floating charge is a class of assets the bank can insist is sold to repay the debt (for example: non-current assets, or receivables).

Hardcore overdraft: An overdraft which has effectively become a permanent part of the capital of the business.

Loan principal: The fixed amount of capital borrowed.

Loan-to-value ratio: The interest rate will also be dependent on the loan-to-value ratio when the loan is for the purchase of an asset.

You may have seen this in the personal mortgage market, where a higher interest applies at higher loan-to-value ratios. If the company takes out a loan for 90% of the asset value, the interest rate is likely to be higher than a loan for 70% of the asset value.

This is because at a lower loan-to-value ratio, the risk to the lender of the borrower defaulting and being unable to recover their loan is also lower.

Loan: An amount of money advanced by a bank to its customer.

Mortgage: A long-term loan secured on property, typically repaid over many years. If the borrower defaults, the lender may sell the property to recover the debt.

Overdraft facility: The amount of potential overdraft that a bank allows a customer.

Overdraft: The amount by which a customer's bank account is in debt.

Personal guarantee: A personal guarantee is where a named individual becomes personally liable in the event the original borrower defaults.

Shares: Units of ownership in a company. Shareholders may receive dividends and have voting rights, depending on the type of shares issued.

Simple interest/Flat rate interest: Interest is charged on the full loan principal at the start of the loan. Also known as flat rate interest.

Variable rate interest: Interest on a loan which changes every time the bank changes its base rate.

Chapter 15: Investment options

Bond: A term given to any interest-paying security, whether it be issued by the government, a company, a bank or other institution. (Gilts are therefore UK government bonds.) Businesses also issue bonds. They are usually for the long term, and usually pay a fixed rate of interest. They may or may not be secured.

Capital return: The increase/decrease in market value of an investment.

Capital risk: The risk that the value of an investment will fall.

Coupon rate: The yearly amount of interest that will be paid on the face value of a security.

Diversification: The process of reducing risk by increasing the number of separate investments in a portfolio.

Equity: An equity investment is generally the purchase of shares in another company.

Financial intermediary: An institution bringing together providers and users of finance.

Gilt-edged securities: Gilt-edged securities or **gilts** are marketable UK government securities. They are fixed interest securities and they form the major part of the fixed interest market. The interest rate on a gilt is also known as a **coupon rate**.

Income return: Interest or dividend received.

Interest yield: The earnings from an investment over a period of time, normally a year.

Liquidity: is the term used for the ease and speed with which an investment can be converted into cash.

Local authority stocks: A type of bond issued by UK local government bodies (such as councils) to raise money for public projects. It pays a fixed rate of interest and has a set redemption date when the original amount is repaid.

Return: Any income and/or capital gain on an investment.

Risk: The chance of making a loss.

Treasury bill: A government short-term debt, maturing in less than one year, and generally issued at a discount.

Index

Tell us what you think

Got comments or feedback on this book? Let us know.
Use your QR code reader:

Or, visit:
https://www.smartsurvey.co.uk/s/W30E6Y/

Need to get in touch with customer service?

www.bpp.com/request-support

Spotted an error?

https://learningmedia.bpp.com/pages/errata